THE
CITY
TAVERN
COOKBOOK

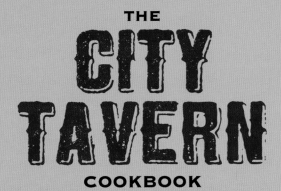

Recipes from the
BIRTHPLACE
of
AMERICAN
CUISINE

WALTER STAIB

with Paul Bauer

Foreword by David McCullough

RUNNING PRESS
PHILADELPHIA · LONDON

I DEDICATE THIS BOOK TO THOMAS JEFFERSON, OUR NATION'S FIRST TRUE
GASTRONOME AND, IN MY OPINION, THE GREATEST CONTRIBUTOR
TO EARLY AMERICAN CULTURE.

© 2009 by Walter Staib

Printed in China

9   8
Digit on the right indicates the number of this printing

Library of Congress Control Number: 2008921273

ISBN 978-0-7624-3417-6

Cover and interior design by Frances J. Soo Ping Chow
Edited by Diana C. von Glahn and
          Kristen Green Wiewora
Photography by William Deering
Food and prop styling by Walter Staib
Typography: Archive Gothic Ornate, Adobe Garamond,
          Abadi, Bauer Bodoni, Buillon Extra Condensced,
          Copperplate, Dead Man's Hand, and Porcelain

Running Press Book Publishers
2300 Chestnut Street
Philadelphia, PA 19103-4371

Visit us on the web!
www.runningpresscooks.com
www.citytavern.com

CONTENTS

ACKNOWLEDGMENTS

First, I would like to thank my wife, Gloria, for being an unwavering partner in my quest to preserve American culinary history at City Tavern.

I would like to thank our nation's foremost historian, David McCullough, for his gracious and insightful foreword.

Many thanks to the United States Department of the Interior, National Park Service, for their unwavering trust and confidence in me as the operator of this unique, historic restaurant.

I am deeply indebted to my assistant and Director of Projects and Marketing, Paul Bauer, who, despite an already onerous workload, undertook the writing of this book. He is the "brains" of my operation and, as always, handled this project with aplomb.

Beth d'Addono and Jennifer Lindner deserve great thanks for having laid solid foundations for this book through their research and writing of *City Tavern Cookbook* and *City Tavern Baking & Dessert Cookbook*.

A very heartfelt thank you to Linda Gentry and Sandy Levins of the Camden County Historical Society for opening wide the doors to Pomona Hall, the beautifully preserved eighteenth-century home of Marmaduke Cooper, for research, and for loaning us priceless objects from their collection for our photo shoot.

Special thanks to my Chef de Cuisine, William Sederman, for his assistance in testing recipes and for keeping up with a very aggressive photo shoot schedule.

Thanks to Bill Deering whose brilliant photography brings this book to life, to Diana von Glahn for her eagle-eyed editing, and to Frances Soo Ping Chow for her inspired design.

Last but certainly not least, I want to thank the entire staff of City Tavern for their daily commitment to the accurate re-creation of history that makes it truly one of a kind.

My most grateful thanks to all of you for realizing my vision!

Chef Staib in the kitchen at Pomona Hall

CITY TAVERN TIMELINE

1772 TO 1773: Fifty-three prominent citizens commission the building of the City Tavern, which is to be "a large and commodious tavern" that will be worthy of Philadelphia's standing as the largest, most prosperous city in the colonies.

DECEMBER 1773: City Tavern opens for business. The building has five levels and includes kitchens, a bar room, two coffee rooms, and three dining rooms; the second largest ballroom in the New World; five lodging rooms and servants quarters. Daniel Smith, its first proprietor, leases the Tavern for £300 per year, an amount roughly equivalent to five years of wages for the common man. He resides there from 1774 to 1778.

MAY 1774: Paul Revere arrives at the Tavern to announce Parliament's closing of the port of Boston. The next day, two to three hundred prominent Philadelphians meet at City Tavern to select a committee of correspondence to draft a letter of sympathy for Revere to take back to Boston.

SEPTEMBER TO OCTOBER 1774: City Tavern is the unofficial meeting place of the delegates before and after sessions of the first Continental Congress, which convened at nearby Carpenters' Hall. George Washington, Thomas Jefferson, John Adams, Richard Henry Lee, and Peyton Randolph are among the participants.

1776 TO 1777: Continental and British troops use City Tavern to house prisoners of war. Military courts-martial are also held there.

JULY 4, 1777: America's first Fourth of July celebration is held at City Tavern.

AUGUST 3 TO 5, 1777: General Washington and his aides-de-camp share table and quarters at City Tavern, making the Tavern the official headquarters of the Continental Army for three days.

DECEMBER 10, 1778: Politician John Jay is elected president of the Continental Congress, while staying as a guest at the Tavern.

1783: The Pennsylvania Society of the Cincinnati is formed at City Tavern in the second floor northwest dining room.

1784: Original subscribers sell City Tavern to Samuel Powel, a prominent Philadelphian and former mayor of the city.

JANUARY 1789: City Tavern's two front rooms become headquarters of the Merchants' Coffee House and Place of Exchange.

APRIL 1789: City Tavern hosts a banquet for George Washington as he passes through Philadelphia on his way to New York for his inauguration.

MARCH 1834: City Tavern's roof catches fire, the building is heavily damaged.

1854: The surviving structure is razed.

1948: Congress authorizes Independence National Historical Park to preserve certain important buildings and sites of significant national importance, encompassing more than forty buildings on forty-two acres, including the site of the original City Tavern.

1975: Historically accurate replication of the original Tavern is completed according to period images, written accounts, and insurance surveys.

1976: The newly rebuilt Tavern opens in time for the bicentennial. The restaurant is managed by a large food service company.

DECEMBER 31, 1992: The restaurant concession at the Tavern closes.

1994: Walter Staib wins congressional approval as operator of the Tavern, which re-opens for business on July 4, featuring eighteenth-century style gourmet cuisine.

FOREWORD

O f all those worthy patriots who gathered for the first Continental Congress in Philadelphia in late summer of 1774—and of those who later fixed their signatures to the immortal Declaration of Independence—none wrote so fully or candidly about the setting of the historic drama, or the human side of life for the protagonists, than did John Adams of Massachusetts. And quite fitting it is that Adams, describing his arrival in Philadelphia for the first time on August 29, 1774, singled out City Tavern for lavish praise. Indeed, to judge by John Adams's diary, the new hostelry on Second Street was the only thing about Philadelphia that made an impression that first day.

Adams and his traveling companions had been on the road since early morning, but "dirty and dusty and fatigued" as they were, they could not resist the Tavern, where, Adams wrote, they received a "fresh welcome," and "a supper . . . as elegant as ever was laid on a table." What time they sat down to eat he did not record, but it was eleven p.m. before they pushed back their chairs and called it a night, all of them, one gathers, departing amply fortified to face whatever might lay in store. For his part, Adams decided that here was the finest tavern in all America.

It was an endorsement few would have disputed, and it came from a man who dearly loved to eat, who all his life loved and appreciated good food, good drink, and good talk around a convivial table.

Philadelphia in the late eighteenth century was the largest, most prosperous city in America, the busiest port, and a cornucopia without equal. Nowhere could one find such bountiful evidence of American abundance; such quantities of fresh fruit and vegetables, fresh fish, meats, sausages, wild game, and cheeses on sale; or such a variety of "elegant" cooking. Delegates from the far-flung colonies, visitors from abroad—visitors of all kinds—marveled at the produce on display at the city's enormous central market. Twice weekly, on market days, German-speaking country people rolled into the city in huge wagons laden with produce, live chickens, ducks, and pigs. One signer of the Declaration of Independence, Stephen Hopkins of Rhode Island, counted seventy farm wagons on Market Street.

Arch Street looking west toward Third Street, with the Second Street Presbyterian Church (demolished in 1838) in mid-ground

In such an atmosphere, not surprisingly, minimalist cuisine was not the fashion. Dinner at City Tavern, or at any of the fine homes of Philadelphia, could include twenty or more different dishes, not counting dessert. As John Adams reported to his wife, Abigail, even "plain Quakers" served ducks, hams, chicken, and beef at a single sitting, while such desserts as served at the home of Mayor Samuel Powel on Third Street were dazzling—custards, flummery, jellies, trifles, whipped syllabubs, floating islands, fruits, nuts, everything imaginable.

But for the delegates to the Congress, City Tavern remained the great gathering place. It was there that Adams and George Washington first met. It was there that so many came and went, not yet figures in history, but flesh-and-blood human beings, let us never forget—Sam Adams, Richard Henry Lee, Patrick Henry, Jefferson, Franklin, Dr. Benjamin Rush. And here they made history, shaped much of the world we live in with what they said among themselves: Bargaining, politicking, speaking their minds, talking small things and large over the rattle of dishes and the steady hubbub of surrounding tables. Nothing of what was said was recorded. No artist is known to have sketched such scenes. Further, the original City Tavern is gone. The present City Tavern, on the same site, is

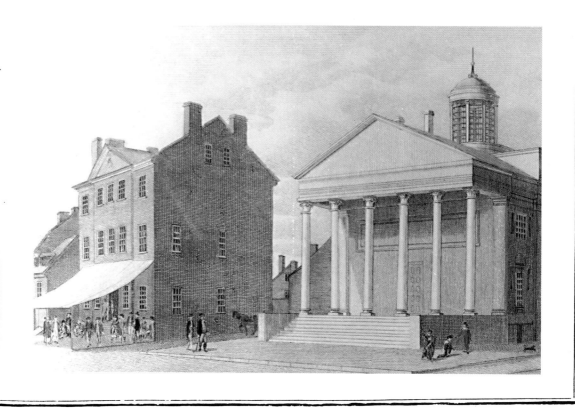

William Birch print of the Bank of Pennsylvania, with the City Tavern and The Three Crowns Tavern at left

an exact reproduction. Still, the feeling of entering another time is strong and appealing, and it makes a visit to City Tavern an essential experience for anyone with even a little interest in history—most especially when the food is served.

The great pull of the place is the same as long before, with the marvelous array of things to eat. Under the direction of chef/restaurateur Walter Staib, the offerings are never static, never routine, any more than in days of old, when the likes of Adams and Washington climbed the marble stairs to the front door. That this sumptuous cookbook contains no less than 200 tantalizing receipts certainly makes the point.

The founding era of America, now more than two centuries past, was a vastly different time from our own. The people, too, were different, and more so than generally understood. Yet it is possible to make contact with them as fellow human beings. We can enter their world, we can come to know them through the letters they wrote, their diaries, the books they read, their music, their architecture, the ways they worshipped, the poetry they loved and learned by heart, and yes, God be praised, by the food they ate.

Besides, with such a guide at hand as this wonderful volume, we are able now to enjoy such singular delights as they knew right in our own homes.

It is all well and good to read that in the eighteenth century the pleasures of the table ranked high among the pleasures of life, but it is quite another thing to savor the real fare itself. To dine as John Adams and his contemporaries once did at City Tavern is to be reminded of how full-flavored life at best must have been for them, and that they themselves, at their best, were anything but dull company.

DAVID McCULLOUGH

PREFACE

When I penned the *City Tavern Cookbook* and *City Tavern Baking & Dessert Cookbook*, I conducted a great deal of research on the cuisine and culinary customs of the eighteenth century. Surprisingly, there was a mountain of information—recipes, anecdotes about dining experiences in prominent homes, menus from the original City Tavern, and so on.

Since that time, my associations with prominent historians like David McCullough, conversations with other experts on the eighteenth century, like Susan Stein at Monticello, and many, many other books on the Founding Fathers have expanded my knowledge beyond what could be contained in those first two volumes. Consequently, I decided to combine both books into one comprehensive volume, add a few more recipes that didn't make the cut before, and include photography as an aid to the modern cook.

Many of the recipes herein were inspired by those in *The Art of Cooking Made Plain and Easy*, written by Hannah Glasse in 1745, along with recipes penned by the first First Lady in her circa 1753 cookbook, *Martha Washington's Booke of Cookery*. Although I strive to preserve the authentic nature of the colonial recipes we use, I have had to adapt some of them to modern tastes and equipment.

Gone are recipes that would have commonly appeared on eighteenth century tables, but would not appeal to the twenty-first century diner. In keeping with increased health awareness, animal fats such as lard and schmaltz have been replaced with healthier alternatives like vegetable oil and vegetable shortening. The sodium and sugar contents of nearly every recipe have also been greatly reduced.

With regard to the photography, I must make the reader aware that although we know that meals were served family-style in the eighteenth century City Tavern, we are still uncertain exactly how dishes would have been presented and served. Even though we used authentic cookware, cooking tools, dishes, and other props, the photos in this book show both family-style and individual platings that are in keeping with today's dining customs.

So how did a German become a custodian of eighteenth-century American culinary history? In 1979, I moved to Philadelphia, taking over as president for the Davre's restaurant chain owned by ARA services. In 1989, I started my culinary consulting business, Concepts By Staib, Ltd. I heard about the City Tavern's closing on New Year's Eve, 1992, and couldn't get the Tavern out of my mind. After inquiring with the National Park Service, which supervises the Tavern, I received a prospectus to apply for its operation. I couldn't believe the lifestyle and level of sophistication those early Philadelphians had. It quickly became clear to me that City Tavern had been, without a doubt, the greatest restaurant in eighteenth-century North America.

The more I learned about City Tavern and its special place in social, political, and gastronomic history, the more I started to believe in its potential. Realizing that, with the right management and cuisine, the Tavern could once again rival any restaurant in America, I began to feel like a culinary crusader, impassioned about keeping America's gastronomic heritage alive. I submitted a proposal.

The first hurdle in my quest to become the Tavern's operator—a process which took six months —was to win the approval of Congress. I was awarded the contract on April 15, 1994, and set about immediately undertaking extensive restorations to bring the Tavern back to its original elegance. The National Park Service's library and archives provided volumes of research material to assist me and my wife, Gloria, with this huge project.

Before we opened our doors on July fourth of that same year, we had completely renovated the kitchen, removed the freezers and the commercial laundry facility, and installed a pastry and bake shop. Independence Historical National Park chief curator, Karie Diethorn, worked closely with us to recreate the most authentic City Tavern experience possible, with slight adjustments to make room for the modern day context. The walls were painted in the Tavern's original colors, the rooms were decorated in reproduction furniture and fabrics, and we dressed our service staff in handmade eighteenth-century attire. We chose reproduction table settings, including candlesticks, plates with a china pattern based on one from 1793, and mid-eighteenth-century style lead-free pewterware for our tabletops. Even our glassware, which was imported from Italy or hand-blown by artisans in West Virginia, was selected to reflect styles used in the late eighteenth century. And for an authentic ambiance, we decided to commission colonial-period "characters" for special events, such as Thanksgiving, and to provide live harpsichord and Irish harp music on weekends.

As critical as the setting was, the most important thing for me as a chef was to work diligently on the food and dining experience. I was fortunate enough to have a head start—a few years earlier—as a consultant to a restaurant of the same period in Richmond, Virginia. There, I had researched colonial culinary and dining traditions with New York food historian Dr. Lorna Sass. It became my mission to recreate the culinary heritage of City Tavern, a one-of-a-kind dining institution.

This experience turned out to be a delightful awakening as I discovered how close to "home" eighteenth-century food was for me. Having grown up in the Old World, where everything was done the old-fashioned way, the original City Tavern recipes were comfortably familiar. Many of them could have come right from my own grandmother's kitchen. At a very young age, I spent a great deal of time in my uncle and aunt's restaurant, Gasthaus zum Buckenberg, complete with its own huge butcher shop. I started out doing odd jobs and was soon learning about food and developing cooking skills. My uncle Karl Hintze was a Master Confissier and Master Pâtissier in Pforzheim both at the Café Frei and at the Café Wagner, and my mother, Herta Staib, was a great baker and chef; the entire family had a passion for baking, cooking, and gardening. We made our own preserves, canned fruits and vegetables, baked our own breads and pastries—all of the techniques that mirrored what the early Americans did back in 1773.

In keeping with Old World tradition, my food philosophy for the Tavern continues to be "from the farm to the table, as fresh as possible." Accordingly, our produce is delivered two to three times a day, breads and pastries are baked each morning, and we use no walk-in freezers—our meats are delivered daily and marinated in the same manner as they were in the early colonial era.

This philosophy is also reflected in our beverage selection. Our beers and ales are custom-brewed for us by a local microbrewery, free of all preservatives and additives, and are served in traditional twenty-ounce British pints. City Tavern offers a unique selection of colonial shrubs, a beverage produced today in the same manner in which it was produced in the eighteenth century.

Thankfully, all our attention to detail has been rewarded with national and international press coverage. On June 29, 1994, days before we opened, City Tavern was the cover story, penned by Florence Fabricant, for the *New York Times Living Section*. That same year, John Mariani of *Esquire* magazine named City Tavern one of the best "new" restaurants in America, and we've continued to garner praise from food professionals and the public alike.

City Tavern is indeed more than a restaurant. It is a piece of history; a living culinary museum that offers diners an experience unavailable anywhere else—insight into America's vast and under-appreciated culinary heritage. I wrote this book to extend that experience to a larger audience, and to solidify City Tavern's place in American gastronomic history.

This collection of more than 200 recipes reflects the kind of food enjoyed by our country's Founding Fathers in the Tavern's heyday—which we faithfully recreate today.

I hope you enjoy this delicious lesson in our country's culinary history.

Cheers! Or as they would have said in colonial days, Huzzah!—a precursor of today's Hurrah!

WALTER STAIB,
CHEF/PROPRIETOR

A TASTE OF HISTORY

APPRECIATING THE EIGHTEENTH-CENTURY TAVERN

A tavern in colonial days was much more than a place to drink a pint of ale. In smaller towns and cities where there were no office buildings or convention centers, taverns met all these needs. Taverns were a town's central place of meeting, a place where stock and ship cargoes were bought and sold, new companies organized, notices posted, and newspapers from home and abroad perused. Taverns were social focal points as well, the place where dinners for fraternal societies were held, political causes championed, and dances and live music enjoyed. Taverns, like eighteenth-century coffee houses, served food and drink, but also offered lodging for visitors passing through the area. City Tavern was the finest tavern of its day, the grandest of all taverns in the New World.

EIGHTEENTH-CENTURY CUISINE: AMERICA'S ORIGINAL FUSION

THE UNINITIATED MAY IMAGINE that the American cuisine served at Philadelphia's original City Tavern in the 1700s was dull, flavorless, and limited. That assumption couldn't be further from the truth. In reality, the bustling nearby port brought a dizzying mix of ethnic groups into the city, each arriving with the culinary tradition of their own heritage. From the British came hearty stews and meat pies, along with scones and breads. The Germans offered their country's tradition of sausages, soups, and baked goods. African and West Indian slaves who arrived in the New World brought with them a food culture that included curries, hot peppers, and exotic spices and fruits.

The French Revolution and the slave rebellion in Hispaniola delivered an influx of French immigrants, among them pastry chefs, confectioners, and a multitude of other food artisans and tradesmen. It was this French influence that brought Philadelphia's cuisine up to European standards.

City Tavern, separated from the Delaware River by just a few short blocks, was a magnet for the ship captains who came to barter their cargo. Depending on the route the captain sailed, he might be offering Madeira from the island of the same name (used as ballast); oranges from Seville; port from Portugal; Nürnberg gingerbread, dried plums, and cherries from Germany; rum, pineapples, and mangoes from Jamaica; or spices from the Spice Islands. Ships arrived about three times a week from the West Indies. Since modern refrigeration did not exist, cargo had to be disposed of quickly before it spoiled, so most goods were auctioned—often at shipside—to eager innkeepers and caterers. Drying, salt curing, and pickling were used to preserve foods over time.

Philadelphia, then the largest city in the New World, and the second largest city in the British Empire, was home to open-air markets that offered the bounty of the area. The Delaware River was brimming with fish and oyster beds. The area's rich agricultural land produced an abundance of natural foods, including wild fruits and berries, game, wildfowl, maple syrup, and honey. From the Native Americans, settlers learned to cultivate corn, sweet potatoes, squash, beans, and wild rice. Local farms produced eggs as well as grains and flour.

This is the stuff of City Tavern's menu, today, as well as then: a cuisine that represents an unparalleled and authentic gourmet dining experience.

CITY TAVERN:
A PIVOTAL SITE IN AMERICAN HISTORY

THE YEAR IS 1774. Storm clouds of revolution were ominously forming in the New World. The people who would become this country's shapers and leaders, men like Thomas Jefferson, Benjamin Franklin, John Penn, and John Adams, were laying the foundation for a document that would become the backbone of a new society. These men spent hours together in heated discussion, arguing, defining, and detailing the basis for this emerging nation.

All of this talk didn't happen on an empty stomach. The food that fueled these intellectual architects was provided by Philadelphia's City Tavern.

Cargo ships at the Dock Street wharf

The "Le Cirque" of its day, modeled after the finest taverns in London, City Tavern was by all historical accounts considered the best restaurant in British North America. Opened in 1773 by fifty-three prominent Philadelphia businessmen and investors, including several signers of the Declaration of Independence, City Tavern was the setting for suppers "as elegant as was ever laid on a table," according to John Adams.

Yet, politics was the true main course on City Tavern's menu. Every Saturday, members of the Second Continental Congress would convene to dine on City Tavern fare. Eight delegates even formed their own "table," opting to frequent the Tavern on a daily basis. Despite such a glorious beginning, City Tavern fell out of favor with the Philadelphia elite in the early 1800s. After an ignoble end—the Tavern acted as a merchant's exchange before catching fire in 1834 and finally being razed in 1854—City Tavern remained a mere footnote in the history books for a century until it was rebuilt and finally reconstructed in its current, authentically beautiful state.

To understand the vigorous role that the Tavern played in eighteenth-century Philadelphia society, you really need to take a historical journey back in time. When City Tavern was conceived in 1772, the city's inns and taverns of the day were roughly hewn, serving primarily as meeting places for merchants to haggle over prices, tip pints of ale, and put up for the night.

The city's elite decided to take matters into their own hands. The original subscribers paid £25* per share to be charter members of the Tavern. Socially connected property owners, office holders, doctors, lawyers, and merchants were among charter members' ranks. Well traveled and schooled in London, these upper crust gents knew what they wanted, and went about getting it. Mixed among the more sober Quakers in the group were raconteurs and gamblers, men accustomed to high living, fine food, and wine. Collectively, the subscribers wanted a place to call their own.

A glance at the subscribers' ranks delivers a Who's Who of eighteenth-century Philadelphia. A few of the more well-known subscribers included Samuel Powel who later became mayor of Philadelphia; Thomas Mifflin, soon to be governor of Pennsylvania; Lt. Governor John Penn; and Samuel Meredith, acclaimed financier who worked tirelessly in government for more than twenty years.

*Translating the Tavern subscription cost into modern currency is challenging since dollars had not yet been "invented" at the time. However, the average laborer in 1762 annually earned £60, of which about £55 was used for food, housing, and other necessities; any colonist paying £25 for Tavern membership certainly lived comfortably. (Source: *Billy Smith's Philadelphia's Laboring People*)

City Tavern Trustee Henry Hill, patriot and Madeira wine importer, would also serve as trustee to Benjamin Franklin's estate when the great man died in 1790. George Clymer, a partner of Samuel Meredith, was among the first to advocate separation from Britain. John Wilcocks was perhaps the most public spirited of the group, serving as trustee of Bray Associates, which provided schooling for black children. John Nixon read the Declaration of Independence in public for the first time. Edward Shippen became a colonial chief justice of the Pennsylvania Supreme Court; Jared Ingersoll, Will Parr, and Benjamin Chew were lawyers and holders of public office. This group naturally sought to emulate the manners, interests, and style of living of their mother country—the Tavern fit perfectly into that picture.

The Tavern's location was prime—two short blocks from the port's wharves in one direction, two long blocks from the courthouse and markets in another, and fronting the city's main north/south thoroughfare, the "Old King's Road" with connections to all principal points.

The Tavern's design may have come from the subscribers themselves—many, including Hill and Powel, had studied architecture and even designed their own homes. It is certain that they networked among themselves and their friends to secure the finest workmanship available. Among the receipts of moneys paid to tradesmen during the building process was £5.12 to Martin Jugiez, a master carver who had also worked on the intricate carvings commissioned for Benjamin Franklin's house.

The Tavern's construction, which took just a year, was completed in November 1773, with the first recorded public event held on January 24, 1774. On that day, a meeting of the St. Georges' Society and the Society of Englishmen and Sons of Englishmen convened, societies established for the assistance of "Englishmen in distress," according to a notice in the *Pennsylvania Gazette*, the city's paper, published, coincidentally, by Benjamin Franklin.

Before City Tavern's arrival on the colonial scene, no place of public accommodation in America had assumed real distinction—the Tavern did for more than two decades. It was appropriate that City Tavern be built in Philadelphia—the colonial center for art, science, education, and commerce and boasting many paved streets lit with lamps, fine public buildings, three libraries, a college, and the first hospital in the New World. If you were active in public, civil, and military life during the Revolutionary period, you entered the Tavern's portals at one time or another. Despite its social status, it was not overpriced—one visitor in 1798 noted that City Tavern, although the "best in town, charges about the same price as the others."

Chestnut Street looking west from Front Street

Little is known about the first innkeeper, Daniel Smith, except that he was British and experienced at his trade. The tavern keeper of that day had to wear many hats, from overseeing the inn's physical upkeep and care to serving as room clerk, bookkeeper, and cashier.

Smith was the first of three innkeepers that tended to the Tavern during its heyday. During the Tavern's "Golden Age," where it was without peer and always at the center of the city's social and political activity, most occasions of note were held in the Long Room. These events included soirées held for heads of state, and more than one lavish dinner for General Washington, including the affair, complete with fireworks, held April 20, 1789, when Washington stopped in Philadelphia on his way to New York to be inaugurated President.

"No man can be a patriot on an empty stomach"
—WILLIAM COWPER BRANN (1855–1898)

IMPORTANT EVENTS HELD AT THE TAVERN

CITY TAVERN'S ROLE as the backdrop for the unfolding of American history is indisputable and well documented. When Paul Revere rode six days from Boston with news that the British had closed the port in retaliation for the famous tea party, he went directly to City Tavern to deliver the news. As the delegates of the first Continental Congress began to arrive in the Fall of 1774, they stopped first at City Tavern. In fact, when John Adams arrived in town, dusty and fatigued from the long ride, he went straight to the Tavern, "the most genteel one in America." George Washington did the same, not proceeding to his lodgings until first supping at City Tavern.

The delegates of the Continental Congress frequented the Tavern the entire time they were assembled, where they often conducted informal discussions outside of the more formal confines of Carpenters' Hall.

When the battles of Concord and Lexington were announced by a rider at City Tavern on April 24, 1775, it became the center of military activity during the war. As battles raged, the funerals of war heroes, such as Colonel John Haslet of Delaware and General Hugh Mercer, took place at the City Tavern, with full military honors.

In 1777, the nation's first Fourth of July celebration was held at the Tavern, "with festivity and ceremony becoming the occasion," according to John Adams. When Washington moved his headquarters to Philadelphia in August of the same year, his letters indicate that he used the Tavern as his informal headquarters—although he would not allow his troops entrance, for fear of their corruption.

When the British retook Philadelphia that fall, innkeeper Daniel Smith welcomed his countrymen with open arms—and an open till. The Tavern was commandeered as a center for officer recreation, including a series of balls where Philadelphia's Tory belles were entertained. The fun was not always so wholesome—record of a horse theft from in front of the Tavern was made in October 1777.

Soon after the Continental Army reoccupied Philadelphia in 1778, Smith returned to England. Gifford Dalley and then George Evans succeeded him as innkeepers. City Tavern once again hosted special events for the upper crust of America and abroad. During Dalley's tenure, the Coffee Room developed into an exchange room and seat of business. When the second Continental Congress convened, a series of dazzling balls and national affairs of state took place, often continuing until the wee hours of the morning. With the establishment of the new political order, Philadelphia was suddenly inundated by politicians needing entertainment, room, and board—exactly the kind of trade most restaurants pray for.

The most lavish party held at the Tavern was most likely the election and installation of the state's chief executive, the president of the Supreme Executive Council in 1778. A party of 270, including ambassadors and ministers of France and Spain, attended. The bill was £2995—only £500 of that for food. The rest was for a stupefying amount of alcohol, including 522 bottles of Madeira, 116 large bowls of punch, nine bottles of toddy, six bowls of sangria, twenty-four bottles of port, and two tubs of grog for artillery soldiers. Understandably, the party turned boisterous—the bill also covered ninety-six broken plates and glasses, as well as five decanters.

In 1785, the Tavern was sold to Samuel Powel, one of the original proprietors, the former mayor of the city and a man of great wealth and social standing. When thirty-nine delegates, representing twelve of the thirteen states, approved a constitution for the United States of America, on September 17, 1787, they then adjourned, according to the record, "to the City Tavern, dined together and took a cordial leave of each other."

From 1785 to 1824, City Tavern served primarily as a hotel, merchants' exchange, and coffee house. The merchants' exchange, a forerunner of the Philadelphia-Baltimore-Washington stock exchange of today, was a bustling center of industry, a lively place where sea captains, insurance salesmen, and farmers haggled and exchanged gossip. The Tavern's fortunes gradually declined in the early 1800s, and in 1834 its roof caught fire, damaging the Tavern irreparably. In 1854, when City Tavern was demolished, the *Pennsylvania Gazette* wrote, "... nobody is going to miss this Tavern except those persons living in the past."

City Tavern Rises Again in the Twentieth Century

FORTUNATELY, THAT PERIOD of the Tavern's obscurity ended when the U.S. Department of the Interior was authorized by the Truman Administration to create Independence National Historical Park, a surviving group of pivotal historic sites that formerly included City Tavern. Although that decision was made in 1948, it took more than twenty-five years of research to recreate the Tavern, brick by brick, according to historic documentation of the original structure. City Tavern finally opened in 1976, just in time for the country's bicentennial celebration.

While there are other restaurants on the Atlantic seaboard that attempt to recapture America's past, only City Tavern has faithfully revisited the high culinary standards of the day. City Tavern is clearly an American original, a restaurant famous both for its Revolutionary cuisine and its formidable place in our nation's history. This unique two-fold attraction appeals to tourists and locals alike and guarantees City Tavern a distinguished place in culinary history, both for its vibrant past and its utterly delicious present.

Touring the Tavern

IN 1975, AFTER PAINSTAKING RESEARCH, the National Park Service rebuilt City Tavern. Today, the Tavern appears essentially as it did 200 years ago, even down to the front awning, which shades the Tavern from the direct summer sun. Every year, 110,000 to 120,000 guests are drawn to City Tavern because of its reputation for fine, authentic colonial dining, as well as for its historic *élan*. At the Tavern, they enjoy a taste of the past in the same atmosphere of gentility and good cheer enjoyed by our nation's founders. Here's a quick "guided" tour through the seven dining and public rooms of this accurately reconstructed inn.

The original City Tavern was comprised of five levels. The cellar housed the kitchens; the first and second floors contained the public areas; the third floor was devoted to lodging rooms; and the attic probably served as servants' quarters. The first and second floors, which we will tour in detail here, were the heart of the Tavern's operation.

West Elevation   *East Elevation*

First Floor

As you walk up a set of marble stairs into the Tavern from Second Street, you first enter a long hallway. On your right is the Subscription Room, so-called because the magazines and newspapers, ships' manifests, and letters of decree to which the Tavern subscribed were located there.

Behind the Subscription Room is the Bar Room, with its high-backed wooden booths and central fireplace. Although it doesn't have a "bar" as we know them today, per se, it does have a narrow, closet-sized room that can accommodate the bartender and, of course, the liquor. It has a window and a Dutch door that doubles as a shelf, with a barred gate that slides down on top of it. In the 1700s, this was commonly used to separate the innkeeper and his liquor from the patrons. Since tempers and political arguments were often stoked by alcohol consumption, whenever the innkeeper felt threatened, he would lower and lock "the bar" to protect himself, thereby explaining the derivation of the modern-day term. Back then, the bar would have functioned as the Tavern's nerve center, where patrons would arrange to rent a room, order a meal, or hear the latest news.

Across the hallway from the Subscription Room is a Coffee Room. From the very beginning of the Tavern's history this Coffee Room was the place where merchants would discuss ship movements and other business over a cup of coffee or stronger drink—one reason why maps remain on the Coffee Room wall today.

The next door is a second Coffee Room that is representative of the Tavern's public dining spaces.

Back in the main hallway, to our left is the back door, which leads out to the porch and garden area, and doubled as the entrance for the gentry class en route to balls and private parties commonly held upstairs.

Second Floor

The stairs in the main hallway lead to the second floor. At the top of the stairs, straight through the hallway, is the Long Room—the scene of countless elegant balls, brilliant musical performances, large meetings, and card games. In fact, it was in the Long Room that Congress held the first Fourth of July celebration in 1777.

Adjoining the Long Room are two private dining rooms. Originally, these rooms would have accommodated clubs or groups desiring privacy. On the left at the top of the stairs, is the Cincinnati

Room (originally called the Northwest Dining Room), named in 1975 in honor of the Pennsylvania chapter for the Society of the Cincinnati, which helped refurbish this room. This organization is composed of direct descendants of the Revolutionary officers who founded the original Pennsylvania chapter at City Tavern in 1783.

Across the hallway is the Charter Room, named in honor of the fifty-three original Tavern subscribers and once reserved for their private use. This room also serves to honors the members of the national Home Fashions League, who contributed toward furnishing the present City Tavern.

Lower Level

The adaptation of City Tavern's cellar provides insight into the historical aspect of food storage, preparation, and service. From 1773 to 1848, the cellar served the vital purpose of being both a work and storage area. Fresh foodstuffs were delivered to the Second Street entrance. At the rear of the building, casks, barrels, and boxes were loaded into the cellar through the cobblestone alley. Because there was access to water pumps on the public street, this area also served for dishwashing.

The back cellar room was used for the long-term storage of bulk foodstuffs such as flour. The larder room located on the southeast corner was possibly used as a storeroom for prepared foods like pickled meat and preserved fruits. From the kitchen on the northeast corner, food was prepared and distributed.

In 1994, the cellar area was opened to the public for dining.

Main staircase to the second floor

CITY TAVERN, PHILADELPHIA. DANIEL SMITH begs leave to inform the PUBLIC, that the Gentlemen Proprietors of the CITY TAVERN have been pleased to approve of him, as a proper person to keep said tavern: in consequence of which he has completely furnished it, and, at a very great expence, has laid in every article of the first quality, perfectly in the stile of a London tavern. . . .

He has also fitted up a genteel Coffee Room, well attended, and properly supplied with English and American papers and magazines.

He hopes his attention and willingness to oblige, together with the goodness of his wines and larder, will give the public entire satisfaction, and prove him not unworthy of the encouragement he has already experienced.

The City Tavern in Philadelphia was erected at a great expence, by a voluntary subscription of the principal gentlemen of the city, for the convenience of the public, and is by much the largest and most elegant house occupied in that way in America.

—Pennsylvania Gazette,
February 16, 1774

INTRODUCTION

W hen City Tavern first opened in Philadelphia in December 1773, it was considered one of the most elegant establishments of its kind in colonial America. The city was growing rapidly in this period, becoming ever more cosmopolitan, wealthy, and politically significant, and its inhabitants and visitors required taverns to suit their social and mercantile needs. In 1756, there were already more than 120 taverns in Philadelphia (more than in New York or Boston). By the mid-1770s, surely even more taverns were needed to serve a city bursting with over twenty-one thousand residents (as many as in New York and four thousand more than in Boston). With the opening of City Tavern, genteel Philadelphians, for the first time, had a place to gather for business, social events, political meetings, and, of course, food and drink, otherwise known in the period as "entertainment." When proprietor Edward Moyston opened the first two front rooms of the City Tavern as a "Merchants' Coffee-House & Place of Exchange" in 1789, it became even more business oriented. Writing in the early 1790s, French visitor Moreau de St. Mery declared it "an extremely useful establishment." The rest of the building, however, remained virtually unchanged, continuing to serve patrons who desired food, drink, and lodging.

Although City Tavern altered and expanded during the nearly twenty years that it remained Philadelphia's most fashionable public house, the information offered in the above advertisement defined the unchanging essence of this establishment. Of course, the sale of food and drink was one among many services City Tavern offered Philadelphians. As one of the most important services, however, the quality of these "entertainments" was implied in the advertisement. Daniel Smith took pride in characterizing his establishment as being "perfectly in the stile of a London tavern"; he emphasized the "goodness of his wines and larder"; and, of course, he described it as "the largest and most elegant house...in America." How does this language relate to the dishes, particularly the desserts, served at City Tavern and in numerous Philadelphia dining rooms during the eighteenth century? It reveals that the sweet preparations were as cosmopolitan, abundant, and "elegant" as the city itself. Set amid the businesses, stores, confectioners' shops, and elite homes that populated the streets just blocks away from the waterfront, City Tavern catered to the fashionable tastes of its patrons, who could obtain the finest imported and prepared foods in shops and private dining rooms throughout Philadelphia. Like imported furniture, silver, ceramics, and so forth, foodstuffs from all over the world arrived daily at the city's ports, ready to be celebrated on fashionable tables. In the same way, just as European craftspeople brought their skills to the colonies and inspired American artisans, so did transplanted European confectioners and cooks not only serve welcoming Americans who patronized their shops and taverns, but also influenced those who cooked in Philadelphia kitchens.

At City Tavern, the sweet dishes served to merchants, Masonic societies, diplomats, and congressmen were much like those prepared in elite households. Seasonal and preserved fruits and vegetables, locally butchered meats and dairy products, fresh breads, nuts, and a wealth of imported spices and exotic ingredients were just some of the products Philadelphians enjoyed. Although tensions ran high between the British and the Americans during the 1770s and 1780s (most of City Tavern's heyday), the cakes, breads, puddings, sweetmeats, and so forth served there and in private homes were based on traditional English cookery. Most colonists could trace their roots back to England, after all, and best enjoyed the dishes with which they were most familiar. The popularity of English cookbooks in Philadelphia and other large cities during the eighteenth century is further testament to Americans' predilection for English cooking.

Although City Tavern served some of the most elegant dishes of the period, it nonetheless employed the frugality that was so admired and necessary during the period. Taverns in many large cities vied for patrons by emphasizing the quality of their "entertainments" in local advertisements. Yet, in the 1770s and 1780s, as the colonies prepared for and went to war with England, even the wealthiest of diners at least occasionally enjoyed simply prepared dishes at home as well as in public houses. On November 17, 1779, for example, a notice appeared in the *Pennsylvania Gazette* describing a governmental procession that was followed by a meal at City Tavern. It stated that only "a cold collation was provided, consistent with that frugality and economy which the situation of our public affairs not only renders necessary but honourable." It is unclear from the notice what time of day this meal took place, but "cold collations" (light meals) were usually served for supper or the evening meal.

An eighteenth—century sweet table

In the eighteenth century, frugality and preparedness were essential to managing a successful kitchen. Although food in Philadelphia was plentiful, households and public houses could not afford to waste it. If the dishes found on menus at City Tavern resembled those served in private Philadelphia homes, so were their methods of storing food similar. Root cellars were vital to the eighteenth-century kitchen. There, packed between layers of sand to keep them cool and, to some extent, out of the reach of vermin, vegetables and some fruits remained fresh during the fall and winter months. Drying, preserving, and pickling were additional methods of storing these items over long periods of time. Poured into ceramic jars and most often covered with paper, jams, preserves, conserves, jellies, and pickles were integral to well-stocked pantries. Households and public houses similarly maintained supplies of meats, which were salted, dried, or pickled, and stored in cellars, larders, or icehouses (Philadelphia having the good fortune of having an abundance of ice). Even butter and eggs could be kept fresh. Butter was generously salted and packed in casks between additional layers of salt or in brine, which were then stored in a cool place. Eggs were preserved with a coating of lime or wax and also kept in a cool storage space. With their skillful knowledge of food preservation and preparation, Philadelphia cooks were able to take full advantage of the city's abundant supply of local and imported ingredients.

If Philadelphia's primarily English character caused it to resemble other eighteenth-century colonial American cities, its general acceptance of other cultural groups made it unique. To be sure, mid- to late-eighteenth-century Philadelphia experienced a veritable acculturation, whereby such groups as the Dutch, Swedes, Irish, Jews, French, and Germans influenced the daily life of this cosmopolitan center. Within this climate of cultural diversity, Philadelphians were exposed not only to a variety of social mores but also to traditions, many of which included foodways. That many kinds of sweet dishes—from gingerbread to crème brûlée to linzertorte to ice cream—were available in eighteenth-century Philadelphia seems obvious today. Yet, only when one understands the degree to which diverse peoples shaped the city is it possible to truly appreciate how their foods became popularized and were incorporated into the culture that was cosmopolitan Philadelphia.

During their travels to the city, many European visitors kept journals in which they described the cultural diversity they witnessed. Writing in the 1790s, Moreau de St. Mery declared of Philadelphia's Caucasian men, "They are made up of English, Scotch, Irish and all the nationalities of Europe." The city, in fact, reflected Americans around the country, who, St. Mery explained, "have extremely diversified European ancestors." Writing in his journal nearly fifty years before St. Mery, Dr. Alexander Hamilton similarly described Philadelphia's eclectic cultural landscape. In 1739, Hamilton left his native Scotland to practice medicine in Annapolis, Maryland. Then, on May 30, 1744, due to health reasons and his interest in the colonies, he began a journey that took him to Maine and then back to Maryland. On Friday, June 8, Dr. Hamilton wrote of dining at a Philadelphia tavern, where he experienced not only the cultural but also the religious diversity of its patrons:

> *I dined att a taveren with a very mixed company of different nations and religions. There were Scots, English, Dutch, Germans, and Irish; there were Roman Catholicks, Church men, Presbyterians, Quakers, Newlightmen, Methodists, Seventh day men, Moravians, Anabaptists, and one Jew. The whole company consisted of 25 planted round an oblong table in a great hall well stoked with flys.*

As they wrote about the city's cultural diversity, many visitors to Philadelphia particularly emphasized the large size of the German community. In addition to the English, Welsh, Irish, and Scots, the Germans were some of the earliest settlers in Pennsylvania, and their numbers continued to increase throughout the eighteenth century. The German community was large outside of the city, but it maintained a strong presence in Philadelphia as well. In June of 1744, Dr. Hamilton wrote in his journal, "The Germans and High Dutch are of late become very numerous here." While visiting Philadelphia in 1765, Scottish traveler Lord Adam Gordon similarly explained in his journal, "The Germans in this province are not under 60,000." Some fifty years later, Moreau de St. Méry expressed similar thoughts. "The population includes many foreigners, especially Germans," he wrote. "Above Third Street in Northern Liberties, as I have said before, there are only Germans. Their peaceful character, their love of work, the similarity of their language to English, which easily lets them understand and be understood—all these things bring them in great numbers to the American continent." As Germans farmed the land and opened businesses in the city, they maintained many of their traditions, including their foodways, which undoubtedly profoundly influenced the food culture of Philadelphia.

Next to the Germans, it was arguably the stylishness, attitudes, and traditions of the French that most colored Philadelphians' way of life. This particularly occurred when France entered the Revolution in 1778. As late as the 1790s, however, Moreau de St. Méry believed, "The misfortunes existing in the colonies have also brought many French to Philadelphia. Twenty-five thousand are estimated to have sought refuge in the United States." As large numbers of French travelers, émigrés, and diplomats passed through and settled in the city, Philadelphians became ever more inspired by their social mores and sense of fashion. The degree to which people were influenced by the French and other cultures was apparent not only in the way they dressed and behaved but also in their ability to communicate with foreigners. While most Philadelphians probably learned German and French out of necessity and convenience, proficiency in the latter was also a sign of gentility. German and French émigrés had little choice; they needed to learn English. It is thus most appropriate that, in the 1780s, a language school opened across the street from City Tavern—the most cosmopolitan and elegant establishment of its kind in the city. The instructor, Mr. Becker, clearly saw a need for such courses and listed the following advertisement in the *Pennsylvania Gazette*:

February 7, 1781…HENRY BECKER, Living Second street, opposite the City Tavern, proposes to wait upon those LADIES and GENTLEMEN that intend to learn the FRENCH, GERMAN AND ENGLISH LANGUAGES, At their respective Houses, any hour of the day, on the most reasonable terms.

N. B. An EVENING SCHOOL will, be opened by said Becker, at his Lodgings, for those that it will not suit to attend in the Day.

Philadelphians expressed their admiration of French culture in many ways. They not only learned the language and adopted various polite French mannerisms but also came to appreciate and desire French foods. Thomas Jefferson was undoubtedly one of the greatest proponents of French cuisine, and, after his term in Paris as Minister Plenipotentiary to the Court of Louis XVI from 1784 to 1788, Americans became more familiar with it than ever before. Before and after the Revolution, they were exposed to many French foods, from wine to cheese to ice cream. One can only imagine the influence that French confectioners, bakers, and chocolatiers had in Philadelphia, as they opened shops to discriminating patrons eager to partake of fashionable delicacies.

French culture was seductive—so much so that even English cookbook author Eliza Smith, writing from London in the early eighteenth century, included French recipes in her otherwise English cookbook, which she wrote "in such a Manner as is most agreeable to English Palates." Sensitive to the animosity that had long existed between England and France and, yet, aware of the British taste for French style, she explained, "I have so far temporized, as, since we have, to our Disgrace, so fondly admired the French tongue, French Modes, and also French Messes, to present you now and then with such Receipts of the French Cookery as I think may not be disagreeable to English Palates."

By the late 1770s, French culture was colorfully influencing daily life in Philadelphia. Local diarists referred to it frequently. On May 3, 1783, young Philadelphia socialite Nancy Shippen described her preparation earlier in the day for a party that took place that evening—one that importantly called for French fashion:

10 o'clock at night—Spent a most delightfull Eveng at Mrs. Powells. I heard in the Morning there was to be a very large Company.—I spent great part of the day in making preparation—I wish'd to look well. Sett off about six oclock —my glass told me I look'd well—was dressed in pink with a gause peticoat —an Elegant french Hat on, with five white plumes nodding different ways—[and] a bouquet of natural flowers.

Another prominent Philadelphian, Elizabeth Drinker, also frequently remarked in her diary upon the French people and events she encountered in the city. Referring to Philadelphia's feting of the recently born Dauphin, on June 15, 1782, she wrote, "Great doings this evening at the French Ambassadors, (who lives at John Dickinsons House up Chesnut Street) on account of the Birth of the Dauphine of France—feasting fire-Works &c, for which they have been preparing for some weeks."

Ironically, while Philadelphians prided themselves on incorporating such things as French mores and foodways into their daily lives, many French visitors chastised them, and Americans in general, for their inferiorities. Among the dining practices they encountered, the French generally found Americans' large consumption of tea ridiculous. Monsieur Roux was one of the many who wrote scathingly of the "immoderate use of tea and coffee at all repasts." The French also believed Americans ate too frequently. Monsieur Chastellux, commenting on dining with a Mr. Brick in Boston, remarked that "supper was served exactly four hours after we had risen from the table. It can be easily imagined that we took practically nothing. Nevertheless, the Americans did very well at it. In general they eat less than we during a single meal, but they eat as often as they wish—a custom which I consider very bad." And the French found foolish Americans' desire to eat copious amounts of meat and small amounts of, what they considered to be, poor quality bread. "They [Americans] eat seven or eight times as much meat as bread," wrote St. Méry, and while the French often complimented the meals they ate in the colonies, they thought little of the bread offered to them. Monsieur de Bourg commented, "Their only grain is Indian corn, which accounts for their eating only that kind of bread—the meanest and worst in the world."

Although this was hardly the case, such a criticism was a common one. Monsieur Revel remarked that some Americans looked unhealthy. "It is possible that their food is partly to blame," he suggested, "for they not only eat no bread, but there are some of them who never even heard of it. They make a sort of biscuit on the hot cinders with corn meal, which they cultivate in great quantities." Some of the worst attacks came from a Monsieur Robin, who not only attributed Americans' physical ailments to the paucity of quality bread, but claimed that American bread could not even satisfy French troops:

> [T]he women, generally very pretty, are often deprived of these precious ornaments (teeth) at eighteen or twenty years of age.... I presume this to be the effect of hot bread.... [Americans], who have such fine wheat, nevertheless do not know the precious art of making it more digestible by kneading and fermentation. Whenever it is required they make a cake which they put to half-cook on an iron plate; the French who went to war in America could not become accustomed to it, and taught them to improve on it a little. It is to be found passable in the inns, but still very inferior to that of our Army.

Despite such criticism, however, the French did offer some compliments. Most referred to Americans' cleanliness, the abundance of food in America, and how well Americans provided for themselves. Monsieur Brissot found that American "kitchens are kept clean, and do not give out the disgusting smell to be found in the best kitchens of France. The dining rooms, which are generally on the ground floor, are also clean and well aired; cleanliness and fresh air is to be found everywhere." Furthermore, with poverty ever increasing in Europe, French visitors were startled at the veritable lack of want in America. Monsieur Beaujour was adamant on this point:

> It must be remarked that the poorest individual, the ordinary day-laborer, is better fed and clad here than in any other country. Every day of their lives they eat more in the United States than in France, and that too of expensive things, and those which elsewhere are considered luxuries. They calculate (based on the receipts of the Custom House) that each man consumes annually ten pounds of sugar, two and a half of coffee, one of tea and about fifteen of molasses.

The many cultures that lived and thrived together in Philadelphia profoundly influenced one another in multiple ways. This diversity gave rise to many shared traditions, one of the most important of which was cookery. Through food, each culture maintained its unique identity while at the same time it inspired others. The continuous arrival of European immigrants, as well as the constant importation of goods from Europe and the Caribbean, exposed Philadelphians to new and exotic foods, which they then incorporated into their own traditional recipes.

An eighteenth-century kitchen

Food in general was important to eighteenth-century Philadelphians, but they arguably revered the preparation of sweet dishes and baked goods in a unique way. As they were in Europe, not only did sweetmeats, cakes, breads, preserves, and the like demand a lot of time and skill to prepare, but the ingredients were very costly as well. Sugar was, for many people, a luxury throughout the eighteenth century; hence the popularity of less expensive maple syrup and molasses in the period. The processes of purchasing, grinding, cooking, and removing the impurities from sugar were also time-consuming. Indeed, if families could afford to do so, they often purchased baked goods and confections from nearby shops.

Although period cookbook authors often encouraged readers to purchase various ingredients or finished dishes in order to save time and money, it is clear that Philadelphians, like their European neighbors, admired the skill required to prepare baked goods and sweet dishes at home. Nearly all households had domestic help; sometimes a woman relied on the abilities of her cook, while at other times she prepared baked goods and other such dishes herself, desirous of displaying her own skills. In many diaries of this period, Philadelphia girls and women recounted such activities as preparing pastry, sweetmeats, and preserving fruit, thus revealing that these were among the most celebrated and important of cooking skills. Eighteenth-century advertisements further emphasize this. On June 4, 1767, Mary McCallister appealed "To the LADIES or [of] PENNSYLVANIA, and the adjacent Provinces" in an advertisement she listed in the *Pennsylvania Gazette*. She detailed her plans to open a boarding school in Philadelphia, where she would teach such classes as:

> *Literature…the English and French Languages, with their proper Accent and Emphasis; Needle Work in Silks, Worsted and Linens.…[T]he Arts of Painting on Glass, Japanning with Prints, Wax and Shell Work…Writing, Arithmetic, Music, or Dancing.…[And] I likewise intend, on a certain Day in every Week, to instruct the Ladies in Pastry, with some other beneficial and amusing Articles, too tedious to mention.*

It is clear that learning how to make proper pastry and "other beneficial…Articles" was as important to a girl's development and to her becoming an accomplished woman as were other artistic endeavors, such as learning a language, needlework, painting, or playing an instrument.

Other advertisements reveal that even though women who managed their households were skilled in the kitchen, they sought domestics who were also knowledgeable about cookery. Women considered trained help highly desirable, as they required little supervision. The woman who listed an advertisement with the *Pennsylvania Gazette* on September 17, 1767, was surely aware of her appealing qualifications. "WANTS a PLACE, in a genteel Family," she wrote, "who is capable of . . . Pastry, in the genteelist Manner; [and] can preserve and pickle." She also added, "She has lived in some of the best Families in London, and in this Country, in that Station"—experiences that would certainly have pleased a Philadelphia family interested in emulating fashionable styles of dining. Yet another advertisement might have appealed to a household or shop owner. On August 5, 1772, the *Pennsylvania Gazette* listed the services of "A LIKELY NEGROE FELLOW, about 23 Years old, has had the Smallpox, can cook, and do all Kinds of Housework, is thoroughly acquainted with the Chocolate Manufactory, in all its Branches." Certainly this man would have been suited to work in one of the city's many chocolate shops, but it is possible he could have been hired to cook for a family as well. These advertisements are significant, as they reveal the sorts of culinary skills Philadelphians most valued.

When City Tavern opened to the public, Philadelphia was already a cosmopolitan city and becoming ever more so. Despite its economic difficulties during the Revolution, Philadelphia saw significant growth in many industries and occupations, especially in the last decades of the century. Food-related businesses experienced this as much as any other. Among the many that existed by 1790, the city had 114 bakers, 26 biscuit bakers, 11 sugar refiners, 9 chocolate makers, 7 sugar bakers, 5 pastry cooks, and 3 cake bakers. City residents were virtually surrounded by culinary artisans, eager to provide their goods and services. In this environment of elegant dining, locally grown and imported foodstuffs, and fashionable taste, City Tavern provided Philadelphians with new dining and socializing experiences. The colonies saw much change in the late eighteenth century, but Philadelphia's City Tavern set standards that public houses up and down the East Coast continued to emulate well into the nineteenth century.

APPETIZERS

I have elected to arrange the chapters of this book in a manner that is more comprehensible to the modern diner—appetizers, soups, salads, main courses, and desserts. Appetizers would have been a foreign concept to colonial diners at City Tavern, rather, they would have been included in what were called the First Plates.

To better understand this seemingly foreign arrangement, one must understand that *service à la francaise*, or French service, was the principal dining style at City Tavern and in the most wealthy, elegant households of the time. Depending on the occasion, two to four courses were served, each course consisting of up to twenty-four dishes laid out around a centerpiece. Items were arranged symmetrically and according to height and importance. Roasts lay on large platters and full soup tureens stood at the ready. At more intimate dinners, the host and hostess would carve the roast and fill soup bowls for their guests. At Monticello, where elaborate but informal dinners were *de rigeur*, guests often helped move the plates from the dumbwaiter to the table, then helped themselves.

So complicated are some renderings of these arrangements, that one wonders whether the cook was an architect as well! In some cases, architects were in fact engaged to lay out the plans, furniture makers were hired to build impressively-shaped tables, and specialty china pieces were commissioned for just the right look.

When all the guests were finished, everything was removed from the table and the table cloth taken up to reveal another table cloth below. Then the process began anew with the second plates and, in some cases, third plates. During dinner, the beverages of choice were typically ale and cider. Wine was drunk only after dinner, when the final tablecloth had been removed and the sweetmeats set up in the same fashion on a separate sweet table.

In *The Art of Cookery Made Plain and Easy*, Hannah Glasse suggests the following first course in her "modern Bill of Fare" for the month of January:

Chestnut Soup, Small Leg of House Lamb, Petit Patties, Boiled Chickens, Chicken and Veal Pie, Cod's Head, Tongue, Rabbits smothered with Onions, Raisolds, Porcupine Beef and Vermicelli Soup.

The working eighteenth–century kitchen at Pamona Hall

Crab Cakes
with Herb Rémoulade

5 tablespoons unsalted butter

½ small onion, finely chopped

¼ green bell pepper, finely chopped

¼ red bell pepper, finely chopped

2 pounds jumbo lump crab meat

½ cup fine dry bread crumbs

¼ cup Homemade Mayonnaise
(page 370)

2 eggs, lightly beaten

2 tablespoons fresh lemon juice
(about 1 small lemon)

½ teaspoon hot sauce

2 teaspoons salt

1 teaspoon freshly ground white pepper

RÉMOULADE

1 small onion, chopped

1 whole kosher dill pickle, chopped

1 bunch fresh basil, stemmed and
chopped (about ½ cup)

½ bunch fresh dill, stemmed and chopped
(about 2 tablespoons)

½ bunch fresh parsley, stemmed
(about 3 tablespoons)

1½ cups Homemade Mayonnaise
(page 370)

2 tablespoons fresh lemon juice
(about 1 small lemon)

1 teaspoon small capers, drained

½ teaspoon Dijon mustard

¼ teaspoon hot sauce

Salt and freshly ground black pepper

Lemon wedges and kale,
for optional garnish

C rab, like lobster, was so plentiful in the New World that it was used as bait and prepared in all manner of dishes, including crab cakes, crab soup, and crab stuffing. Most recipes similar to modern crab cakes called for the crab to be mixed with vegetables and bread crumbs, then stuffed back into the crab shell and roasted over an open fire. Understanding the difficulty this would pose to modern chefs, the recipe has been amended to this more familiar preparation.

MAKES 12 TO 15 CAKES, 2 CUPS RÉMOULADE;
SERVES 4 TO 6

PREPARE THE CRAB CAKES: Heat 1 tablespoon of the butter in a small skillet, add the onion and bell peppers, and sauté for 5 minutes, until soft and translucent and any liquid they release has evaporated. Set aside and let cool completely.

Pick over the crab meat to discard any cartilage and pieces of shell. Transfer the crab meat to a medium-size mixing bowl. Add the cooked onion and bell peppers, the bread crumbs, mayonnaise, eggs, lemon juice, hot sauce, salt, and pepper. Mix well. Shape the mixture into 12 to 15 (2-inch) round cakes. Place the crab cakes on a large baking sheet. Cover and refrigerate for 2 hours to allow the crab cakes to firm.

PREPARE THE RÉMOULADE: In a food processor bowl, purée the onion, pickle, and fresh herbs. Transfer purée to a medium-size mixing bowl. Add the mayonnaise, lemon juice, capers, mustard, and hot sauce. Mix well. Season with salt and pepper to taste. Cover with plastic wrap and refrigerate until chilled (about 2 hours). Will keep in the refrigerator for up to 3 days.

When ready to serve the crab cakes, preheat the oven to 350°F.

Heat the remaining 4 tablespoons of butter in a large skillet over medium heat. Place the crab cakes in the skillet with space between each and cook until golden brown on each side.

Transfer the crab cakes to a baking sheet and bake them for 10 to 15 minutes, until crisp.

Serve with Herb Rémoulade and garnish with lemon wedges and kale, if desired.

Cornmeal Fried Oysters
with Herb Rémoulade

T he rivers around Philadelphia teemed with oysters, making them quite possibly the greatest staple of the eighteenth-century diet. The earliest cookbooks, including Martha Washington's *Booke of Cookery*, were full of oyster recipes, from stuffings for fowl to easy starters like this one. Cornmeal, a plentiful and a common ingredient of the day, was used for skillet breads, stuffings, and breading seafood, including oysters.

SERVES 4 TO 6, WITH 2 CUPS RÉMOULADE

Place the flour, eggs, and cornmeal in separate dishes. Dip each oyster, first into the flour, then the eggs, then the cornmeal to evenly coat. Place the coated oysters on a baking sheet and refrigerate until ready to fry.

Pour the oil into a deep-fat fryer or 4-quart heavy saucepan. Heat the oil over high heat to 350°F (if you drop a small amount of the cornmeal mixture into the oil and it sizzles, it's hot enough). To prevent the coated oysters from sticking together, carefully drop them into the heated oil one at a time. Fry the oysters, a few at a time, for 2 minutes, until golden. Using a slotted spoon, remove the oysters from the oil and place them on a baking sheet lined with paper towels to absorb any excess oil.

To serve, arrange the oysters on individual plates and serve with the Herb Rémoulade.

Garnish with the lemon wedges.

½ cup all-purpose flour

4 eggs, lightly beaten

1½ cups yellow cornmeal

24 extra-large Bluepoint oysters, shucked (see Chef's Note)

1 quart vegetable oil, for frying

Herb Rémoulade (page 44)

Lemon wedges, for garnish

CHEF'S NOTE

Oysters can be tricky to open; doing so safely requires a special glove, a special knife, and a practiced hand. I recommend buying oysters already shucked from your favorite fishmonger.

Chestnut Fritters

In colonial times, it was generally believed that American chestnuts were sweeter and of a higher quality than their European cousins. Yet another free food that literally grew on trees and seemingly fell from the sky in abundance, chestnuts were used equally abundantly by colonial cooks who prized them for their ability to last through the winter. While they were chiefly featured in sweet dishes and desserts, they were also commonly used in savory preparations, like soups, stews and stuffings.

Advance preparation required.

SERVES 8

Preheat the oven to 450°F.

With the point of a small paring knife, make a crisscross cut through the flat side of each chestnut and place them on a baking sheet. Bake for 35 minutes.

Let the chestnuts cool, then peel and chop them finely. Set aside.

Heat 1½ tablespoons of the butter in a small skillet over medium heat, add the shallots and cook for 2 minutes, until golden brown.

In a large mixing bowl, combine the cooked shallots, the chopped bacon, parsley, five-spice powder, coriander, and salt and pepper to taste. Add the chopped chestnuts. Process until fine in a food processor.

Cut each slice of bacon in half and lay the halves on your workspace, overlapping to make an X. Place two tablespoons of the shallot mixture in the center of each bacon X and fold the ends over the center to enclose the filling.

Flatten each fritter with the palm of your hand, then place them on a baking sheet. Cover with plastic wrap and refrigerate for 10 to 20 minutes.

Preheat the oven to 375°F.

Heat the remaining 6½ tablespoons of butter and the oil in a large sauté pan over medium heat. Place the fritters ¼ inch apart in the skillet and cook for 2 minutes on each side, until golden and crisp.

Transfer the fritters to a baking sheet. Bake for 5 to 10 minutes.

To serve, sprinkle the fritters with the chives and a generous amount of black pepper. Garnish with the watercress.

1½ pound chestnuts (about 27)

¼ pound (1 stick) unsalted butter

4 shallots, chopped

2 pounds lean raw bacon,
finely chopped

1 bunch fresh parsley, chopped
(about 6 tablespoons)

1 teaspoon five-spice powder

Pinch of ground coriander

Salt and freshly ground black pepper

16 slices lean raw bacon

3 tablespoons vegetable oil

1 bunch fresh chives,
finely chopped (about 6 tablespoons),
for garnish

4 sprigs fresh watercress,
for garnish

Smoked Brook Trout
on Potato Pancakes

4 medium red skinned potatoes, peeled

1 cup all-purpose flour

1 cup whole milk

2 eggs

10 tablespoons unsalted butter

1 teaspoon chopped fresh parsley

1 teaspoon salt

½ teaspoon freshly ground black pepper

½ cup mayonnaise

1 teaspoon freshly grated horseradish
(see Chef's Note)

2 pounds smoked brook trout

Chopped parsley, for garnish

Dill sprigs, for garnish

In addition to pickling, smoking was one of the most popular methods of preservation available to colonists. Rocky streams that meandered through the countryside offered an abundant supply of trout, so it rapidly became a common sight on early American dinner tables. Pairing smoked fish with potato pancakes is a Southern German tradition that made its way to the colonies with some of the very first German settlers. Different from the potato-only pancakes made in Northern Germany, this recipe incorporates flour. The same recipe is still made today in the Pennsylvania Dutch and Amish communities in Lancaster, Pennsylvania.

SERVES 4 TO 6

Place the potatoes in a large saucepan filled with lightly salted water, bring to a boil over high heat, and boil until the potatoes are just tender, about 15 minutes. Drain the potatoes and set them aside to cool slightly.

To make the pancakes, combine the flour, milk, eggs, 8 tablespoons of the butter, parsley, salt, and pepper in a medium-size mixing bowl and whisk until there are no lumps. Grate the potatoes into the batter and mix to combine.

To make the pancakes, heat a large nonstick skillet over medium heat. Add 1 teaspoon of the butter to coat the pan and spoon 1 tablespoon of the batter into the skillet for each pancake. Space them out about ¼-inch apart. Cook for 2 minutes on each side, until brown. Repeat with the remaining butter and batter. Transfer the pancakes to a plate and keep warm in a 275°F oven.

In a small mixing bowl, stir together the mayonnaise and horseradish.

Place a dollop of the mayonnaise-horseradish mixture on top of each pancake and top with a piece of trout. Garnish each pancake with a sprig of dill. Serve immediately.

CHEF'S NOTE

You may also use prepared horseradish in this recipe. Place 2 teaspoons in a cheese-cloth or clean towel and squeeze out the excess liquid before incorporating it into the mayonnaise.

Welsh Rabbit

Interestingly, Welsh rabbit contains absolutely no rabbit. Among poor people in England, who couldn't afford regular cuts of meat, rabbit became the meat of choice because it could be hunted or trapped in the vast forests owned by the nobility. Legend has it that the Welsh were not even allowed to catch rabbits on noble lands, so cheese became their version of rabbit. Hence, the name Welsh rabbit came into existence. Nowadays, we see this dish referred to as Welsh Rarebit, which came about as an attempt to explain away the lack of rabbit.

SERVES 6

Preheat the oven to 350°F.

Slice the baguette on a bias into ¼-inch-thick slices and place them on a baking sheet. Bake until slightly golden, about 5 to 8 minutes. Remove from the oven and let cool.

Preheat the broiler.

In a small mixing bowl, combine the cheese, beer, paprika, salt, and pepper to make a slightly moist mixture. Mound the mixture on top of each bread slice and place under the broiler, until melted.

To serve, place on a large serving platter and garnish with the parsley.

1 French Baguette (page 320)

1 pound Cheddar cheese, shredded

2 ounces porter or other dark beer

Pinch of paprika

Pinch of salt

Pinch of white pepper

1 small bunch fresh parsley

Basil Shrimp

———◆———

Shrimp was in abundance in the New World and was often grilled on skewers over an open fire. This recipe uses fresh basil, an ingredient that would only have been available during the eighteenth century from a summer garden.

As Culinary Ambassador to the City of Philadelphia and Commonwealth of Pennsylvania, I have had many occasions to break bread with former Philadelphia Mayor and current Pennsylvania Governor, Edward G. Rendell, a man who really loves to eat. Every time he visits City Tavern he requests this dish—it's his favorite, and he can easily finish a dozen shrimp in one sitting.

MAKES 16 SHRIMP; SERVES 4

Preheat the oven to 375°F.

To butterfly the shrimp, make a deep slit along the back of each, not all the way through. Rinse the shrimp; pat dry. Place one basil leaf inside the slit in each shrimp. Wrap a slice of bacon around each shrimp and secure with a toothpick.

In a medium-size stockpot or saucepan, heat the oil over high heat to 350°F. When the oil is hot, carefully add the shrimp a few at a time. Deep-fry them for 2 to 3 minutes, until crisp.

Using a slotted spoon, remove the shrimp from the oil and place on a tray lined with paper towels to absorb any excess oil.

In an ovenproof skillet, combine the barbecue sauce, horseradish, and hot sauce. Add the shrimp and heat in the oven for 5 minutes, basting the shrimp often, until the shrimp is heated through.

Serve on a platter garnished with lemon wedges and extra basil leaves.

16 jumbo shrimp (thawed if frozen), peeled and deveined

16 fresh basil leaves (preferably purple), plus more for garnish

16 slices applewood-smoked bacon (see Resources, page 378) or regular bacon

16 flavorless wooden toothpicks

2 cups vegetable oil

12 ounces barbecue sauce

4 teaspoons grated horseradish

2 dashes hot sauce

Lemon wedges, for garnish

Fried Asparagus

1½ pounds asparagus,
stems peeled and trimmed

2¼ cups all-purpose flour

3 eggs, beaten

1¼ cups whole milk

1½ tablespoons clarified butter
(see Chef's Note) or olive oil

⅛ teaspoon freshly grated nutmeg

⅛ teaspoon salt

⅛ teaspoon freshly ground
white pepper

4 cups vegetable oil, for frying

Herb Rémoulade (page 44)

In Thomas Jefferson's notes for the President's House, he mentions instructions for frying asparagus, but they are included in the list of desserts. Although no exact recipe survives, surely asparagus would have been served as a first or second course dish at Monticello, as Jefferson mentions numerous plantings of asparagus between 1767 and 1816 in his *Garden Book*. Asparagus was quite a common vegetable in colonial times, given its relatively short growing time. On March 27, 1794, Jefferson notes "The first plant of asparagus up." Less than one week later, on April 8, he enjoys "our first dish of Asparagus."

Serves 6

In a large saucepan, bring 2 quarts of lightly salted water to a boil over high heat. Place the asparagus in the water and cook until just tender, about 2 to 3 minutes.

Drain. Add enough cold water to cover the asparagus. Let stand for about 5 minutes, until the asparagus is cool. Drain again, and pat the asparagus dry with towels.

In a large mixing bowl, whisk together the flour, eggs, milk, clarified butter, nutmeg, salt, and pepper.

Heat the oil in a deep-fat fryer or 4-quart heavy saucepan over high heat to 350°F.

Dip the asparagus in the batter, shaking off any excess, then carefully drop them into the heated oil a few stalks at a time. Fry until golden brown. Using a slotted spoon remove the asparagus from the oil and place on a baking sheet lined with paper towels to absorb any excess oil.

Serve the asparagus on a platter with the Herb Rémoulade on the side.

CHEF'S NOTE

Clarified butter (also called drawn butter or *ghee*) is easy to prepare. Because it is free of milk solids, it has a higher smoking point than regular butter (meaning it doesn't burn as quickly), has a longer shelf life, and a lighter flavor. To prepare it, slowly melt unsalted butter in a saucepan and gently simmer until the white milk solids have sunk to the bottom of the pan and the clear, clarified butter remains on top. Skim any foam that rises to the surface, carefully pour the clarified butter into a jar, and store in the refrigerator.

Vol-au-Vent
with Sweetbreads

T his sweetbread recipe is an exact copy of Hannah Glasse's "A Third Way of Making a White Fricassee," which is intended for chicken. However, a follow up recipe, "To fricassee Rabbits, Lamb, Sweetbreads, or Tripe" suggests "Do them in the same way." Although her recipe is not served in a vol-au-vent, fricassees and stews were occasionally served in vol-au-vents, as evidenced by Martha Washington's recipe "To Make Puff Kids," which she suggests using for "pasties, dishes and patty pans." According to the *Old English Dictionary*, the word "kids" refers to a pannier, or basket, indicating that what Martha made was what we now call a vol-au-vent.

SERVES 8

TO MAKE THE VOL-AU-VENT: Roll out one puff pastry sheet to about ⅛ inch thick, dock (prick) it all over using the tines of a fork, and cut the pastry into 8 rounds, using a 4-inch round cutter. (Alternatively, turn a 4-inch-diameter bowl upside down on the pastry and cut around the rim using a paring knife.) Arrange the rounds on a parchment paper–lined baking sheet, and reserve in the refrigerator.

Roll out a second sheet of puff pastry to about ½ inch thick, and cut out 8 more 4-inch rounds. Using a 3-inch round cutter, cut the centers from each of these rounds to create ½-inch rings.

Prepare an egg wash by whisking together the eggs, 1 tablespoon water, and the salt in a small bowl. Brush the ⅛-inch-thick, 4-inch rounds with the egg wash, and place one pastry ring on top of each round, making certain that the edges are precisely aligned. Brush again with egg wash. Repeat egg wash with 3-inch rounds and refrigerate for 30 minutes.

Preheat the oven to 425°F.

Using a paring knife, make incisions, about ¼ inch apart, around the perimeter of each vol-au-vent, brush again with egg wash, and bake until golden brown, about 20 minutes. Remove from the oven, and reserve on a rack to cool. (If storing, wrap the baked vol-au-vent tightly in aluminum foil or seal in an airtight container.)

(continued)

VOL-AU-VENT

2 pounds Puff Pastry (page 373)

3 large eggs

⅛ teaspoon salt

SWEETBREADS

3 pounds veal sweetbreads

1 onion, peeled and studded with three whole cloves

1 bay leaf

½ pound (2 sticks) unsalted butter, softened

8 ounces white button mushrooms, cut into ¼-inch pieces

1 cup all-purpose flour

½ cup heavy cream

4 egg yolks, lightly beaten

Juice of 2 large lemons (about ¼ cup), strained

Salt and freshly ground white pepper

Chopped fresh parsley, for garnish

Lemon wedges, for garnish

TO MAKE THE SWEETBREADS: Place the sweetbreads in a large saucepan, cover with cold salted water, and add the studded onion and bay leaf. Bring to a boil over medium-high heat, and lower the heat to medium-low. Simmer for 30 to 45 minutes, skimming any foam that rises to the surface, until the sweetbreads are fully cooked and easily pierced with a knife. Drain the sweetbreads, reserving the cooking liquid, and set in cold water to cool. Peel off the outer membrane, pull apart the pieces where they naturally separate, and reserve in the refrigerator.

Strain the cooking liquid, return it to the saucepan, and bring to a boil over high heat. Lower the heat to medium, and simmer until reduced by three-quarters. Reduce the heat to medium-low, and maintain the liquid at a simmer.

Heat 2 tablespoons of the butter in a large sauté pan over medium heat. Add the mushrooms and sauté until any liquid they release has evaporated, about 3 to 5 minutes. Remove from the heat, and reserve momentarily.

In a small bowl, knead together the flour and remaining butter to form a paste (*beurre manié*). Drizzle about ⅓ cup of the hot sweetmeat liquid into the paste, mixing constantly. Stir this thinned paste into the simmering liquid, and simmer for about 15 minutes, or until the sauce is smooth and velvety. Strain the sauce again through a fine mesh strainer, and return it once more to the pan. Bring the sauce to a simmer over medium-low heat (careful to keep it from boiling) and add the sweetbreads. Drain the mushrooms of any excess liquid and add them to the sauce.

Whisk together the cream and the egg yolks in a medium-size bowl, gradually fold into the sauce, and simmer for about 3 minutes (again being careful to keep it from boiling or the egg yolks might curdle). Stir in the lemon juice, and season with salt and white pepper.

To serve, place each vol-au-vent in the center of a plate, fill with the sweetbreads, top with a 3-inch center, and garnish with parsley and a lemon wedge.

*18th century china cupboard
in the kitchen at Pomona Hall.*

Escoveitch Salmon

•═══•

Escoveitch is a West Indian preparation typically used in the preparation of almost any type of fish. Nowadays, it is a freshly made preparation, but in colonial times, it was used as a means of preserving fish, as the acid in the vinegar would cure the fish and keep it for long periods of time. In *The Virginia Housewife Or, Methodical Cook*, Mary Randolph shares a recipe "To Caveach Fish," which, like the recipe below, suggests serving the dish at room temperature.

SERVES 4

2 (8-ounce) salmon fillets

1 lime

½ cup all-purpose flour

1 tablespoon oil

1 tablespoon unsalted butter

1 cup white vinegar

⅛ teaspoon salt

⅛ teaspoon sugar

2 medium carrots, peeled and finely julienned

1 red bell pepper, finely julienned

1 green bell pepper, finely julienned

1 yellow bell pepper, finely julienned

1 habañero pepper, sliced into thin rings (see Chef's Note)

1 large yellow onion, sliced into thin rings

6 whole allspice berries

1 small bunch fresh parsley, for garnish

Slice each fillet into 4 slices on a bias. Place the salmon in a medium-size shallow dish. Add water to cover and squeeze the lime juice into the water. Gently "wash" the fillets with the lime water. Discard the water and pat the salmon dry.

Dip the fillets into the flour to coat evenly, shaking off any excess.

Heat the oil and butter in a large skillet over medium heat. Add the salmon fillets and cook until slightly browned on both sides, about 2 minutes per side.

Remove the salmon and place it on a serving platter or divide among individual plates.

In a medium-size saucepan, combine 1 cup water, the vinegar, salt, and sugar, and bring to a boil over medium-high heat. Add the carrots, bell peppers, habañero, onion, and allspice berries, and cook for about 2 to 3 minutes, until heated through. Remove the habañero slices and discard.

To serve, spoon the vegetables and sauce over the salmon, and garnish with parsley.

CHEF'S NOTE

With one or two rare exceptions, habañero peppers are the hottest peppers on earth. Wear rubber gloves when slicing them and don't touch your skin or eyes. Wash all implements thoroughly in very hot, soapy water.

Smoked Pheasant
en Croûte

1 tablespoon unsalted butter

1 yellow onion, finely chopped

2 shallots, finely chopped

1 garlic clove, chopped

1 pound smoked, cooked pheasant (or turkey) meat, finely chopped (see Resources, page 378)

2 cups finely diced wild mushrooms

½ cup dry white wine, such as a Sauvignon Blanc

1½ tablespoons chopped fresh parsley

1 sprig fresh thyme

Salt and freshly ground black pepper

½ cup Demi-Glace (page 367)

1 sheet of Quick Puff Pastry (see Chef's Note)

1 egg, lightly beaten

1 cup Madeira Wine Sauce (page 368)

In early America, the Pennsylvania woods were full of game, which was a staple in households and taverns alike. Pheasant was most popular among these many "free" food sources, so it was prepared in numerous ways—roasted, stewed, boiled or braised—and was often made into a savory pie using "puff paste" as the crust. This method, which requires the pheasant filling to be cooked twice, ensured not only that the pheasant was tender, but that it was free of any bacteria.

MAKES 18 (3-INCH) TURNOVERS; SERVES 6

Melt the butter in a medium-size saucepan over medium heat, add the onion, shallots, and garlic, and sauté for 3 to 4 minutes, until translucent. Stir in the pheasant and mushrooms. Add the wine to deglaze the pan, loosening any browned bits on the bottom of the pan with a wooden spoon. Add the parsley and thyme. Cook the mixture over medium heat for about 5 minutes, until it becomes dry. Season to taste with salt and pepper.

Add the demi-glace, reduce the heat, and let the mixture simmer for about 3 minutes, until it reduces and becomes thick. Transfer to a medium-size bowl and reserve.

Preheat the oven to 350°F.

On a lightly-floured surface, roll out the puff pastry sheet. Cut the pastry into 18 (3½-inch) squares. Brush the edges of the squares with the beaten egg.

Divide the pheasant mixture into 18 equal portions. Place one portion in the center of each puff pastry square. Fold each square over diagonally to form a triangle and press the edges firmly to seal. Pierce the pastry with a fork so the steam can escape. Place on a baking sheet and bake for 10 to 15 minutes, until golden brown. Serve with Madeira Wine Sauce.

CHEF'S NOTE

Commercially made puff pastry is available in the frozen foods section of most supermarkets.

Forced Cabbage

The word "forced" is an anglicized version of the French culinary term *farci*, which means "stuffed." Nearly every European culture can claim a version of this basic dish, but the two most common versions represented in colonial cookery seem to have descended from the recipes brought by English and German settlers. In *The Art of Cookery Made Plain and Easy*, Hannah Glasse's recipe for "A forced Cabbage" calls for the incorporation of veal, which seems quite extravagant for the time, considering its relatively high cost. This version, containing pork and beef, is much more traditional.

SERVES 6

Melt the butter in a small skillet over medium heat. Add the onion and sauté for 3 to 5 minutes, until softened and translucent. Reserve, and cool completely.

In a medium-size mixing bowl, combine the onion, the pork, beef, egg yolks, scallion, parsley, rice, salt, and pepper, and reserve in the refrigerator.

Preheat the oven to 350°F.

Bring a large saucepan of lightly salted water to a boil over high heat. Reduce the heat to medium high and maintain at a hearty simmer.

Gently drop the cabbage into the water and simmer until the outer leaves are slightly softened, about 2 to 3 minutes. Remove the softened outer leaves and drain on a towel. Continue this process, simmering the cabbage and removing the leaves until you have accumulated at least 24 leaves.

Coat a shallow baking dish with nonstick cooking spray.

Place 2 leaves, slightly overlapping, on a work surface. Place ⅛ cup of the stuffing in the center and fold the leaves over the stuffing to seal tightly (the rolls should be about the size of a Chinese spring roll). Place the stuffed leaves seal side down in the prepared baking dish. Repeat the process with the remaining leaves and stuffing.

Bake until firm to the touch, about 20 minutes.

To serve, place two cabbage rolls on each plate and serve, or top with demi-glace, if desired.

1 tablespoon unsalted butter

½ yellow onion, finely chopped

½ pound ground pork

½ pound ground beef

3 egg yolks

1 scallion,
trimmed and finely chopped

1 tablespoon chopped fresh parsley

1 cup cooked long grain white rice

Salt and freshly ground black pepper

1 medium head green cabbage, cored

Demi-glace, for serving
(optional) (page 367)

Mustard Eggs

Nearly every colonial household owned at least one hen, so eggs were plentiful in supply and prepared in numerous ways. This rich and lively cousin to deviled eggs was inspired by a recipe for "Stuffed Eggs" written by Martha Washington's sister, Anna Maria Dandridge, in 1756. Surprisingly, Miss Dandridge never shared this recipe with her more famous sister, as no similar egg recipe appears in Martha's *Book of Cookery*. Traditionally, the eighteenth-century chef would have roasted the eggs in the hot ashes of the kitchen fireplace, but cooking them in boiling water produces the same result.

SERVES 6

Preheat the oven to 350°F. Line a baking sheet with aluminum foil.

Shell and halve the hard-cooked eggs lengthwise.

Remove the egg yolks and reserve. Place the egg whites on the prepared baking sheet and set aside.

Heat 1 tablespoon of the butter in a small skillet over medium heat. Add the shallots and cook for 2 minutes, until golden brown. Reserve.

In the bowl of an electric mixer fitted with a paddle attachment (or a food processor bowl), mix the reserved egg yolks, cooked shallots, cream, chives, tarragon, and mustard into a paste. Season with salt and pepper to taste.

Fill a pastry bag with the mixture, leaving enough room to close and twist the top of the bag. Pipe the mixture into the egg white halves. Dot each egg white half with a piece of the remaining 1 tablespoon butter, sprinkle with paprika, and bake for 5 to 8 minutes, until browned on top.

Serve with Mustard Sauce, if desired.

6 extra-large eggs, hard-cooked (see Chef's Note)

2 tablespoons unsalted butter

4 medium shallots, chopped

3 tablespoons heavy cream

3 tablespoons chopped fresh chives

3 tablespoons chopped fresh tarragon

2 tablespoons Dijon mustard

Salt and freshly ground white pepper

¼ teaspoon Hungarian paprika

¼ cup Mustard Sauce (page 370)

CHEF'S NOTE

To make no-fail hard-cooked eggs, place the eggs in a small saucepan and cover with boiling water. Bring back to a boil. Boil for 8 minutes. (In the Black Forest, we traditionally add 1 tablespoon white vinegar to the water. In case the eggs crack during cooking, the vinegar seals the egg. However, the vinegar is not necessary.) Remove from the heat, drain, and place the eggs under cold running water. When cool, peel and discard the shells.

Shrimp Toast

2¼ cups all-purpose flour

3 eggs, beaten

2¼ cups whole milk

1½ tablespoons clarified butter
(see Chef's Note page 54) or olive oil

1 tablespoon finely chopped fresh basil

1 tablespoon finely chopped fresh parsley

1 tablespoon stemmed and
finely chopped fresh thyme

1 tablespoon finely chopped fresh chives

Pinch of freshly grated nutmeg

Pinch of salt

Pinch of freshly ground white pepper

8 tablespoons (1 stick) butter

6 (1-inch-thick) slices Sally Lunn Bread
(page 318) (see Chef's Note)

1 clove garlic, minced

1 small shallot, minced

1½ pounds extra-small shrimp

¼ cup dry white wine,
such as Sauvignon Blanc

1 cup Béchamel Sauce,
warmed (page 369)

2 tablespoons chopped fresh parsley,
for garnish

The colonial recipe for this dish was called "To butter Shrimps," and it was most often served over a "sippet," the colonial term for fried bread, similar to Italian crostini. Versions of buttered shrimp differ, however. Martha Washington merely buttered them and finished them with pepper. This recipe more closely follows the version found in Eliza Smith's *The Compleat Housewife: Or Accomplishd Gentlewoman's Companion*, the first cookbook ever published in the colonies in 1742.

SERVES 6

In a large mixing bowl, whisk together the flour, eggs, milk, clarified butter, basil, parsley, thyme, chives, nutmeg, salt, and pepper.

Heat 6 tablespoons of the butter in a large skillet over medium heat. Dip the bread slices into the batter and place in the pan, cooking until both sides are well browned, about 3 minutes per side. Remove and keep warm.

Heat the remaining 2 tablespoons butter in a separate pan over medium heat. Add the garlic and shallot and sauté for 3 to 5 minutes, until translucent. Add the shrimp and sauté for 3 to 5 minutes, until they are completely pink.

Add the wine to deglaze the pan, loosening any browned bits on the bottom of the pan with a wooden spoon. Cook for 3 minutes, until the wine is reduced by half.

Stir in the Béchamel Sauce and remove from the heat.

Cut a 2-inch-diameter round hole from the center of each piece of bread and place on individual plates. Spoon the shrimp into the holes and over the bread and garnish with parsley.

CHEF'S NOTE

You can use any thickly-sliced bread or plain Texas Toast
in this recipe, as well.

Pickled Herring

———◆———

Pickled herring is another dish that was firmly rooted in English and German traditions and made its way onto the pages of colonial cookbooks due to its practicality. Similar to "caveach," or escoveitch, in its use of vinegar as a preservative, pickled herring is one of the few food sources that would last through the winter in cool, dry root cellars. This recipe is inspired by one found in *The Lady's Companion* (1753), but the inclusion of the herring roe has been omitted.

Overnight preparation required.

SERVES 8

Place the herring fillets in a large bowl and cover with cold water. Refrigerate for 12 to 24 hours, changing the water twice. Rinse the fillets under cold running water and pat them dry. Slice into 1-inch pieces and reserve.

Combine the wine, vinegar, bay leaf, peppercorns, allspice, dill seeds, cinnamon stick, and sugar in a medium-size saucepan and bring to a boil over medium-high heat, stirring to dissolve the sugar. Once the sugar has been incorporated, remove from the heat and cool to room temperature.

In sterilized mason jars, alternate layers of herring and onions, then cover with the pickling brine and seal. Refrigerate for one week before serving.

When ready to serve, drain the herring and place on a platter. Serve the potatoes, red onion, capers and sour cream in individual bowls on the side.

2 pounds salt herring fillets

1 cup dry white wine,
such as Sauvignon Blanc

1 cup white vinegar

1 bay leaf

¼ teaspoon whole
black peppercorns, cracked

¼ teaspoon whole allspice, cracked

¼ teaspoon dill seeds

½ cinnamon stick

⅓ cup sugar

1 medium red onion, sliced

1 pound small Yukon Gold potatoes,
boiled (see process, page 219)

1 medium red onion, finely chopped

¼ cup small capers, drained

¼ cup sour cream

Marinated Asparagus

———◆———

Although Hannah Glasse offers a similar recipe she calls "Asparagus dressed the Italian Way," poached asparagus dressed with vinaigrette has existed in French culinary culture for the past few centuries. Thomas Jefferson enjoyed this recipe for asparagus while he was Minister to France and, given how much asparagus he grew in his gardens at Monticello, he surely would have instructed his French-trained chef, James Hemings, to prepare it for his American guests.

SERVES 6

In a large saucepan, bring 2 quarts of lightly salted water to a boil over high heat. Place the asparagus in the water and cook until just tender, 2 to 3 minutes.

Drain. Add enough cold water to cover the asparagus. Let stand about 5 minutes, until the asparagus is cool. Drain again, and pat the asparagus dry with paper towels.

In a medium-size mixing bowl, whisk together the vinegar, oil, thyme, parsley, egg, onion, and capers, and salt and pepper to taste.

Place the asparagus on a serving platter. Pour the vinaigrette evenly over the asparagus and serve.

1½ pounds asparagus, stems peeled and trimmed

2 tablespoons red wine vinegar

½ cup vegetable oil

Pinch of fresh thyme

Pinch of chopped fresh parsley

1 large egg, hard-cooked and chopped (see Chef's Note, page 63)

½ red onion, finely chopped

1 tablespoon fine capers, drained

Salt and freshly ground white pepper

Duck Liver Pâté

⬦•••⬦

5 pounds boneless duck meat, skinned, fat trimmed, and cut into ¼-inch pieces

1 cup imported Madeira

¾ cup brandy

1 tablespoon vegetable oil

1 tablespoon unsalted butter

1 pound lean bacon, finely chopped

1 pound boneless pork shoulder, fat trimmed and cut into ¼-inch pieces

2 bay leaves

1 pound fresh chicken livers

3 garlic cloves, chopped

4 sprigs fresh thyme, chopped (about 1 teaspoon)

4 egg whites

4 teaspoons salt

2 teaspoons freshly ground black pepper

1 pound lean bacon

The appreciation Americans have for this French and Southern German delicacy reflects the strong influence the French had on the colonial culinary repertoire. To make pâté, City Tavern chefs would have relied on the wild ducks found a stone's throw away along the banks of the Delaware river. Original recipes call for fat back, which can sometimes be difficult to find for modern cooks. For the sake of ease, bacon is substituted here, with no detriment to the overall flavor.

Overnight preparation required.

Serves 10 to 12

Place the duck meat in a large mixing bowl. Add the Madeira and brandy. Cover and marinate in the refrigerator overnight, stiffing periodically.

Heat the oil and butter in a large skillet over high heat. Add the chopped bacon and, stirring constantly, sauté about 3 minutes, until the fat is cooked out.

Add the pork shoulder and the bay leaves and cook for 5 to 8 minutes, until the mixture is reduced and there is no liquid in the pan.

Add the chicken livers and sauté about 5 minutes, until the mixture once again becomes dry.

Remove from the heat and add the garlic and thyme.

Remove the bay leaves and stir in the egg whites. Transfer the mixture to a food processor bowl and process into a paste (the mixture should be smooth but have some consistency). Add the salt and pepper and mix well. Reserve.

Remove the duck meat from the marinade and discard the marinade. Sprinkle the duck meat with additional pepper.

Line the bottom and sides of a 9 x 4-inch loaf pan with bacon slices, allowing at least 2 inches overhang so you can fold the bacon over the top of the liver mixture. Place the duck meat on the bottom. Press the liver mixture on top of the duck meat. Cover with foil and refrigerate for at least 10 hours or overnight.

When ready to bake the mixture, preheat the oven to 375°F.

Place the foil-covered loaf pan into a larger, higher-sided ovenproof dish. Pour boiling water into the larger dish to within ½ inch of the top of the loaf pan.

Bake for about 1 hour and 40 minutes, until the pâté shrinks from the sides of the pan and liquid rises to the top.

Remove the loaf pan from the larger dish and cool on a wire rack for 10 minutes.

Cut a piece of cardboard to fit the inside of the loaf pan and cover the cardboard with foil. Place it on top of the pâté and weigh it down with a heavy weight (such as a large can of tomatoes). Refrigerate for at least 8 hours.

When ready to serve, remove the foil-lined cardboard. Invert the pâté onto an oblong serving plate and cut into ¼-inch-thick slices.

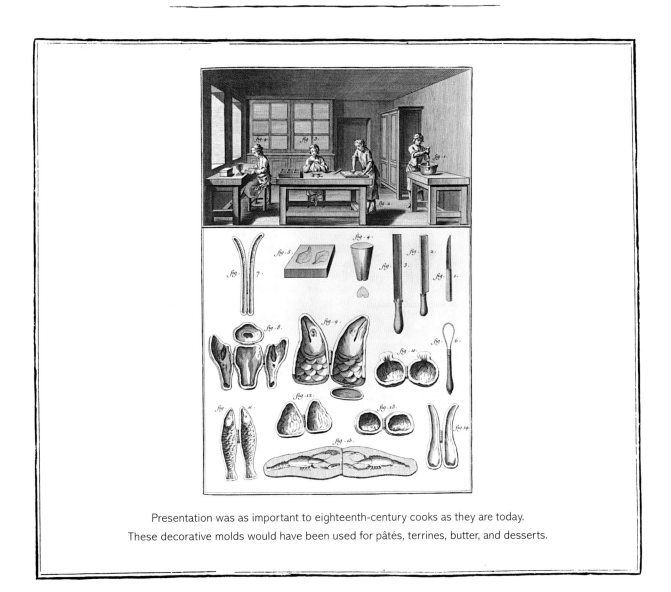

Presentation was as important to eighteenth-century cooks as they are today. These decorative molds would have been used for pâtés, terrines, butter, and desserts.

SOUPS, STEWS, AND CHOWDERS

Given that most colonial meals had to be made in a large pot hanging over an open fire, soups, chowders, and bisques were the most convenient dishes to cook. A nourishing meal could be made from very few ingredients, and, when necessary, served as a one-pot, one-course meal in households of meager means. Because of the portability of the cooking equipment required, soups, such as the West Indies Pepperpot Soup that kept George Washington's rag-tag army alive during the long winter at Valley Forge, were commonly made in military encampments.

Interestingly, soup itself was also portable in eighteenth-century America, as evidenced by various recipes for "Pocket Soup" that appear in the cookbooks of the era. In 1729, William Byrd, Esquire, of Westover, Virginia recommends his favorite pocket soup recipe to foresters in his *History of the Dividing Line*: "This Glue is so strong, that two or three Drams, dissolv'd in boiling Water, with a little Salt, will make half a Pint of good Broth, & if you shou'd be faint with Fasting or Fatigue, let a small Piece of this Glue melt in your Mouth, and you will find yourself surprisingly refreshed."

Chowder—named from the French *chaudière* after the pot in which it was traditionally made—referred to a fish stew that originated in fishing towns along the Brittany and Bordeaux coastlines in France, and Cornwall in England. Recipes for chowder differed from soups in that they called for the addition of salt pork, required the ingredients to be layered in the pot, rather than stirred together as in a traditional soup, and were thickened with biscuits, the equivalent of today's crackers. The first line of an interesting and poetic recipe for fish chowder that appeared in the *Boston Evening Post* on September 23, 1751, illustrates this point perfectly: "First lay some Onions to keep the Pork from burning / Because in Chouder there can be not turning." The earliest settlers brought this recipe to New England, only to find that their Native American contemporaries had already been making a similar dish for ages. Eventually, the chowder recipe was disseminated among the colonies and later evolved to include the most abundant native foods available, such as clams and even vegetables and starches like corn and potatoes.

In the 1790s, French citizens fleeing the terror of their own revolution brought to America the smooth, cream-infused bisques that were *de rigeur* in French cuisine. Before that time, only the most elite, well-traveled Americans, such as Benjamin Franklin, John Adams, and Thomas Jefferson, had the privilege of enjoying this refined version of a classically meager dish. Since the original manager of City Tavern "engaged English and French Cooks of approved abilities," it is uncertain whether or not their first taste of this dish would have been at the Tavern or in Paris.

Whatever the case, we do know that all three of these types of soup would have been included in the first plate offerings at City Tavern, elegantly presented in china terrines with sterling silver ladles.

West Indies Pepperpot Soup

¾ pound salt-cured pork shoulder, diced (see Chef's Note)

¾ pound salt-cured beef shoulder, diced (see Chef's Note)

2 tablespoons vegetable oil

1 medium white onion, chopped

4 garlic cloves, chopped

¼ habañero pepper, seeded and chopped (see Chef's Note, page 58)

1 cup chopped scallions

1 pound taro root, peeled and diced

1 gallon Beef Stock (page 363)

2 bay leaves

1 teaspoon chopped fresh thyme

1 tablespoon freshly ground allspice (see Chef's Note)

1 tablespoon freshly ground black pepper, plus more

1 pound callaloo or collard greens, rinsed and chopped (see Chef's Note)

Salt

Sweet Potato & Pecan Biscuits, for serving (page 306)

During the long winter at Valley Forge, George Washington instructed his cook to make this soup to nourish and warm his starving, freezing troops. Though this West Indian dish may seem out of place in colonial American life, it was in fact quite common in and around Philadelphia, the last stop for ships traveling the Southern Trade Route. English ships returning from the islands transported slaves and exotic foodstuffs, so West Indian cookery found its way into the very fabric of Philadelphia life. It is assumed that Washington was familiar with pepperpot soup long before he camped at Valley Forge. During his only trip abroad in 1751, Washington visited his brother Lawrence in Barbados, where he enjoyed *Cohobblopot*, a version of pepperpot soup made with okra. The recipe below is the grandfather to the more widely recognized Philadelphia Pepperpot Soup, and is made from an authentic West Indian recipe more than 300 years old.

SERVES 10

In a large stockpot, sauté the pork and beef in the oil over high heat for 10 minutes, until brown.

Add the onion, garlic, and habañero pepper, and sauté for 3 to 5 minutes, until the onion is translucent. Add the scallions and sauté for 3 minutes. Add the taro root and sauté for 3 to 5 minutes more, until translucent. Add the stock, bay leaves, thyme, allspice, and pepper. Bring to a boil over high heat. Reduce the heat to medium and cook for about 30 minutes, until the meat and taro root are tender.

Stir in the callaloo. Reduce the heat and simmer for about 5 minutes, until the callaloo is wilted. Season with salt and pepper to taste.

Serve in a tureen or divide among individual soup bowls. Serve with Sweet Potato Biscuits, if desired.

CHEF'S NOTES

To salt-cure pork and beef shoulder, choose meat that appears well-marbled, then rub with coarse (kosher) salt and refrigerate for at least three days. Wash the salt off the meat before cooking as directed.

The heat factor of peppers is measured by Scoville heat units. A jalapeño has 80,000 Scoville heat units while habañeros from Jamaica or Mexico's Yucatan Peninsula have been found to have 550,000 Scoville heat units. Always wear rubber gloves when handling this fiery pepper.

The allspice must be freshly ground, or the flavor will be compromised.

The only substitution you can make in this recipe and still achieve the intended flavor is to use collard greens instead of callaloo, the leafy top of the taro root.

Beef Barley Soup

On June 18, 1795, Thomas Jefferson entered "cut barley at Shad-well" into his *Farm Book*. As opposed to George Washington, who grew barley to feed the whiskey stills in his distillery, Jefferson seems to have grown barley for consumption. When settling back into Monticello in 1809, he wrote a letter to Gordon Trokes & Co. requesting ten pounds of pearl barley for Monticello. Though colonial cooks used barley in a number of ways, it was most often served in soup. Colonial cooks typically made their barley soup with vegetables and mutton, but would have substituted beef when mutton wasn't available.

SERVES 6

1 tablespoon vegetable oil

1 pound beef chuck, trimmed and cut into ½-inch pieces

2 cloves garlic, finely chopped

2 large yellow onions, finely chopped

1 small celery root, diced

2 large carrots, peeled and diced

2 bay leaves

1 cup sliced button mushrooms

¾ cup pearl barley

¼ teaspoon dried thyme

2 tablespoons chopped fresh parsley

Salt and freshly ground black pepper

In a large pot, heat the oil over medium heat, then add the beef and cook until browned on all sides, about 15 minutes.

Add the garlic and cook for 1 to 2 minutes, until slightly golden. Add the onions and cook for 3 to 5 minutes, until translucent. Add the celery root and carrots and cook until slightly soft, about 10 minutes.

Pour in 2 quarts water, add the bay leaves, and simmer over low heat for about 1 hour, or until the meat is tender.

Stir in the mushrooms, barley, and thyme, and cook until the barley is tender, about 15 to 20 minutes.

Just before serving, add the parsley and season with salt and pepper to taste. Serve in a tureen or divide among individual soup bowls.

CHEFS NOTE

For a richer flavor, add a couple of beef marrow bones or neck bones when the water is added. Also, if you use leftover beef for this soup, substitute beef stock for the water.

Corn & Crab Chowder

2 tablespoons unsalted butter

1 cup chopped carrots

1 cup chopped celery

1 cup chopped onion

1 quart Vegetable Stock (page 363)

1 tablespoon chopped shallots

1 tablespoon chopped fresh basil

1 teaspoon chopped fresh thyme

1 teaspoon sweet paprika

3 garlic cloves, chopped

3 large russet potatoes (about 1 pound),
peeled and diced

10 ears fresh white corn,
kernels cut from cobs

2 cups heavy cream

¼ cup cornstarch

¼ cup dry white wine,
such as Sauvignon Blanc

1 pound crabmeat

Chopped chives or green onions,
for garnish

Herb Croutons, for serving (page 371)

Sixteenth-century American colonists were introduced to corn by Native Americans who had mastered its cultivation nearly five hundred years before. By the eighteenth century, colonists were well versed in the many uses of corn, and added it to many of their traditional European recipes. Catherine Moffatt Whipple, the daughter of a wealthy Portsmouth, New Hampshire, merchant, left behind the recipe for corn chowder, upon which the recipe below is based. Given the abundance of fresh seafood that appeared on the tables of New England colonists, Mrs. Whipple surely would have stirred crabmeat into this dish on special occasions.

SERVES 8 TO 10

Melt the butter in a medium-size stockpot over medium heat, add the carrots, celery, and onion, and sauté for 5 minutes, until the onions are translucent.

Add the stock, shallots, basil, thyme, paprika, and garlic. Bring to a boil, then stir in the potatoes and corn kernels and bring back to a boil.

Stir in the cream. Reduce the heat and simmer, stirring occasionally, for 10 to 15 minutes, until the vegetables are tender and the soup is heated.

In a small bowl, combine the cornstarch and wine and mix until velvety smooth. Add some of the boiling soup to the cornstarch mixture and stir until the mixture is thin. Gently stir the mixture into the soup. Cook until bubbly.

Pick over the crabmeat to discard the cartilage and pieces of shell. Stir the crab into the soup. Serve hot, garnished with chives and Herb Croutons.

CHEF'S NOTE

For an even more wonderful flavor, add 1 pound of chopped, cooked lobster or shrimp, or 1½ pounds of chopped, cooked chicken breast to the chowder when the crab is added to the soup.

As with most cream-based soups, you can substitute half-and-half for the cream without giving up too much flavor or consistency. I don't recommend using whole or skim milk, but this is only a guideline. Experiment to find a balance between flavor and healthfulness to match your tastes.

Chicken Noodle Soup

I n colonial times, chickens were kept mainly for their eggs, which were prized for baking. Older chickens that no longer produced eggs were then cooked in stews and soups like this one. These chickens normally were fattier than younger hens, and colonial housewives used this to their advantage by rendering the fat to use as a flavorful alternative to butter or lard in other dishes. Adding egg noodles to the soup, a traditional German preparation, lent texture and served as a means of transforming the soup into a more hearty meal that could feed an entire family.

SERVES 6 TO 8

Melt the butter in a medium-size saucepan over medium heat, then add the onion and sauté for 3 to 5 minutes, until softened and translucent. Add the celery and carrots, and sauté for 3 to 5 minutes more, until softened.

Stir in the stock and thyme, and bring to a boil over high heat. Reduce the heat to low, and simmer for about 30 minutes, until the stock is reduced by one-third.

Remove and discard the thyme and add the chicken and egg noodles. Simmer for 10 to 15 minutes, until heated. Season with salt and pepper to taste.

Serve the soup in a tureen or in individual bowls garnished with parsley.

1 tablespoon unsalted butter

1 medium onion, chopped

3 celery ribs, chopped

2 large carrots, peeled and chopped

3 quarts Chicken Stock (page 364)

1 sprig fresh thyme

1 pound boneless chicken (white or dark meat), cooked and chopped

8 ounces Egg Noodles (page 212), cooked and drained

Salt and freshly ground black pepper

Chopped fresh parsley, for garnish

Pumpkin Chowder

———

When the colonists arrived in North America, they found the Native Americans cultivating pumpkins. The flavorful fruit was embraced by the settlers, who used it in everything from pie to soup. Pumpkin soup was a staple in the West Indian diet and, like pepperpot soup, the recipe made its way to the colonies via the ships that sailed the Southern Trade Route. This recipe is a "colonialized" version of the West Indian original.

SERVES 8

1 large pumpkin (about 6 pounds)

1 large onion, chopped

¼ habañero pepper
(see Chef's Note, page 58)

2 bay leaves

1 garlic clove, chopped

5 cups heavy cream

1 cup dry white wine, such as Sauvignon Blanc or dry sherry

Salt and freshly ground black pepper

2 cups Herb Croutons (page 371), for serving

2 tablespoons finely chopped fresh chives, for garnish

Cut the pumpkin into 8 wedges; remove and discard the seeds and membranes. Scoop out the pumpkin flesh and reserve. Discard the rind.

Cut the flesh into cubes and transfer them to a large stockpot; add enough salted water to cover. Add the onion, habañero pepper, bay leaves, and garlic. Bring to a boil over high heat.

Reduce the heat to medium and cook for 30 minutes, until the pumpkin is fork-tender. Remove from the heat. Remove and discard the bay leaves. Transfer the pumpkin mixture to a medium-size saucepan. Stir in the cream and wine. Simmer for about 20 minutes, until the soup is creamy and heated through. Season to taste with salt and pepper.

To serve, divide the soup among soup bowls. Sprinkle with the Herb Croutons and chives.

Snapper Turtle Soup

Colonial housewives were adept at preparing turtle, and they left very detailed instructions on when and how to kill and cook them. In *The Virginia Housewife*, Mary Randolph advises, "kill it at night in winter, and in the morning in summer." She then provides a long recipe that would certainly intimidate even advanced cooks. In *The Art of Cookery Made Plain and Easy*, Hannah Glasse does the same, mentioning that her recipe is "for a turtle of sixty pounds weight" and suggesting the use of curry powder to enhance the flavor. Most recipes, however, call for sherry or Madeira to heighten the flavor profile. Nowadays, turtle can easily be found through specialty markets or online vendors, making this soup much easier to prepare and enjoy.

SERVES 6 TO 8

Heat 1 tablespoon of the butter in a 5-quart stockpot over medium heat, then add the turtle meat. Cook, stirring frequently, for 3 minutes, until brown. Add the carrots, onion, celery, shallots, and garlic. Sauté for 5 minutes, until the vegetables become soft. Add the stock, 1 cup of the sherry, the thyme, parsley, bay leaf, and cloves. Bring to a boil. Reduce the heat and simmer for 1½ hours, until the turtle meat begins to fall apart.

Remove the soup from the heat and strain it through a fine wire sieve or cheesecloth into a large bowl. Reserve the stock.

Remove and discard the bay leaf. Place the turtle meat and vegetables in a food processor bowl. Process until the mixture has a coarse consistency.

Return the stock and turtle-vegetable purée to the stockpot. Bring to a boil.

Stir in the tomato paste.

Heat the remaining 4 tablespoons of butter in a separate medium-size saucepan over low heat. Add the flour and mix well. Cook for 15 minutes, then slowly stir the mixture into the soup until combined. Reduce the heat to medium and cook for 5 minutes, until heated through.

Stir in the remaining ½ cup sherry (or else pour it into a cruet and serve alongside the soup at the table). Season with salt and pepper to taste.

Serve immediately in a tureen or divide among individual soup bowls. Garnish with the chopped eggs.

5 tablespoons unsalted butter

1 pound skinless and boned turtle meat, cubed (see Resources, page 378)

1 cup chopped carrots

1 cup chopped onion

1 cup chopped celery

2 medium shallots, chopped

2 garlic cloves, chopped

3 quarts Beef Stock (page 363)

1½ cups dry sherry or imported Madeira

4 sprigs fresh thyme

1 bunch fresh parsley, chopped (about 6 tablespoons)

1 bay leaf

1 teaspoon ground cloves

¾ cup tomato paste

¼ cup all-purpose flour

Salt and freshly ground black pepper

3 hard-cooked eggs (see Chef's Note, page 63), yolks and whites separated and chopped, for garnish

Oxtail Soup

───◆───

½ cup dried lentils

3 pounds beef oxtails,
cut into 1-inch pieces

6 tablespoons unsalted butter

1½ cups chopped onions

1 cup chopped carrots

1 cup chopped celery

1 tablespoon chopped garlic

¾ cup tomato paste

2 cups red Burgundy wine

2 quarts Beef Stock (page 363)

¼ cup chopped fresh parsley

1 teaspoon chopped fresh rosemary

1 bay leaf

¼ cup all-purpose flour

Salt and freshly ground black pepper

The ox was an important animal to early Philadelphians, who used it as a beast of burden as well as in the fields. Because meat of any kind was at a premium, nothing, including tough ox meat, was wasted. Even the relatively tough, but very flavorful, tail of the ox was used. Colonials relied on their knowledge of slow braising and stewing as a way of tenderizing the meat. This is a classic English recipe for hearty oxtail soup, which can be flavored with Madeira, as was the traditional fashion.

Overnight preparation recommended.

Serves 6 to 8

To pre-soak the lentils, place them in a colander and rinse thoroughly with water to clean. Place the lentils in a large bowl and cover with water. Let stand at room temperature for at least 8 hours or overnight.

Drain and thoroughly rinse the lentils; reserve. Preheat the oven to 400°F.

Place the oxtail pieces in a roasting pan and roast, stirring the meat frequently to prevent burning, for about 35 minutes, until dark brown. Drain the roasting pan and discard any pan drippings. Let the meat cool for 15 minutes.

Heat 2 tablespoons of the butter in a large stockpot over medium heat, add the onions, carrots, celery, and garlic, and sauté for 5 minutes, until the onions are translucent. Add the oxtails and the tomato paste. Add the wine to deglaze the pan, loosening any browned bits on the bottom of the pan with a wooden spoon. Cook over high heat, stirring occasionally, for about 10 minutes, until the mixture is reduced by half.

Add the stock, parsley, rosemary, and bay leaf. Bring to a boil over high heat. Reduce the heat to medium and cook for 1½ hours.

After 1 hour and 15 minutes, cook the reserved lentils in a medium-size saucepan in boiling, lightly salted water for 10 to 15 minutes, until tender. Drain and add to the meat mixture. Cook over low heat for 25 minutes, until the meat falls off the bones. Remove and discard the bones.

Heat the remaining 4 tablespoons of butter in a separate medium-size saucepan over low heat, add the flour, and mix well. Cook for 15 minutes.

Bring the soup to a boil over high heat. Slowly stir in the flour-butter mixture until combined. Reduce the heat to medium and cook for 5 minutes more, until the soup is heated through. Season with salt and pepper to taste. Serve hot.

Tripe Soup

Tripe, the honeycombed lining of a cow's stomach, has a long history of use in Spain, France, and Italy. Never willing to waste a single part of a valuable animal, colonials consumed tripe after the slaughter, usually in soups and stews, so it could be slow cooked to a buttery tenderness.

Overnight preparation recommended.

SERVES 6

To pre-soak the beans, place them in a colander and rinse thoroughly with water to clean. Place the beans in a large bowl and cover with water. Let stand at room temperature for at least 8 hours or overnight.

Drain and thoroughly rinse the beans. Place them in a stockpot, and add enough salted water to cover. Cook over medium heat for 45 minutes, until tender. Drain and reserve.

In the same stockpot, add the tripe and enough lightly salted water to cover. Bring to a boil over high heat, then reduce the heat to low, and simmer about 30 minutes until the tripe is tender. Strain the mixture through a fine wire sieve or cheesecloth and discard the liquid. Let the tripe cool for 15 minutes, then cut it into ½-inch strips. Reserve.

Melt the butter in the stockpot over medium heat, add the carrots, leeks, celery, and garlic, and sauté for 5 minutes, until soft. Add the tripe and beans and sauté for 5 minutes more. Add the stock, wine, and bay leaf. Bring to a boil over high heat. Reduce the heat. Add the tomato paste, parsley, and thyme, and simmer for 30 to 45 minutes, until the beans fall apart.

Serve in a soup tureen or divide among soup bowls. Sprinkle with the Parmesan cheese.

¾ cup dried cannellini beans

1 pound honeycomb beef tripe

2 tablespoons unsalted butter

1 cup chopped carrots

1 cup leeks, cut into julienne strips

1 cup chopped celery

1 tablespoon chopped garlic

1½ quarts Beef Stock (page 363)

1 cup red Burgundy wine

1 bay leaf

¾ cup tomato paste

1 tablespoon chopped fresh parsley

1 large sprig fresh thyme, chopped (about 1 teaspoon)

¼ cup grated Parmesan cheese, for serving

CHEF'S NOTE

Tripe is readily available in many supermarkets, especially those that cater to an ethnic clientele.

Madeira Onion Soup

2 quarts Chicken Stock (page 364)

½ pound (2 sticks) unsalted butter

4 pounds (about 16) yellow onions, thinly sliced

3 tablespoons all-purpose flour

1 loaf French bread, cut into 10 (¼-inch) slices

1 cup Rainwater-style Madeira

4 cups grated Swiss cheese

2 large eggs

Salt and freshly ground black pepper

Although the average cook in the eighteenth century would not have "wasted" good Madeira in food, America's aristocrats, such as Thomas Jefferson, certainly would have enjoyed the indulgence. Onion soup was among the many French recipes Jefferson copied when in Paris, featured as part of his "Observations on Soups." This recipe employs "rainwater" Madeira, which came from the barrels of Madeira that were loaded onto the decks of trade ships. Rain water seeped into the barrels and mixed with the Madeira to create a lighter, drier flavor, which contrasts perfectly with the sweetness of the onion and richness of the cheese.

Serves 10

In a 3-quart stockpot, bring the stock to a boil over high heat. Remove from the heat and reserve.

Heat half of the butter in a large skillet over medium heat, add the onions, and cook for about 15 minutes, until golden brown.

Sprinkle the flour over the onions and stir until a paste forms. Slowly stir about 2 cups of the hot chicken stock into the onion mixture until the paste becomes a thin, smooth liquid. Transfer the onion mixture to the remaining stock in the stockpot. Simmer for 30 minutes.

Preheat the oven to 400°F.

Heat the remaining butter in a 12-inch skillet over low heat, add the bread slices, half at a time, and cook for 5 minutes on each side, until crisp.

Pour ½ cup of the wine into a 3-quart ovenproof soup crock or casserole.

Add the bread and sprinkle with half of the cheese.

In a small bowl, beat the eggs and the remaining ½ cup wine until completely combined. Pour into the onion mixture, stirring constantly. Do not boil. Pour the onion mixture into the soup crock and sprinkle with the remaining cheese. Bake for about 20 minutes, until golden brown.

CHEF'S NOTE

If you prefer, you can substitute 1 quart dry white wine, such as Sauvignon Blanc, for half of the quantity of Chicken Stock (making a mixture of 1 quart white wine and 1 quart stock) and applejack for the Madeira. Adjust the amount of applejack to suit your own taste.

Potato-Leek Soup

M arjoram, a Mediterranean herb considered by the ancient Greeks to be a symbol of happiness, has a wonderful but delicate flavor. Interestingly, this herb was commonly called for in eighteenth-century recipes, yet it is rarely used in today's recipes. Thomas Jefferson grew it in abundance at Monticello, eventually including it among the plants he grew in his new "orangery" or greenhouse. When construction on George Washington's greenhouse was finished, he was sent "tufts of knotted marjoram" by Mrs. Margaret Carroll, a family friend in Baltimore.

SERVES 8

Melt the butter in a large stockpot over low heat, add the leeks, and sauté for 10 minutes, until soft.

Add the stock and potatoes and cook for about 30 minutes, until the potatoes are fork-tender.

In a medium-size saucepan, sauté the onion and bacon over medium heat for 5 minutes, until the onion is golden brown. Drain off the bacon drippings. Add the onion mixture and the marjoram to the soup, and season with salt and pepper to taste.

Serve in a soup tureen or divide among individual soup bowls. Sprinkle with the Herb Croutons.

---

3 tablespoons unsalted butter

5 leeks (white part only), rinsed well and chopped (about 5½ cups)

1½ quarts Chicken Stock (page 364)

6 medium red skinned potatoes (about 2 pounds), peeled and chopped

1 medium yellow onion, chopped

½ cup (9 slices) chopped lean bacon

1 teaspoon dried marjoram

Salt and freshly ground black pepper

2 cups Herb Croutons (page 371), for serving

Oyster Stew

2 cups whole milk

1 pint fresh select oysters
(or 25 to 30 Bluepoint oysters),
shucked

1½ tablespoons unsalted butter,
softened

Salt and freshly ground
black pepper

All along the Eastern seaboard, oysters were plentiful in the eighteenth century, which explains why they were popular in Philadelphia. Philadelphians consumed so many oysters, the shells were used as street paving, for artificial wharves along the Delaware, and even as ballast for ships. It's no surprise, then, that oysters were prepared in many different ways—roasted, fried, stewed, and so on. A recipe for oyster stew shows up in virtually every cookbook of the era. The most interesting recipe was Martha Washington's, which called for the addition of "beaten & sifted ginger" at the end.

SERVES 4

In a small saucepan, bring the milk to a boil over medium heat, cover, and keep warm.

Place the oysters with their liquid in a medium-size saucepan. Cook over medium heat for 3 to 5 minutes. Keep an eye on the oysters; when the edges begin to curl, add the milk. Add the butter and stir to combine. Season with salt and pepper to taste.

CHEF'S NOTE

Add 2 dashes hot sauce or a pinch of hot red pepper flakes for an extra bite.

Split Pea Soup

◦—◦◦◦—◦

1 pound dried split peas

6 medium red skinned potatoes
(about 2 pounds), peeled and cubed

4 tablespoons unsalted butter

½ pound (9 slices) lean bacon,
finely chopped

1 large white onion, chopped

2 garlic cloves, chopped

3 quarts Chicken Stock (page 364)

1 cup heavy cream

Salt and freshly ground black pepper

Fried Leek Garnish, optional
(page 89)

The split pea is actually a field pea, a variety of yellow or green pea grown specifically for drying. Dried peas and beans were an important staple for the colonists, because they could be stored easily and would last indefinitely. They also traveled well, making them a common item for cooking on the wagon trails. Using the peas to make split pea soup was very common in colonial times. Cookbooks of the era refer to these as white peas, presumably for the light color they develop when dried. Martha Washington used "white pease" in her recipe "To Make Pease Porrage Of Old Peas," which includes coriander and mint, which were thought to guard against indigestion and "windiness."

Overnight preparation recommended.

SERVES 10 TO 12

To pre-soak the peas, place them in a colander and rinse thoroughly with water to clean. Place the peas in a large bowl and cover with water. Let stand at room temperature for at least 8 hours or overnight.

Drain and thoroughly rinse the peas; reserve.

In a small saucepan, cook the potatoes in enough boiling, lightly salted water to cover for 10 to 15 minutes, or until the potatoes are fork-tender. Drain and reserve.

Melt the butter in a large stockpot over medium heat, add the bacon and sauté for 3 minutes. Add the onion and garlic and sauté about 3 minutes more, until golden brown. Add the split peas and stock. Bring to a boil over high heat. Reduce the heat to medium and cook for about 1½ hours, until the split peas have dissolved.

Press the split pea mixture through a fine sieve into a large bowl. Discard the bacon and return the mixture to the stockpot. Add the potatoes and cream, and season with salt and pepper to taste.

To serve, divide among individual soup bowls. Garnish with the Fried Leek Garnish, if desired.

Fried Leek Garnish

Leeks would have been left in the garden all winter, then harvested and fried in lard to lend color to drab winter dishes.

1 medium leek,
rinsed well to remove sand

1 cup vegetable oil, for frying

Cut the leek lengthwise into ½-inch-long strips, julienne as fine as possible, and thoroughly pat dry between paper towels.

Heat the oil in a medium-size saucepan over medium heat to 350°F.

Carefully add the leek and cook for several minutes, until golden brown. Be careful not to let the leek burn. Using a slotted spoon, remove the leek and place it on a paper towel to absorb any excess oil.

The Tavern staff is dressed exactly as their counterparts were two centuries ago, as servants to the upper class. A colonial observer could tell the class of a servant by the material of his buttons, with wood buttons indicating the lowest strata, working up to bone and ivory buttons. City Tavern staff fasten their breeches with metal buttons, indicating that the original servants were placed somewhere in the middle of the servant class social ladder.

Cabbage & Turnip Soup

2 tablespoons unsalted butter

1 tablespoon vegetable oil

1 cup finely chopped lean salt pork
or slab bacon

1 medium white onion, chopped

1 cabbage (about 3 pounds),
trimmed and coarsely chopped

4 large carrots, peeled and quartered

3 large turnips, quartered

3 peppercorns, crushed

2 quarts Chicken Stock (page 364)

½ cup heavy cream

2 egg yolks

Salt and freshly ground black pepper

Many eighteenth-century recipes call for salt pork, which in colonial times was preserved in root cellars for the entire winter, to be used to give the flavor and benefit of animal fat when meat was a rare commodity. Salt pork was used to flavor everything from soups to stews to sauces. The recipe below is the traditional German version of this soup, but many variations existed, with each cook making her own adjustments according to personal taste. In *The Frugal Colonial Housewife*, Susannah Carter wrote a recipe "To Make Turnip Soup," but her version has neither salt pork nor cabbage.

SERVES 8

Melt the butter and oil in a large stockpot over medium heat. Add the salt pork and sauté for 3 minutes. Add the onion and sauté about 3 minutes more, until translucent. Add the cabbage, carrots, turnips, and peppercorns. Add the stock and bring to a boil over high heat. Reduce the heat and simmer for about 1½ hours, until the vegetables are soft and the turnips are dissolved.

Just before serving, whisk together the cream and egg yolks in a small bowl, until velvety smooth. Stir the mixture into the hot soup. (Do not bring to a boil again.) Season with salt and pepper to taste.

Serve in a soup tureen or divide among individual soup bowls.

Clam Chowder

⸻

Clam chowder, originally named "la chaudiere" for the huge French copper fish cauldron in which it was cooked, originated in America in the Massachusetts colonies. The chowder was placed in the big stew pot and hung over the fire on an iron crane, where it could cook for hours. Clam chowder in New England was a bit stronger than similar chowders made in the mid-Atlantic and southern colonies, as it called for more clam "liquor," or juice. A recipe from Mary Cowgill Corbit of Delaware cautions against using too much—"We think it too strong, but do as you like about it."

SERVES 8

To clean clams still in the shell, scrub them thoroughly, soak to remove any sand, rinse, and drain well. Repeat soaking, rinsing, and draining two more times.

Place the clams in a stockpot.

In a small saucepan, heat the wine and pour over the clams. Cover the stockpot and cook the clams over high heat for about 15 minutes, until the clams open. Discard any clams that do not open.

Transfer the open clams and the wine mixture to separate bowls. Let the clams cool for 10 minutes. Using a paring knife, remove the clams from their shells and use kitchen shears to trim off the clam beards. Chop the clams into ¼-inch pieces and reserve.

In the stockpot, cook the bacon over medium heat for 5 minutes, until crisp. Add the onions and sauté for 3 minutes. Add the potatoes, bell peppers, and reserved wine mixture. Cook over medium heat for about 15 minutes, until the potatoes are tender.

Stir in the clams, cream, and hot sauce.

Melt the butter in a separate medium-size saucepan over low heat, add the flour, and mix well. Cook for 15 minutes. Stir the flour mixture into the clam mixture until fully incorporated. Heat for 5 minutes. Season with salt and pepper to taste.

Garnish the soup with the chives.

30 large fresh cherrystone clams
or 10 ounces cooked clams
(see Chef's Note)

1½ cups dry white wine,
such as Sauvignon Blanc

½ pound (9 slices) lean bacon,
finely chopped

4 medium yellow onions, finely chopped

6 medium red skinned potatoes,
peeled and chopped

2 medium green bell peppers,
finely chopped

1 cup heavy cream

1 teaspoon hot sauce

4 tablespoons unsalted butter

¼ cup all-purpose flour

Salt and freshly ground black pepper

1 bunch fresh chives, finely chopped
(about 6 tablespoons), for garnish

⸻

CHEF'S NOTE

If you are using cooked clams, which you can purchase canned or fresh at supermarket fish counters, begin the recipe by cooking the bacon.

Add 1 dash Worcestershire sauce or 2 pinches red pepper flakes for added flavor.

White Bean & Bacon Soup

W hite beans, like all dried beans, last forever, are easy to store, and provide an important source of nutrition during the winter months. Most eighteenth-century housewives wouldn't have used chicken stock as a base for this soup because meat was too dear, but the chefs at City Tavern, where cooking was elevated to the highest standards, certainly would have.

Overnight preparation recommended.

SERVES 8 TO 10

To pre-soak the beans, place them in a colander and rinse thoroughly with water to clean. Place the beans in a large bowl and cover with water. Let stand at room temperature for at least 8 hours or overnight.

Drain and thoroughly rinse the beans. Place them in a large stockpot, add the stock, and bring to a boil over high heat.

Reduce the heat to low and cook for about 1 hour, until the beans are soft.

Melt the butter in a large skillet over medium heat, add the onions and garlic and sauté for 5 minutes, until light brown. Add the tomatoes, bacon, and marjoram, and sauté for 3 to 5 minutes more, until the tomatoes begin to dissolve. Add the tomato mixture to the beans in the stockpot. Simmer the soup for about 10 minutes, until the tomatoes are soft. Season with salt and pepper to taste.

Just before serving, stir in the parsley.

1 pound dried navy beans

2½ quarts Chicken Stock (page 364)

4 tablespoons unsalted butter

2 medium yellow onions, chopped

3 garlic cloves, chopped

8 large plum tomatoes (1 pound), seeded and chopped

½ pound slab bacon, cut into ¼-inch cubes

1 teaspoon dried marjoram

Salt and freshly ground black pepper

2 bunches fresh parsley, finely chopped (about 12 tablespoons)

Lentil Soup

½ cup dried lentils

2 medium yellow onions, chopped

2 large carrots, peeled and chopped

2 garlic cloves, chopped

¼ cup olive oil

2½ quarts Chicken Stock (page 364)

1 bay leaf

1 sprig fresh thyme

Salt and freshly ground black pepper

L entils were a common item in the eighteenth-century storehouse, where they were kept in burlap bags, along with other items kept in bulk, such as dried beans and rice. Early German settlers prepared lentils frequently—and to this day lentil soup is a common item on Amish and Pennsylvania Dutch menus. Adding a bit of chopped sausage or virtually any kind of smoked cut of pork will boost the flavor of this hearty soup. The traditional preparation calls for a shot of vinegar right before serving.

Overnight preparation recommended.

SERVES 8 TO 10

To pre-soak the lentils, place them in a colander and rinse thoroughly with water to clean. Place the lentils in a large bowl and cover with water. Let stand at room temperature for at least 8 hours or overnight.

Drain and thoroughly rinse the lentils; reserve.

In a large stockpot, sauté the onions, carrots, and garlic in the oil over medium heat, stirring frequently, about 4 minutes, until tender.

Add the lentils, stock, bay leaf, and thyme. Bring to a boil over high heat. Reduce the heat to medium and cook for about 1 hour, until the lentils have dissolved. Season with salt and pepper to taste.

Serve in a soup tureen or divide among individual soup bowls.

Mushroom Bisque

The Pennsylvania woods are renowned for their many varieties of mushrooms. No doubt enterprising settlers would gather mushrooms and go into the city to peddle them to restaurants and inns, where they would be incorporated into all kinds of dishes, including this French-style soup. City Tavern, with its sophisticated menu that demanded a wide range of ingredients, was certainly a prime market for this emerging cottage industry of vendors hawking everything from mushrooms to herbs, vegetables, meats, and fresh fish.

SERVES 10 TO 12

Melt the butter in a Dutch oven over medium heat, add the mushrooms and sauté for 5 minutes. Remove from the heat and set aside to cool for 15 minutes.

Transfer the mushrooms to a food processor and process until finely chopped. Reserve.

In a large stockpot, combine the stock, bay leaf, and garlic. Bring to a boil over high heat until the mixture is reduced by half, about 45 minutes. Add the sherry and cream, remove the bay leaf, and cook for about 30 minutes, until the soup reduces again by half.

Add the mushroom purée and bring the soup to a boil over high heat. Lower the heat and simmer for 10 minutes, until heated through. Season with salt and pepper to taste.

Serve immediately in a soup tureen or divide among individual soup plates. Garnish with the parsley.

2 tablespoons unsalted butter

12 cups (2 pounds) assorted
fresh mushrooms (button, porcini, or
chanterelles), cleaned and chopped

4 quarts Vegetable Stock (page 363)

1 bay leaf

2 large garlic cloves, minced

1 cup dry sherry

2 quarts heavy cream

Salt and freshly ground white pepper

Fresh parsley, chopped, for garnish

Nearly half the mushrooms Americans eat come from the state of Pennsylvania.

Lobster Bisque

◆━━━━◆

This rich, buttery bisque came to the New World from France, where lobsters—better known as *langouste*—were the spiny, clawless variety found in the temperate coastal waters of the Mediterranean. French immigrant chefs had no problem recreating the dish in Philadelphia, since North Atlantic or Maine lobsters were considered commonplace and were readily available. This preparation would have elevated the common lobster, which was considered a poor person's food, to new culinary heights.

SERVES 6 TO 8

Heat 2 tablespoons of the butter in a stockpot over medium heat, add the celery, carrots, and onion, and sauté for 5 minutes, until tender. Add the cognac to deglaze the pan, using a wooden spoon to scrape any bits from the bottom of the pan. Add 3 quarts water, the lobster shells, tomato paste, bay leaf, thyme, and peppercorns. Bring to a boil over high heat. Reduce the heat and simmer for 6 hours.

Strain the stock through a fine sieve or cheesecloth into a large bowl. Discard the shells and vegetables. Return the stock to the stockpot and add the cream.

Heat the remaining 4 tablespoons of butter in a separate medium-size saucepan over low heat, add the flour and mix well. Cook for 5 minutes.

Bring the stock to a boil over high heat, then slowly stir in the flour-butter mixture until fully incorporated. Heat thoroughly for 5 minutes. Season with salt and pepper to taste.

Serve immediately in a soup tureen or divide among individual soup bowls.

6 tablespoons unsalted butter

4 celery ribs, chopped

2 large carrots, peeled and chopped

1 medium white onion, chopped

1 cup cognac

5 pounds lobster shells
(heads and bodies, without tails)

2 tablespoons tomato paste

1 bay leaf

1 sprig fresh thyme

1 teaspoon black peppercorns

1 cup heavy cream

¼ cup all-purpose flour

Salt and freshly ground black pepper

CHEF'S NOTE

Adjust the amount of cognac to suit your own taste. I also love to add a little Madeira just before serving; the mix of flavors is sensational.

In the early 1880s, lobster's wholesale price was only 6 cents a pound.

SALADS AND RELISHES

The concept of salad in eighteenth-century Philadelphia was slightly different from what we have come to know in the twentieth century. Salads weren't typically the tender green tosses of mesclun and baby greens we favor today. Although versions of these lettuces did exist—like tennis-ball, the grandfather of butterhead lettuce, and ice lettuce, a forerunner to our iceberg—they weren't readily available to the public. They would have been available to elites who purchased seeds in their travels and grew small amounts in their kitchen gardens.

In his gardens at Monticello, Thomas Jefferson grew both of these early types of lettuce from seeds he imported from Europe. Also noted in his *Garden Book* are various cresses that he called white lettuce, white loaf lettuce, and Dutch brown lettuce, which is similar to the red oak leaf lettuce available today.

Jefferson was also most likely the first American to dress salads with olive oil and vinegar, a practice he learned while living in Paris when he served as Minister Plenipotentiary. Although he regularly imported oil and wine vinegar from France, he occasionally had to conduct his search domestically. On April 16, 1810, Jefferson wrote to his grandson, "We are out of salad-oil, and you know it is a necessity of life here. Can any be had in Richmond?"

For the average colonial, however, salads were closer to what we today call composed salads—seasoned mixes of root vegetables, cabbage, kale, dried peas, legumes, and beans—the composition of which depended on the seasonal availability of the ingredients. Beets, potatoes, carrots, lentils, and other crops that stored well in root cellars were incorporated into salads during the winter months, and fresh ingredients like corn, scallions, cucumbers, and other seasonal vegetables were used in the summer.

Salads were served as part of the first plates course, except among the British, who were in the habit of eating salads in the late afternoon, during tea.

The practice of making relishes, invented as a means of preserving fruits and vegetables, can be traced back to the West Indies. Ships engaged in trade between Great Britain and the Islands incorporated relishes into their cargoes of tropical fruits and spices. The practice continued in the colonies, and relishes filled out first plate offerings in households and taverns alike.

Celery Root Salad

1 large celery root

¼ cup lemon juice
(about 1 large lemon), strained

¾ cup Homemade Mayonnaise
(page 370)

2 tablespoons Dijon mustard

1 tablespoon heavy cream

½ teaspoon curry powder

½ teaspoon Worcestershire sauce

Salt and freshly ground white pepper

1 butterhead (Boston or Bibb) lettuce,
cored and rinsed, for serving

2 tablespoons chopped walnuts,
for garnish

Celery root was commonly grown in colonial times because, if properly picked and stored, it could last the whole winter. Although today it is the stalk that is the favored part of this vegetable, colonials used the root as well. The most common use of celery appears to have been to make celery sauce, which was a common accompaniment for fowl dishes. Colonial cooks differ, however, as to which part of celery is best to use for this sauce. In her book, *The Art of Cookery Made Plain and Easy*, Hannah Glasse cooked the root with cream, mace, and nutmeg, whereas Mary Randolph instructed the cook to use the green stalks in her cookbook, *The Virginia Housewife*.

SERVES 4

Peel the celery root and cut it into 2-inch-long strips (the finer, the better). Place the strips in a medium-size bowl and coat thoroughly with the lemon juice. Cover with plastic wrap and refrigerate for 45 minutes, until completely chilled.

In a small mixing bowl, blend together the mayonnaise, mustard, cream, curry powder, and Worcestershire sauce. Add to the celery root, mix well, and season with salt and pepper to taste.

To serve, arrange the lettuce leaves on salad plates. Divide the celery root mixture among the plates and garnish with the walnuts.

CHEF'S NOTE

If you like a richer curry flavor,
increase the curry powder to suit your taste.

Apple & Walnut Salad

This salad makes the most of a tried-and-true pair: apples and walnuts, which were both indigenous to Pennsylvania. In colonial times, it was one of the few fresh salads that could be eaten in the winter. Even though the apples may have shriveled over time in the cellar, once the skins were removed, the flesh would be sweet and intact. Though this salad would have been common throughout the apple-growing regions of the continent, the addition of curry powder here would indicate that this recipe came from a seaport town, where the use of curry powder came into vogue as a result of close contact with ships carrying the necessary spices from the West Indies.

SERVES 4

In a medium-size mixing bowl, toss the apple slices with the lemon juice.

In a small mixing bowl, combine the walnuts, mayonnaise, cream, Worcestershire sauce, and curry. Pour the mayonnaise mixture over the apples and toss gently to coat. Season with salt and pepper to taste. Cover and refrigerate for 1 hour, until well chilled.

Just before serving, garnish with the parsley.

4 large apples,
peeled, cored, and thinly sliced

¼ cup fresh lemon juice
(about 1 large lemon), strained

½ cup chopped walnuts

¼ cup Homemade Mayonnaise
(page 370)

2 tablespoons heavy cream

¼ teaspoon Worcestershire sauce

⅛ teaspoon curry powder

Salt and freshly ground white pepper

Fresh parsley, chopped, for garnish

CHEF'S NOTE

To turn this side dish into a wonderful main course,
add diced chicken, pineapple chunks, and cooked long-grain rice.
To intensify the curry flavor, add double the amount.

Spiced Pepper Slaw
with Warm Bacon Dressing

½ medium head green cabbage,
finely shredded (about 4 cups)

1 tablespoon salt

2 medium green bell peppers,
finely chopped (about 1½ cups)

½ teaspoon hot red pepper flakes

1½ slices lean bacon, chopped

1 scallion, finely chopped
(about 2 tablespoons)

2 tablespoons red wine vinegar

1 tablespoon chopped fresh parsley

1½ teaspoons whole-grain mustard

½ teaspoon cayenne pepper

¼ teaspoon sugar

¼ cup olive oil

Salt and freshly ground black pepper

Cabbage grows mainly during cool seasons, like spring and fall, and in the more temperate climates found in Southern states it can even be grown in winter. Colonial cultivators took full advantage of any growing time available to them, so cabbage was a big staple in the colonial diet. Back then, this dish would have either been eaten when cabbage was freshly picked and ingredients like fresh peppers were available as well, or prepared later on in the winter with preserved cabbage.

Serves 4

Place the cabbage in a large mixing bowl and sprinkle with the salt. Cover with plastic wrap and refrigerate for about 1½ hours to remove excess water from cabbage.

Thoroughly rinse and drain the cabbage, pressing it lightly to remove any additional water. Return it to the bowl and stir in the bell peppers and red pepper flakes.

In a small saucepan, cook the bacon over medium heat for 3 minutes, until crisp. Remove the bacon from the pan and drain on paper towels.

In the same skillet over medium heat, cook the scallions in the bacon drippings for 1 minute, until lightly brown. Add the vinegar to deglaze the pan, loosening any browned bits on the bottom of the pan with a wooden spoon. Remove from the heat.

In a medium-size mixing bowl, combine the parsley, mustard, cayenne pepper, sugar, and the hot vinegar mixture. Slowly add the olive oil, whisking constantly. Add the warm dressing immediately to the cabbage mixture. Toss to mix.

Season with salt and pepper to taste. Sprinkle the reserved bacon on top of the salad before serving.

Dandelion Salad

Dandelions come into season from late March into early April, depending on where they're grown. According to the *Dictionary of American Regional English*, Pennsylvanians colloquially called dandelion greens salad "Dutch Salad" because these greens were favored by German immigrants. Colonials knew to choose young, tender wild dandelion leaves, because once the dandelions started to flower, the leaves became bitter and virtually inedible.

SERVES 8

Pat the dandelion greens dry with paper towels. Tear into bite-sized pieces. Place the greens in a large mixing bowl.

In a medium-size saucepan, cook the bacon over medium heat for 3 minutes, until crisp. Pour the fat in a thin stream over the dandelion greens. Toss to mix.

Add the balsamic vinegar to the bacon in the saucepan, and pour over the dandelion greens. Add the garlic and toss to mix. Season with salt and pepper to taste.

2½ pounds fresh
dandelion greens, rinsed

6 slices lean bacon, cut into thin strips

¼ cup balsamic vinegar

2 garlic cloves, chopped

Salt and freshly ground black pepper

CHEF'S NOTE

If you pick your own dandelion greens, be sure to pick them from an area
that hasn't been sprayed with chemicals.

Potato Salad

---

12 medium Yukon gold potatoes

1 large yellow onion, finely chopped

¼ cup red wine vinegar

¼ cup vegetable oil

1½ to 2 cups Beef Stock (page 363)

Salt and freshly ground white pepper

Chopped fresh chives, for garnish

Potatoes were one of the few vegetables that could be stored in colonial root cellars and eaten all year long. This recipe would have made its way to the Colonies from Germany, carried in the recipe books of Germans who settled in the cooler northern locales, like Pennsylvania. This recipe is inspired by one for "Hot Potato Salad" left behind by Magdelena Hoch Keim, the daughter-in-law of Johannes Keim, a Rhinelander, and one of the first Germans to answer William Penn's invitation to settle a "utopian colony" in the New World.

SERVES 6

In a large saucepan, cook the potatoes in enough boiling, lightly salted water to cover for 20 to 25 minutes, until just tender. Drain the potatoes and cool slightly. Peel and cut the potatoes into ¼-inch-thick slices.

In a medium-size mixing bowl, combine the potatoes, onion, vinegar, and oil, tossing gently to coat. Pour in the stock a little at a time, mixing gently until it is absorbed. (The salad should be moist but not drenched.) Season with salt and white pepper to taste.

Sprinkle with the chives. Serve immediately while still warm.

Cabbage Salad

———◆◆◆———

Cabbage, which wintered well, was a staple for the early settlers. A terrific source of nutrients, especially with winter's limited menu, cabbage was eaten braised, in salads, and as sauerkraut. The addition of lean bacon, garlic, and olive oil dressing to this cabbage salad elevates it heads above the average slaw.

SERVES 8

Heat 1 tablespoon of the olive oil and the butter in a large skillet over medium heat. Add the bacon and sauté for 3 minutes, until crisp.

Add 2 tablespoons of the vinegar, then the cabbage. Increase the heat to high and cook for 3 minutes, until the cabbage begins to wilt. Remove from heat.

In a large bowl, combine the mustard, the remaining 2 tablespoons vinegar, and the remaining 6 tablespoons oil. Pour the mustard mixture over the cabbage mixture. Toss to coat. Season with salt and pepper to taste.

Just before serving, add the garlic and parsley. Toss to mix.

7 tablespoons olive oil

2 tablespoons unsalted butter

9 slices lean bacon, chopped

4 tablespoons white wine vinegar

1 medium green cabbage,
shredded or sliced into narrow strips
(about 8 cups)

1 tablespoon Dijon mustard

Salt and freshly ground black pepper

2 garlic cloves, finely chopped

1 small bunch fresh parsley, chopped

Lentil Salad

——◆——

SALAD

4 cups dried French lentils
(see Chef's Note)

2 carrots, peeled and julienned

1 medium yellow onion, chopped

2 large garlic cloves, chopped

1 bay leaf

3 sprigs fresh thyme

1 teaspoon salt

½ teaspoon freshly ground black pepper

9 slices lean bacon, chopped

DRESSING

1 red onion, finely chopped

½ cup olive oil

¼ cup red wine vinegar

1 bunch fresh chives, chopped
(about 6 tablespoons)

2 tablespoons Dijon mustard

3 garlic cloves, chopped

1 teaspoon salt

½ teaspoon freshly ground black pepper

This sophisticated French salad would have been common only at a restaurant as upscale as City Tavern—the typical colonial housewife would have never made this dish. The Tavern chefs constantly incorporated French and European dishes into the menu, and strove to use creatively the ingredients that were at hand, such as dried beans and lentils. The lentils in this recipe are the smaller French lentils, which were most likely discovered in France and introduced to the colonies by Thomas Jefferson, who grew them in his garden at Monticello.

SERVES 8

TO PREPARE THE SALAD: Pre-soak the lentils by placing them in a colander and rinsing them thoroughly with water to clean. Place the lentils in a large bowl and cover with water. Let stand at room temperature for at least 8 hours.

Drain and thoroughly rinse the lentils; reserve.

In a large saucepan, combine the lentils, carrots, onion, garlic, bay leaf, thyme, salt, and pepper. Add enough water to cover. Bring to a boil over high heat. Reduce the heat, cover the pan, and simmer for about 10 minutes, until the lentils are tender, but not overcooked. Check frequently for doneness during cooking.

Drain the lentil mixture in a colander and transfer to a large bowl. Remove the thyme and bay leaf. Cover and refrigerate the lentil mixture for 1 hour, until chilled.

In a small saucepan, cook the bacon over medium heat for about 3 minutes, until crisp. Remove the bacon from the saucepan and drain on paper towels.

TO PREPARE THE DRESSING: In a large bowl, combine the onion, oil, vinegar, chives, mustard, garlic, salt, and pepper. Add the lentil mixture to the dressing and mix gently. Season with additional salt and pepper to taste. Let stand at room temperature for about 30 minutes to allow the flavors to develop. Before serving, adjust seasoning to taste.

CHEF'S NOTE

Turn this salad into a main dish by stirring in some chopped roast pork or cooked sausage and diced, cooked potato. Serve on lettuce leaves.

Because this recipe requires a shorter-than-average cooking time, we soak the lentils to ensure an al dente texture.

Cucumber & Cream
Salad

---

1 large European seedless cucumber
or 4 small cucumbers, peeled
and thinly sliced (about 4 cups)

½ cup sour cream

1 medium red onion, finely chopped

1 tablespoon cider vinegar

⅛ teaspoon paprika

Dash of cayenne pepper

Salt and freshly ground black pepper

Fresh chives, chopped, for garnish

In days gone by, this dish was only served during the warm months when cucumbers were in season. We can only imagine how much cooks and diners alike anticipated the fresh, tender bounty of summer after a winter of eating dried and root vegetables. If the paprika and cayenne pepper seem out of place in a colonial recipe, one need only turn to Hannah Glasse, who made a warm version of this salad, "To Ragoo Cucumbers," with cayenne pepper!

SERVES 4

Place the cucumber in a medium-size mixing bowl and sprinkle with salt. Cover with plastic wrap and refrigerate for about 1 hour, until chilled and the liquid has drained from the cucumbers.

Thoroughly rinse the cucumbers with cold water and gently squeeze out all of the excess water.

In a small mixing bowl, stir together the sour cream, onion, vinegar, paprika, and cayenne pepper until combined. Add to the cucumber and mix well. Season with salt and pepper to taste. Garnish with the chives.

Roasted Red & Golden Beet Salad

Beets aren't a favorite American vegetable nowadays, but considering the qualities of what colonial chefs would consider the perfect vegetable, beets ranked very high on the list. They stored well over the winter and were extremely versatile in soups, salads, and relishes. Even then, Mary Randolph noted in *The Virginia Housewife* that red beets "are not so much used as they deserve to be." However, she seems to have made good use of them, noting after one recipe for boiling beets that they are "an excellent garnish, and easily converted into a very cheap and pleasant pickle."

1 pound whole fresh red beets, stems trimmed ½ inch above the beets

1 pound whole fresh golden beets, stems trimmed ½ inch above the beets

1 cup olive oil

½ cup finely chopped onions

¼ cup rice wine vinegar

1 tablespoon chopped fresh parsley

Juice of ½ lemon

½ teaspoon red pepper flakes

1 tablespoon Dijon mustard

Salt and freshly ground black pepper

½ cup roughly chopped walnuts

2 hard-cooked eggs, sliced (optional)

SERVES 6

Preheat the oven to 350°F.

Separate the beets according to color and place them in separate shallow baking dishes. Roast for 30 to 45 minutes (the golden beets will cook more quickly because of their size), or until they can be penetrated with slight resistance, from a sharp knife. Set aside to cool enough to handle.

Use a small paring knife to remove the beet skins and cut the beets into 1-inch cubes. Reserve.

In a medium-size mixing bowl, combine the oil, onions, vinegar, parsley, lemon juice, red pepper flakes, mustard, and salt and pepper to taste. Stir in the beets, walnuts, and hard-cooked eggs, cover the bowl with plastic wrap, and refrigerate for about 2 hours, until the salad is marinated and thoroughly chilled. Adjust seasoning to taste.

Serve chilled.

Green Bean Salad

Every gardener knows that green beans are among the easiest crop to grow—and that they can take over a garden in no time. Early settlers, who did without green vegetables for much of the year, must have welcomed this hardy crop with great eagerness, using green beans fresh, as in this recipe, dried, or pickled in precious preserves for winter. In his *Garden Book*, Thomas Jefferson makes several mentions of planting "long haricots," the very thin French style of green bean, but, surprisingly, he leaves not even one recipe for them. Given his long *séjours* in France, we can infer that he would have enjoyed them prepared in the classical French manner below.

SERVES 8

Bring a large saucepan of salted water to a boil over high heat. Add the haricots verts and cook for 10 to 15 minutes, until just firm but tender. Drain the haricot verts and place them in a large bowl. Add the mushrooms and shallots and mix gently.

In a small bowl, whisk together the oil, vinegar, and mustard until blended. Pour over the haricot vert mixture and toss gently to coat. Season with salt and pepper to taste.

Serve at room temperature.

CHEF'S NOTE

If you can't get walnut oil, substitute olive oil.
Balsamic vinegar can also be used in place of the red wine vinegar, if you like.

2½ pounds fresh haricots verts, trimmed

5½ cups sliced fresh button mushrooms (about 1 pound)

3 medium shallots, chopped

6 tablespoons walnut oil

3 tablespoons red wine vinegar

2 teaspoons Dijon mustard

Salt and freshly ground black pepper

Tomato & Basil Salad

4 vine-ripened or heirloom tomatoes, cored and sliced into thin wedges

1 small red onion, finely chopped

About ⅓ cup fresh basil leaves, thinly sliced into strips about 2 inches long and ⅛-inch wide

1 small clove garlic, finely chopped

½ cup red wine or balsamic vinegar

½ cup olive oil, sunflower oil, or walnut oil

Salt and freshly ground black pepper

1 head Boston Bibb lettuce

Fresh basil leaves, for garnish

Tomatoes were slow to gain popularity in the New World because many believed that this member of the nightshade family was poisonous. However, Thomas Jefferson, who was introduced to tomatoes in France, where they were called "love apples," championed them tirelessly. He was the first American to plant what he called "tomatas," and quickly set about copying down recipes for their use. He served them at Monticello and in the White House, virtually forcing friends and guests to shrug off their prejudices and give them a try. He even went so far as to eat a tomato in public to prove that they weren't poisonous.

SERVES 4

Combine the tomatoes, onion, basil, and garlic in a large bowl, toss with the vinegar and oil to coat, and season with salt and pepper.

Arrange about 2 lettuce leaves on each serving plate (try to form them into a "bowl"), spoon some of the tomato salad into the leaves and garnish with basil.

CHEF'S NOTE

For a lovely light summer salad, serve this with thinly sliced fresh mozzarella cheese.

Romaine Lettuce
with Red Burgundy Wine-Dijon Vinaigrette

Roquefort cheese was introduced to the New World by the French, quite possibly either by Benjamin Franklin or Thomas Jefferson, both of whom served as Minister to France, and both of whom adored cheese of all types. Ever searching for culinary balance, the French traditionally paired Roquefort's pungent flavor with French Dijon mustard and tart wine vinegar, a preparation which surely would have graced the tables of Franklin's Philadelphia home at 141 High Street (now Market Street) and Jefferson's beloved Monticello.

MAKES 2 CUPS VINAIGRETTE;
SERVES 6

In a medium-size mixing bowl, whisk together the vinegar, wine, mustard, and sugar. Slowly add the olive oil, whisking constantly. Season with salt and pepper to taste.

When ready to serve, whisk the dressing. Pour over the romaine lettuce and toss to coat. Crumble the Roquefort over the salads.

¼ cup red wine vinegar

¼ cup red Burgundy wine

1 tablespoon Dijon mustard

1 teaspoon sugar

1½ cups olive oil

Salt and freshly ground white pepper

2 heads romaine lettuce,
rinsed and torn

1 cup crumbled Roquefort,
for serving

Butterhead Lettuce
with Raspberry Shrub Vinaigrette

———◦•◦———

½ cup raspberry shrub
(see Resources, page 378)

2 teaspoons balsamic vinegar

1 teaspoon sugar

1 teaspoon Dijon mustard

1½ cups olive oil

Salt and freshly ground white pepper

3 heads butterhead (Boston or Bibb)
lettuce or mixed greens, rinsed and torn

Edible unsprayed flowers,
for garnish

In his *Garden Book*, Thomas Jefferson mentions several plantings and harvests of Tennis-ball lettuce, a parent of butterhead lettuce, at Monticello. He also grew Brown Dutch lettuce, similar to Oak Leaf, and "Ice" lettuce, which is presumed to be a parent of modern iceberg lettuce. However, the Tennis-ball variety seems to have been preferred and more widely known because it didn't "require so much care and attention." Its seeds were brought over from France and Germany, and its tender leaves were enjoyed in the late spring and early summer seasons.

MAKES 2 CUPS VINAIGRETTE;
SERVES 6

In a medium-size mixing bowl, whisk together the raspberry shrub, balsamic vinegar, sugar, and mustard. Slowly add the olive oil, whisking constantly. Season with salt and pepper to taste.

When ready to serve, whisk the dressing. Pour over the lettuce or mixed greens and toss to coat. Garnish with edible flowers, if desired.

Garnishing salads with fresh, edible flowers is by no means a twenty-first century idea. Thomas Jefferson grew corn flowers and nasturtium for just that purpose. In fact, he so enjoyed the peppery, watercress-like taste of nasturtium in salads that by 1824 his nasturtium bed had increased to 1,800 square feet. Sophisticated colonial cooks also used edible orchids, pansies and chrysanthemum petals in salads and as garnishes for dishes of every type.

Cranberry Relish

3 cups fresh cranberries
(about 12 ounces)

½ cup sugar

2 tablespoons grated orange rind

Cranberry bogs, which were found mainly in the New England colonies, greeted the settlers when they first arrived to the New World. As such, cranberries became a great part of the colonial diet, especially in Massachusetts. In addition to pies, tarts, and preserves, colonial cooks made cranberry sauce as we know it today. John Adams mentions cranberry sauce in a diary entry on April 8, 1787. "Arrived at Dr. Tufts where I found a fine Wild Goose on the Spit and Cramberries stewing in the Skillet for Dinner." He further adds that Dr. Tufts invited him "to dine upon wild Goose and Cramberry Sause."

MAKES 2 CUPS; SERVES 8

In a stainless steel or enameled saucepan, combine the cranberries, sugar, orange rind, and ½ cup water. Bring to a simmer over medium-low heat. Cook, stirring occasionally, for about 5 minutes, until the cranberries burst.

Remove from the heat and let cool. Store in a tightly sealed plastic or glass container and refrigerate for up to 8 weeks.

Cranberries, together with grapes and blueberries, are among the few fruits native to North America.

Pineapple Relish

Pineapples were a symbol of hospitality in the eighteenth century and remain so today. It seems that when a ship's captain returned home from a West Indian voyage, he would place a pineapple on a stick in front of his door as a signal to friends and neighbors that he had returned and was welcoming visitors. The incorporation of habañero pepper, which would have been among captains' cargoes, follows the traditional West Indian preparation of this flavorful relish.

MAKES 4 CUPS; SERVES 6 TO 8

In a medium-size mixing bowl, combine all of the ingredients. Cover and refrigerate for about 2 hours, until completely chilled.

Serve chilled as an accompaniment to meats, poultry, or fish.

Store in a tightly sealed plastic or glass container and refrigerate for up to 8 weeks.

1 large fresh pineapple, peeled and finely chopped (see Chef's Note)

1 medium white onion, very finely chopped

¼ cup honey

¼ cup pineapple juice

¼ cup rice wine vinegar

¼ habañero pepper, finely chopped (see Chef's Note, page 58)

¼ teaspoon ground allspice

Salt and freshly ground white pepper

CHEF'S NOTE

TO PREPARE A PINEAPPLE: Cut the top and bottom off, then remove the outer skin with a chef's knife. Cut the pineapple in half lengthwise and then in half again. Cut out and discard the core. Dice the remaining fruit.

Mango & Papaya Relish

In the 1700s, ships typically pulled into the harbor loaded with tropical fruits that had to be used immediately. The colonial cook's primary means of preserving fresh fruits and vegetables included sun-drying, making jams and chutneys, and cooking them into relishes, such as this one.

MAKES 6 CUPS; SERVES 8 TO 12

In a medium-size mixing bowl, combine all of the ingredients. Cover with plastic wrap and refrigerate for about 2 hours, until thoroughly marinated.

Store in a tightly sealed plastic or glass container and refrigerate for up to 8 weeks.

3 medium papayas, peeled and chopped

2 medium mangoes, peeled and chopped

1 medium red onion, chopped

½ cup honey

¼ cup rice wine vinegar

1 teaspoon chopped fresh cilantro leaves

½ teaspoon ground star anise

Spicy Corn Relish

◦—◦◦◦◦•◦◦◦—◦

After a long winter full of dark, drab dishes made from the contents of the root cellar, colonial cooks tended to splurge a bit when the first fruits of their garden labor came to the kitchen. Fresh, sweet corn was available again, and red and green peppers could be used to make bright, colorful dishes, and fresh herbs and spices brought renewed excitement to their palates.

MAKES 6 CUPS; SERVES 12

Bring a large saucepan of lightly salted water to a boil over high heat. Add the corn and cook for 5 to 7 minutes, until tender. Do not overcook.

Drain the corn and place it in a medium-size mixing bowl. Add the remaining ingredients except for the sprig of thyme and mix well. Season with salt and pepper. Cover and refrigerate for about 30 minutes, until chilled. Store in a tightly sealed plastic or glass container and refrigerate for up to 8 weeks.

Corn was introduced to the colonists by Native Americans, who held it sacred, and used it as the foundation of their diet. Fresh *maize* or corn was also dried or parched so that it could be stored and used later in stews and other cooked dishes. Corn also could be pounded or ground to make a substitute for flour.

10 ears fresh white corn, kernels cut from cobs

1 medium red bell pepper, finely chopped

1 medium green bell pepper, finely chopped

1 medium white onion, finely chopped

¼ cup rice wine vinegar

¼ cup olive oil

2 medium scallions, finely chopped (about 3 tablespoons)

1 garlic clove, finely chopped

½ bunch fresh chives, finely chopped (about 3 tablespoons)

½ bunch fresh cilantro, finely chopped (about ¼ cup)

1 teaspoon ground cumin

1 teaspoon red pepper flakes

1 sprig fresh thyme, for garnish

Salt and freshly ground black pepper

Onion & Raisin
Relish

•❦•

1½ pounds pearl onions
(preferably small)

5 cups dry white wine,
such as Sauvignon Blanc

1 cup raisins

1 cup olive oil

½ cup red wine vinegar

3 tablespoons tomato paste

½ bunch fresh savory

1 sprig fresh thyme
or 1 teaspoon dried thyme

2 bay leaves

5 garlic cloves, finely chopped

1 teaspoon dried rubbed sage

½ teaspoon red pepper flakes

Salt and freshly ground black pepper

Sweet and savory flavors make perfect complements in this chunky German-style relish made with pearl onions. In *American Cookery*, Amelia Simmons offered the following advice on onions: "If you consult cheapness, the largest are best, but if you consult taste and softness, the very smallest are the most delicate, and used at the finest tables."

MAKES 6 CUPS; SERVES 12

Place the onions in a large saucepan and fill with water to cover. Bring to a boil over high heat and boil for 5 minutes, then drain and reserve. With a small paring knife, make a crisscross cut in the stem end of each onion.

In a large saucepan, combine the onions, wine, raisins, oil, vinegar, tomato paste, savory, thyme, bay leaves, garlic, sage, and red pepper flakes. Bring to a boil over high heat. Reduce the heat and simmer, stirring frequently, for 35 to 50 minutes, until the liquid is evaporated, leaving a most chutney-like mixture. Set aside to cool.

Season with salt and pepper to taste.

Store in a tightly sealed plastic or glass container and refrigerate for up to 4 weeks.

In colonial times, relishes and other types of preserves would have been kept away from sunlight and stored in a cool, dry pantry.

Peach Chutney

Chutney was brought to America by the British, who had learned to make the spicy condiment from the East Indians. It was made with a variety of fruits as a way of preserving perishable fruit, such as peaches, past their normal seasonal prime. Peach chutney would have appeared on tables in southern colonies, where peaches grew in abundance. Sarah Gibbons Telfair—wife of Edward Telfair, a wealthy Savannah, Georgia, merchant who was among those gathered at City Tavern to draft the response to the Intolerable Acts—included tomato, cayenne pepper, and chili powder in her recipe for peach chutney.

Makes 3 cups; Serves 6

In a large saucepan, sauté the onion in the oil over medium heat for 3 minutes, until translucent. Stir in the peaches, bell pepper, honey, vinegar, brown sugar, and nutmeg. Bring to a boil over high heat. Reduce the heat and simmer, stirring occasionally, for 8 to 10 minutes, until liquid is reduced. Let cool.

Store in a tightly sealed plastic or glass container and refrigerate for up to 8 weeks.

1 medium red onion,
halved lengthwise and sliced

1 tablespoon vegetable oil

4 medium fresh peaches,
peeled and cut into wedges
(about 4 pounds)

1 red bell pepper, chopped

½ cup honey

½ cup white wine vinegar

1 tablespoon light brown sugar

¼ teaspoon freshly grated nutmeg

CHEF'S NOTE

To ensure that chutneys and relishes maintain a long shelf life,
always use a clean utensil when serving and store in the refrigerator.

MAIN DISHES

In the eighteenth-century City Tavern, today's main dishes appeared both as "first plates" and "second plates," although in greater number in the second plates. Some colonial menus even show main course dishes, such as "Rabbit Fricaseed, Larks à la Surprise, and Buttered Crab," appearing as third plates. At large parties at the Tavern, it was not unusual to see a display of up to twenty dishes per course. These feasts would typically last from three to four hours and reflected the cultural diversity of Philadelphia. Diners enjoyed typically English beef chops, pork roasts, veal loins, whole fish, and seafood; German organ meat delicacies like tripe and heart, smoked meats, and sausages; and French pâtés and terrines made from wild game birds, venison, and rabbit. Though these would have been sliced and served in smaller portions than we enjoy today, they would have been presented artfully on large platters, decorated with fresh fruits and vegetables, and garnished with bunches of fresh herbs.

While the main dishes herein have been adjusted to suit modern portion sizes and cooking methods, the point must be made that colonial cooks managed to create these very complicated and sophisticated main dishes despite the limited types of cooking equipment available. Some very ingenious thinking led to helpful inventions. A swinging arm allowed the cook to adjust the temperatures at which the food was cooked by moving the pot nearer to or away from the fire. Fireplaces were also equipped with various pulley and ratchet systems to raise and lower pots for the same effect. To avoid burning or overcooking, large roasts were placed in front of the fire, rather than over it, and a shield placed on the outward-facing side was used to reflect heat back onto the roast. Drip pans were installed below to capture juices, which were then used to baste meats or fowl, or to make sauces and gravies. Rotisseries were cranked by hand, usually by one of the cook's children, and some were even designed to be operated by dogs. Ever the inventor, Thomas Jefferson installed a spit-jack that used a clock-type movement with weights to turn the spit automatically. His stew stove, the grandfather of our modern stoves, was a waist-high counter of brick with individual openings and grates below. The temperature of each "burner" could be adjusted simply by changing the amount of coals placed in the grate.

Cooking pots were typically made of cast iron, which held the heat and distributed it evenly. They used large cauldrons and kettles, and frying pans called *spiders* because of their long legs and handles. There were also French *daubières*, pots with concave lids onto which burning coals could be heaped to ensure even cooking. Copper pots, though they existed, would have only been used in the wealthiest households. Thomas Jefferson had several specialized copper pieces shipped to Monticello from Paris: saucepans, kettles, skillets, *tourtières* (tart pans) and *poissonières* (long, narrow fish poachers), that were used on the stew stove to recreate the delicate French dishes he preferred.

A typical eighteenth-century dining room.

Braised Oxtail

---

2 tablespoons vegetable oil

3 pounds oxtail,
cut into 2-inch pieces

1 clove garlic, chopped

2 medium yellow onions, chopped

2 large carrots, peeled and chopped

1 large celery root, chopped

2 cups dry red wine,
such as Burgundy

8 sprigs thyme

1 teaspoon dried marjoram

1 quart Demi-Glace (page 367)

In many cultures, both Eastern and Western, it was believed that eating the tail of the ox would convey an ox-like strength and endurance to the diner. For colonials, it was more a matter of necessity, as no part of the animal was wasted after the slaughter. The meager pieces of meat found on the oxtail are very flavorful, but tough, so they must be braised or stewed to achieve the desired tenderness.

Serves 4

Heat the oil in a large pot over medium heat. Add the oxtails and cook for about 5 to 8 minutes per side, until well browned. Drain the excess grease from the pan, leaving enough in the pan to coat the bottom.

Add the garlic and cook for 1 to 2 minutes, until golden. Add the onions, carrots, and celery root, and cook for about 5 to 10 minutes, until the onion is translucent and the carrot and celery root are softened.

Pour in the wine, thyme, and marjoram, and cook for 15 to 20 minutes, until the liquid is reduced by half. Add the demi-glace, reduce the heat to low and cook for 1 to 1¼ hours, until the meat is tender and falling off the bone. Remove the thyme stems before serving.

Stuffed Roasted Quail

———✦———

Quail were among the many game birds that inhabited the forests around Philadelphia and beyond. As such, there were countless recipes for roasting quail in colonial cookbooks. Some called for the quail to be stuffed with herbs and beef suet, presumably to keep the breast meat juicy. Other recipes called for an oyster stuffing, which was a common ingredient in the preparation of stuffed fowl. Yet others required a simple bread or cornbread stuffing. The quail were then either roasted on a spit or in a beehive oven.

SERVES 4

Place the cornbread in a large bowl.

Heat ½ tablespoon of the oil in a large skillet over medium-low heat, add the onions and bacon, and sauté for 10 to 15 minutes, until the onions are golden and the bacon crisp. Add the garlic, thyme, marjoram, sage, salt, and pepper, and sauté for 5 minutes, until the garlic is golden. Add the wine and cook for about 5 minutes, until the liquid is evaporated. Add this mixture to the cornbread in the bowl.

Heat the remaining ½ tablespoon oil in the same skillet over high heat, add the mushrooms, and sauté for 5 to 8 minutes, until browned and the liquid is evaporated. Add to the cornbread mixture and add the parsley, pecans, and raisins. Mix well. Add enough of the stock to moisten the mixture, but be careful not to make it soggy. Cover and refrigerate for 1 hour.

Preheat the oven to 425°F.

Rinse the quail inside and out, and pat dry with paper towels. Season their insides with half of the thyme, sage, and salt and pepper. Stuff with the cornbread stuffing and tie their legs together with kitchen twine. Season their outsides with the remaining sage, thyme, and salt and pepper. Place in a large, shallow baking dish.

Roast for 15 minutes, until brown, then baste with the pan drippings and cover with foil. Lower the oven temperature to 350°F and roast for an additional 10 minutes, until the thigh bones can be wiggled easily. Remove and snip the twine from the legs.

Combine the demi-glace and Madeira in a small saucepan and cook over medium heat for 5 to 8 minutes, until the mixture is completely warmed through. Remove from the heat and whisk in the butter.

Place the quail on a large serving platter or divide among individual plates and top with the Madeira Demi-Glace.

CORNBREAD STUFFING

1 recipe Cornbread (page 309), cooled and cut into ½-inch cubes

1 tablespoon olive oil

2 onions, chopped

6 slices bacon, diced

3 garlic cloves, chopped

1 tablespoon fresh thyme leaves

1 teaspoon dried marjoram

1 teaspoon dried sage

1 tablespoon salt

1 tablespoon freshly ground black pepper

½ cup dry white wine, such as Sauvignon Blanc

4 cups sliced mushrooms (about 12 ounces)

½ cup chopped fresh parsley

½ cup chopped pecans

1 tablespoon chopped raisins

¾ cup Chicken Stock (page 364)

QUAIL

12 (4- to 6-ounce) quail, breastbones removed

2 tablespoons dried sage

2 tablespoons dried thyme

Salt and freshly ground black pepper

MADEIRA DEMI-GLACE

1½ cups Demi-Glace (page 367)

¼ cup Rainwater-style Madeira

2 tablespoons unsalted butter

Rice-Stuffed
Roasted Pheasant

2 (2½ pound) pheasants

1 (750 ml) bottle dry red wine, such as Burgundy

6 whole peppercorns

1 bay leaf

1 sprig thyme

1 sprig sage

1 tablespoon dried sage

1 tablespoon dried thyme

Salt and freshly ground black pepper

4 cups Wild Rice Stuffing (page 228)

1 pound bacon or fatback, sliced

1½ cups Demi-Glace (page 367)

¼ cup Rainwater-style Madeira

2 tablespoons unsalted butter

Colonial cooks differentiated between male pheasants ("cocks"), female pheasants ("hens"), and young pheasants ("poults"). Hannah Glasse gives the following recommendations for choosing pheasants: "The spurs of the pheasant cock, when young, are short and dubbed; but long and sharp when old; when new, he has a firm vent, when stale, an open and flabby one." Pheasants were also always roasted with their heads on, turned toward the back for presentation. Modern cooks need not bother with such concerns, as many specialty purveyors will choose an appropriate fowl and butcher it according to twenty first–century tastes.

Overnight preparation required.

SERVES 4

Rinse the pheasant inside and out, and pat dry with paper towels.

Combine the pheasants, wine, peppercorns, bay leaf, sprig of thyme, and sprig of sage in a high-sided casserole dish. Cover and refrigerate overnight, turning periodically.

When ready to cook the pheasants, remove them from the marinade and pat them dry with paper towels. Discard the marinade.

Preheat the oven to 425°F.

Season the cavities with half of the dried sage and dried thyme, and salt and pepper. Stuff the cavities with the Wild Rice Stuffing, then tie the legs together with kitchen twine. Season the outsides of the pheasants with the remaining dried sage, dried thyme, and salt and pepper. Place the pheasants breast-up on a rack in a roasting pan. Lay the bacon over the breasts.

Roast for 30 minutes, until the pheasants become brown, then baste with the pan drippings and cover with foil. Lower the oven temperature to 350°F and roast for an additional 45 minutes, until the thigh bones can be wiggled easily. Remove the bacon and discard and roast for an additional 5 minutes, until the skin is crispy. Remove from the oven and snip the twine from the legs.

Combine the demi-glace and Madeira in a small saucepan and cook over medium heat for about 5 to 8 minutes, until completely warmed through. Remove from the heat and whisk in the butter.

Place the pheasants on a large serving platter or carve. Divide among individual plates and top with the Madeira Demi-Glace.

Beef Tongue
in Caper Sauce

———•◦•———

Again, never willing to waste one single part of the cow after the slaughter, eighteenth-century cooks developed many recipes for beef tongue. It was pickled, roasted, stuffed, stewed, potted, and even rubbed with charcoal to preserve it in the same manner as Westphalia ham. When he was president, Thomas Jefferson employed a French maître d'hotel named Etienne Lemaire, who kept shopping lists and detailed the president's dining habits in his diaries. It seems beef tongue was among Jefferson's favorite breakfast foods and given his deep connection with France (and Lemaire's natural culinary leanings), we assume that it would have been prepared in the French manner, as included here.

SERVES 4

Pierce the onion with the cloves. In a large pot of lightly salted water, add the onion, beef tongue, and pickling spice, and simmer over low heat until firm, periodically skimming off any foam that rises to the top, about 1½ hours.

Remove and let cool in the stock, making sure that the tongue remains completely covered by the stock.

Once the tongue is cool, peel off the skin and trim off any excess fat. Place the tongue back into the stock and cook over medium heat for about 10 to 15 minutes, until warmed through. Remove the tongue from the stock and slice on a bias into ¼-inch-thick pieces.

In a medium saucepan, combine the Béchamel Sauce and ¼ cup of the stock from the tongue, and cook over low heat until warmed completely through. Stir in the capers and caper brine.

Place the Homemade Egg Noodles on a large serving platter and fan the tongue out overtop. Top with the sauce and garnish with the parsley.

1 yellow onion

6 whole cloves

1 (2½-pound) beef tongue

2 tablespoons pickling spice

2 cups Béchamel Sauce (page 369)

2 tablespoons capers

1 tablespoon caper brine

Homemade Egg Noodles
(see page 212), for serving

1 small bunch fresh parsley,
for garnish

Braised Pork Shank

———•—•—•———

This dish comes from the German tradition of the Schlachtfest, or slaughter fest. When a pig was slaughtered, it was a family event. All the cooks in the family had to be gathered together to make sure that every part of the pig could be pickled, preserved, salted, roasted, or made into sausages before any of it went to waste. Because of its practicality, this custom spread rapidly from German settlers in Pennsylvania to the other colonies, making the particular dishes that accompanied it, such as this braised pork shank, common in many colonial households.

4 (10- to 12-ounce) pork shanks, skin on

Salt and freshly ground black pepper

Sauerkraut, for serving (page 211)

SERVES 4

Preheat the oven to 325°F.

Sprinkle the shanks with salt and pepper and place them in a roasting pan. Pour water around the shanks to a depth of ¼ inch.

Roast the shanks for about 30 to 40 minutes, until the water has evaporated and the skin is crispy.

Increase the oven temperature to 375°F and roast for about 1½ hours more, checking frequently to make sure the grease does not overflow the pan, until the meat has shrunk back from the bone by about 1 inch.

To serve, place a bed of sauerkraut on a large platter and top with the pork shanks.

Roasted Sweetbreads

Ever-frugal colonial housewives learned to make sweetbreads in all manner of ways. In the *Art of Cookery Made Plain and Easy*, Hannah Glasse advises readers that "There are many ways of dressing sweetbreads: you may lard them with thin strips of bacon, and roast them with what sauce you please; or you may marinate them, cut them into thin slices, flour them and fry them. Serve them up with fried parsley, and either butter or gravy. Garnish with lemon." Following her advice, here they are roasted and finished in the French manner with red wine demi-glace.

Overnight preparation required.

SERVES 4

In a large mixing bowl, combine the sweetbreads with enough cold water to cover. Cover with plastic wrap and soak in the refrigerator overnight.

Preheat the oven to 325°F.

Drain the sweetbreads, pat dry with paper towels, and place in a roasting pan. Sprinkle with the salt, pepper, thyme, and sage and coat with the oil.

Roast for 45 minutes.

Cover the pan with aluminum foil and roast for 15 minutes more, until firm.

Heat 2 tablespoons of the butter in a medium saucepan over medium heat, add the shallot, and sauté for 3 minutes, until translucent. Add the mushrooms and cook for 5 to 8 minutes, until the liquid they release has evaporated.

Add the wine and cook for 5 to 8 minutes, until the liquid is reduced by half.

Stir in the demi-glace and cook until heated through. Remove from the heat and whisk in the remaining butter.

Serve the sweetbreads over mashed potatoes on a large platter and top with the sauce.

8 (6- to 8-ounce) sweetbreads, cleaned

Salt and freshly ground black pepper

¼ teaspoon dried thyme

¼ teaspoon dried sage

2 tablespoons vegetable oil

4 tablespoons butter

1 small shallot, finely chopped

½ cup morel mushrooms, rinsed very well

2 cups dry red wine, such as Burgundy

2 cups Demi-Glace (page 367)

1 recipe Mashed Potatoes (page 219), for serving

Veal Olives

FILLING

1 pound jumbo lump crabmeat

½ cup fine dry bread crumbs

⅛ cup mayonnaise

1 egg, lightly beaten

⅛ green bell pepper,
finely chopped

⅛ red bell pepper, finely chopped

¼ small onion, finely chopped

1 tablespoon fresh lemon juice
(about 1 small lemon)

¼ teaspoon hot sauce

1 teaspoon salt

½ teaspoon freshly ground
white pepper

VEAL

1 tablespoon butter

6 (6- to 8-ounce) veal cutlets

Salt and freshly ground white pepper

SAUCE

2 cups Sherry Cream Sauce (page 368)

1 tablespoon cornstarch

The recipe for veal olives does not contain olives at all; rather, it gets its name from the fact that the veal scaloppine look like large olives when they are rolled around the stuffing. Owing to the high cost of veal in colonial days, this recipe appears in only the cookbooks of the upper crust. Accomplished, wealthier cooks like Martha Washington and Hannah Glasse stuffed their veal olives with forcemeat, oysters, or seafood, and served them in a rich, spiked cream sauce with truffles and mushrooms.

Advance preparation required.

SERVES 6

PREPARE THE FILLING: Pick over the crabmeat to discard the cartilage and pieces of shell. Transfer the crabmeat to a medium mixing bowl. Add the bread crumbs, mayonnaise, egg, bell peppers, onion, lemon juice, hot sauce, salt, and pepper. Mix well. Refrigerate for at least 1 hour to set.

Preheat the oven to 475°F. Spread the butter evenly over the bottom of a large, shallow baking dish.

Pound the veal scallops until very thin, then season with salt and pepper.

Divide the filling into 6 equal amounts and place in the center of each veal cutlet. Roll the cutlet gently around the filling. Place the veal rolls in the prepared baking dish and bake for 10 to 15 minutes, until the stuffing is completely cooked through.

PREPARE THE SAUCE: Heat the Sherry Cream Sauce in a small saucepan over medium heat.

In a separate bowl, whisk together the cornstarch and 3 tablespoons water to make a slurry. Whisk the slurry into the sauce and cook for 3 to 5 minutes, until thick.

Place the stuffed veal on a serving platter or divide among individual plates and top with the sauce.

Roasted Oysters

Since everyone in the eighteenth century had a fireplace, roasting was a very common preparation of this ubiquitous food source, quite possibly ranking third to eating them raw and frying them. Oysters were a very cheap meal, and roasting them was so easy, it didn't require any culinary talent on the part of the cook. Roasted oysters were a dinner that even the men of the house could make, if they so desired!

Serves 4

Preheat the oven to 475°F.

Place a layer of rock salt on a baking sheet. Remove the top shells of the oysters and arrange them on the salt. Dot each oyster with ½ teaspoon of the butter and drizzle with ½ teaspoon of the wine.

Bake for 3 to 4 minutes, until the edges of the oysters curl.

Rock salt

2 dozen Blue Point Oysters

4 tablespoons butter

¼ cup dry white wine

CHEF'S NOTE

You can also cook these oysters on a grill over high heat.

Shrimp
in Saffron Cream

2 pounds raw jumbo shrimp,
peeled and deveined

¼ cup Worcestershire sauce

Juice of 1 lemon

4 tablespoons unsalted butter

1 medium shallot, finely chopped

1 cup sliced button mushrooms

1 cup dry white wine,
such as Sauvignon Blanc

1 cup heavy cream

Pinch of saffron threads

1 tablespoon all-purpose flour

Salt and freshly ground
white pepper to taste

2 tablespoons anisette, such as Pernod

1 tablespoon finely chopped parsley

Though the bulk of the world's saffron is grown in Spain, saffron was grown in England from Medieval times until well past the eighteenth century in the town of Saffron Walden in Essex. English settlers familiar with its many uses brought saffron to the colonies. Cookbooks of the colonial era indicate that the English tended to use saffron more in sweet dishes, like saffron cake, and to color marzipan. It is the Spanish, and later the French, whose savory saffron recipes began to infiltrate eighteenth-century American culinary culture.

Advance preparation required.

SERVES 4

Wash the shrimp thoroughly in cold running water and pat them dry with paper towels. Combine the shrimp, Worcestershire sauce, and lemon juice in a mixing bowl and toss. Cover and refrigerate for 1 hour.

Melt 3 tablespoons of the butter in a large skillet over medium heat. Add the shrimp and cook for 2 to 3 minutes per side, until completely pink. Remove and reserve.

Add the shallot to the skillet and sauté for 2 to 3 minutes, until translucent. Add the mushrooms and sauté until the liquid they release has evaporated, 5 to 8 minutes. Add the wine to deglaze the pan, stir in the cream and saffron, and cook for 5 to 8 minutes, until the liquid in the pan is reduced by one-quarter.

In a small bowl, knead together the remaining tablespoon of butter and the flour (*beurre manié*). Whisk the *beurre manié* into the cream a little bit at a time, until the sauce is thick. Reduce the heat to low, return the shrimp to the skillet and cook for 2 to 3 minutes, just until warmed through. Season with salt and pepper to taste. Stir in the anisette and parsley just before serving.

Honey-Glazed
Roasted Duckling

Raised by slave families and sold to Thomas Jefferson for a modest price, ducks made regular appearances on the tables at Monticello. This preparation would have been a particular favorite of Jefferson's because of the addition of pecans. In his *Notes on the State of Virginia*, Jefferson records the planting of "paccan" or "Illinois nut" trees at Monticello and expounds on the benefits of eating these delicious nuts in other writings.

SERVES 6

Preheat the oven to 425°F.

Rinse the ducks thoroughly with cold water and pat dry with paper towels. Rub the cavities with salt, pepper, and thyme, and stuff with the apples, onions, celery roots, and parsley stems. Tie the legs together with kitchen twine.

Place the ducks breast side up on a rack in a large roasting pan. Roast for 45 minutes, until golden brown. Remove from the oven and allow to rest for about 15 minutes.

Slice the ducks in half down the breastbone and remove the breastbone and backbones.

Reduce the oven temperature to 350°F.

Lay the duck halves flat on a baking sheet. Brush the honey over the skin of the ducks and sprinkle with the pecans. Roast for 5 minutes more, until the honey has melted and coated the skin.

Place each duck half on a bed of Herbed Barley and top with Peach Chutney.

3 (6-pound) whole ducks
Salt and freshly ground black pepper
1 teaspoon dried thyme
3 Granny Smith apples, quartered
3 yellow onions, quartered
3 celery roots, quartered
3 small bunches parsley stems
1 cup honey
½ cup chopped pecans
Herbed Barley, for serving (page 226)
½ cup Peach Chutney, for serving (page 123)

Chicken Madeira

6 (6- to 8-ounce) skinless, boneless chicken breast halves

1½ cups Rainwater-style Madeira (see Chef's Note)

½ cup vegetable oil

½ bunch fresh basil, chopped (about ¼ cup)

1½ tablespoons chopped fresh parsley

1 teaspoon chopped fresh rosemary

1 sprig fresh thyme

2 garlic cloves, chopped

2 medium shallots, chopped

Salt and freshly ground black pepper

½ cup all-purpose flour

1 tablespoon unsalted butter

2 cups sliced button mushrooms

½ cup dry red wine, such as Burgundy

2 cups Demi-Glace (page 367)

The island of Madeira's location, 400 miles off Portugal's coast in the middle of the Atlantic Ocean, made it a popular hub in colonial trade routes. The diplomatic alliance between England and Portugal, Madeira's ruling nation, is the oldest in the world, dating back to the Middle Ages and strengthened over the centuries by sporadic royal marriages. Consequently, Madeira wine, which was originally stocked in the ships' holds for ballast, could be purchased tax-free in the colonies, making it a relatively inexpensive alternative to unpotable drinking water. It was consumed in surprisingly large quantities and was used frequently in sweet and savory recipes.

Overnight preparation recommended.

SERVES 6

In a medium bowl, combine the chicken, 1 cup of the Madeira, the oil, basil, parsley, rosemary, thyme, garlic, shallots, and a sprinkling of salt and pepper. Cover with plastic wrap and marinate in the refrigerator at least 6 hours or overnight.

Remove the chicken from the marinade and discard the marinade. Pat the chicken dry with paper towels.

Dredge the chicken in the flour and shake off any excess.

Melt the butter in a large skillet over medium heat and add the chicken breasts. Cook for 3 to 4 minutes per side, until browned. Add the mushrooms and sauté about 2 minutes, until golden. Add the remaining ½ cup of Madeira and the wine to deglaze the pan, loosening any browned bits on the bottom of the pan with a wooden spoon. Cook for 3 minutes, until the sauce reduces slightly.

Stir in the demi-glace and bring to a boil over high heat. Reduce the heat and simmer for 3 to 5 minutes, until reduced and thickened.

CHEF'S NOTE

The unique process that makes Madeira so flavorful involves heating and aging in oak casks, as well as the addition of brandy. Madeira ranges in flavor from dry, pale, and crisp, to full-bodied and very fruity. For cooking purposes, I prefer Rainwater Madeira, a soft, medium-dry Verdelho-style Madeira that has undergone a clarifying process to create a more golden color.

Pan-Seared Venison Medallions
with Bourbon-Mushroom Sauce

───◆◆◆───

Venison, though commonly thought of as deer meat, actually applies broadly to the meat of other wild game, including elk and moose. In early colonial days, all of these animals were plentiful in the untamed forests of Pennsylvania, so it was consumed regularly by even the poorest families. However, by as early as 1800, it had rapidly grown scarce, becoming the most expensive meat one could purchase, at thirteen cents per pound. What had been an everyday meal just a few years before was now considered a delicacy, affordable only to the wealthiest Americans.

Overnight preparation required.

SERVES 4 TO 6

Slice the venison into ¼-inch-thick medallions (about 3 ounces each). Place the medallions in a medium-sized shallow dish and add the wine, shallots, garlic, rosemary, and sage. Cover with plastic wrap and marinate in the refrigerator for 8 hours or overnight.

Remove the venison from the marinade and discard the marinade. Pat the venison dry with paper towels.

Melt the butter in a large skillet over high heat, add the venison, and cook for 3 minutes on each side (for medium-rare), until brown. Remove the venison from the pan and keep warm.

Add the leek to the pan and sauté for about 2 minutes, until soft. Add the mushrooms and sauté for about 3 minutes, until soft. Add the bourbon to deglaze the pan, loosening any browned bits on the bottom of the pan with a wooden spoon. Stir in the demi-glace, reduce the heat, and let the mixture simmer for about 3 minutes, until the demi-glace comes to boil. Season with salt and pepper to taste.

To serve, fan out the venison on a bed of Herbed Barley and top with the mushroom mixture.

1½ pounds venison tenderloin, fat trimmed and silver skin removed (see Resources, page 378)

2 cups red Burgundy wine

3 medium shallots, chopped

2 garlic cloves, finely chopped

1 sprig fresh rosemary, leaves pulled

1 teaspoon dried rubbed sage

2 teaspoons unsalted butter

1 medium leek (white part only), well rinsed, cut into 2-inch lengths, and finely julienned

1½ cups sliced button mushrooms

½ cup bourbon

2 cups Demi-Glace (page 367)

Salt and freshly ground black pepper

Herbed Barley, for serving (page 226)

Beef Medallions
with General Washington Tavern Porter

4 pounds beef tenderloin, fat trimmed
and silver skin removed

4 cups General Washington Tavern Porter
(see Resources, page 378) or
other dark beer

1 teaspoon salt

1 teaspoon freshly ground black pepper

2 tablespoons unsalted butter

4 medium shallots, finely chopped

4 bunches mustard greens
(about 1½ pounds), rinsed

½ bunch fresh parsley, chopped
(about 3 tablespoons)

1 sprig fresh thyme

2 cups Demi-Glace (page 367)

Mashed Potatoes, for serving (page 219)

Ales, especially dark "small" ales made from molasses, were used frequently in colonial cooking. When used as a marinade, a dark ale (or porter), tenderized and added flavor to the rather bland, tough, grass-fed beef that typically came from cows that were too old to give milk. Although higher quality beef was available, it was costly, and therefore only available to the very wealthy. Etienne Lemaire, Thomas Jefferson's *maître d'hotel* at the President's House, notes in his Day Book that he purchased 120 pounds of beef at the beginning of each week at nine cents per pound. Even with a presidential salary of $25,000 per year—seemingly a fortune in the early 1800s—Jefferson could scarcely afford this regular expenditure.

Overnight preparation required.

Serves 6

Slice the beef into ¼-inch-thick medallions (about 3 ounces each). Place the medallions in a large shallow dish and add 3 cups of the porter, the salt, and pepper. Cover with plastic wrap and marinate in the refrigerator for at least 4 hours or overnight.

Remove the beef from the marinade and discard the marinade. Pat the beef dry with paper towels.

Melt the butter in a large skillet over high heat, add the beef, and cook for 2 minutes on each side, until brown. Remove the beef from the skillet and keep warm.

Reduce the heat to medium, add the shallots, and cook for 2 to 3 minutes, until translucent. Add the mustard greens, parsley, and thyme, and sauté for 2 minutes, until the greens are wilted.

Add the remaining 1 cup porter to deglaze the pan, loosening any browned bits on the bottom of the pan with a wooden spoon. Stir in the demi-glace and cook over medium to high heat for about 5 minutes, until the liquid is reduced by half.

To serve, arrange a bed of mashed potatoes in the center of each plate. Top with the mustard greens, arrange the beef medallions atop the greens and drizzle the sauce over the beef medallions.

Baked Veal Chop

English colonists were familiar with veal because in England, where pasture land was scarce, young calves were routinely slaughtered for meat. In America, grazing land was plentiful and cows were prized for their dairy production, making eating veal a rarity usually reserved for holidays or special occasions. We know from Etienne Lemaire's notes that veal was served regularly at the President's House during Thomas Jefferson's terms. Given Jefferson's love of French cuisine (and his French maître d'hotel), we assume that this elegant French preparation of *côtelettes de veau*, would have been among the veal recipes served to his guests.

SERVES 8

Preheat the oven to 375°F.

Sprinkle the chops with salt and pepper. Place the flour in a medium-sized shallow bowl and dip each chop into the flour evenly to coat, shaking off any excess flour.

Heat 2 tablespoons of the butter and the oil in a large skillet over medium heat, add half of the chops, and cook for 5 to 8 minutes on each side, until brown. Repeat with the remaining chops. Reserve.

Discard the oil from the skillet and add the remaining 2 tablespoons butter and the onions. Sauté for 3 minutes, until golden brown.

In a large baking dish, place half of the cooked onions. Place the veal chops on top of the onions. Add the thyme, cilantro, 1 teaspoon salt, and ½ teaspoon pepper. Cover with the remaining onions and the Parmesan cheese. Pour in the wine and Chicken Stock.

Bake for about 20 minutes, until a meat thermometer inserted in the veal registers 140°F (for medium).

To serve, arrange the veal chops and onion mixture on a large platter and garnish with the dill.

8 (10- to 12-ounce) veal chops from the rack, cut 1-inch thick and Frenched (see Chef's Note)

1 teaspoon salt, plus more as needed

½ teaspoon freshly ground black pepper, plus more as needed

1 cup all-purpose flour

4 tablespoons unsalted butter

3 tablespoons vegetable oil

6 medium yellow onions, finely chopped

3 sprigs fresh thyme, leaves pulled

1 tablespoon chopped fresh cilantro

1 cup grated Parmesan cheese

1 cup dry white wine, such as Sauvignon Blanc

1 cup Chicken Stock (page 364)

1 sprig fresh dill, for garnish

CHEF'S NOTE

Frenching is a process whereby the meat trimmings are removed from between the bones; any butcher should be familiar with the procedure.

Roasted Leg of Lamb

—❖—

4 to 7 pounds leg of lamb

4 garlic cloves, cut into slivers

2 sprigs fresh thyme

¼ pound (1 stick) unsalted butter

5 large yellow onions, sliced

2 to 3 pounds Yukon gold potatoes,
very thinly sliced

Salt and freshly ground black pepper

1 cup dry white wine,
such as Sauvignon Blanc

Sprig of rosemary, for garnish

Colonial cooks also relied on their knowledge of specialized cooking methods and preparations to counter the potential negative affects of the equipment limitations they faced. Larding, a process whereby thin strips of salt pork or bacon were woven through the outer flesh of a roast, kept meat juicy and infused it with added flavor. To the same end, fowl and meats were stuffed with moist, often fat-infused, stuffings to keep delicate breast meat juicy from the inside.

At the original City Tavern, large cuts of meat, such as leg of lamb, were reserved for bigger parties that were held for special occasions. This would have been the case in larger households as well. In *American Cookery*, Amelia Simmons included a recipe for Roasted Spring Lamb: "Lay down to a clear good fire that will not want stirring or altering, baste with butter, dust on flour, baste with the dripping, and before you take it up, add more butter and sprinkle on a little salt and parsly shred fine." Here, the recipe has been adapted to follow a similar French recipe that uses the juices of the lamb to flavor the potatoes during cooking.

Advance preparation required.

SERVES 8

Place the lamb in a medium-sized shallow dish. Using a small paring knife, cut shallow slits in the lamb. Insert the garlic slivers into the slits. Place the sprigs of thyme over the lamb, cover, and refrigerate for 4 to 8 hours, allowing the flavors to marry.

Preheat the oven to 450°F.

Melt 4 tablespoons of the butter in a Dutch oven over high heat, add the lamb, and cook on all sides for 10 minutes, until brown. Place the Dutch oven in the oven and roast for 30 minutes.

Melt the remaining 4 tablespoons butter in a large skillet over medium heat, add the onions, and sauté for 5 minutes, until translucent. Transfer the onions to a large roasting pan. Add the potatoes and sprinkle with salt and pepper. Place the lamb on top of the potato mixture and add the wine.

Roast for about 30 minutes, until the wine has evaporated.

Reduce the oven temperature to 350°F and roast for 30 to 40 minutes more, until a meat thermometer inserted in the lamb registers 145° to 150°F (for medium-rare).

To serve, cut the lamb into ¼-inch-thick slices. Arrange the potato mixture on a serving platter and top with the lamb slices.

Garnish with the rosemary.

Crown Roast of
Pork Madeira

———◆———

From the founding of Jamestown in 1607 until well into the nineteenth century, pigs were so plentiful that they actually wandered the streets of Philadelphia, New York, and Boston, like today's stray cats. Their foraging destroyed shellfish beds in the Massachusetts Bay Colony, and New Yorkers actually built a wall to keep them at bay. Since pork was so readily available, there are countless recipes for pork in colonial cookbooks. Hannah Glasse includes fourteen recipes for pork in *The Art of Cookery Made Plain and Easy*, among which are recipes for pickling, making sausages, pies, stocks, hams, and roasts. Together with dried fruits, Madeira was often used in sauces for pork because its sweetness paired well with and enhanced the meat's subtle flavor.

Overnight preparation required.

SERVES 6 TO 8

Place the pork loin in a large casserole dish. Add the Madeira, onions, garlic, bay leaf, and thyme. Cover with plastic wrap and marinate in the refrigerator, turning occasionally, overnight.

Preheat the oven to 375°F.

PREPARE THE STUFFING: Bring the milk to a boil in a small saucepan over high heat. Place the bread cubes in a large bowl and pour enough of the milk over the bread, tossing to coat the cubes, until the bread is just moistened (you might not need all of the milk). Set aside while preparing the other ingredients.

Heat a medium sauté pan over medium-high heat, add the bacon, and sauté until crisp and golden. Remove the bacon to paper towels to drain.

Melt the butter in a medium sauté pan over medium-high heat, add the onions, and sauté for 2 to 3 minutes, until translucent and slightly softened. Stir in the parsley and sauté for 1 minute more. Remove from the heat, and set aside to cool.

Toss the bacon, onion mixture, eggs, egg yolks, chopped herbs, and nutmeg together with the moistened bread, season with salt and pepper, and set aside for about 30 minutes.

Remove the pork loin from the marinade and reserve the marinade. Place the pork loin in a large roasting pan, bones standing up. Bend the loin into

1 (6- to 8-pound) bone-in pork loin

2 cups imported Madeira

7 medium yellow onions, sliced

8 garlic cloves, chopped

1 bay leaf

1 sprig fresh thyme

Salt and freshly ground black pepper

STUFFING

1 cup milk

2 medium 1- to 2-day-old
French Baguettes (about 1 pound),
cut into ¼-inch cubes (page 320)

1½ pounds bacon, chopped

2 tablespoons unsalted butter

2 medium onions, finely chopped

2 bunches fresh parsley, finely chopped

4 whole eggs

4 egg yolks

½ cup mixed chopped fresh herbs,
such as tarragon, basil, thyme, and chives

¼ teaspoon freshly grated nutmeg

Salt and freshly ground black pepper

2 cups dry red wine, such as Burgundy

7½ cups sliced mushrooms
(about 1½ pounds)

2 cups Demi-Glace (page 367)

1 cup heavy cream

Salt and freshly ground pepper

Scallions (green part only),
chopped, for garnish

———— *(continued)* ————

a circle and tie with kitchen twine. Sprinkle it with salt and pepper. Mound the stuffing into the center of the pork loin.

Bake for about 1 hour, until the stuffing is brown. Cover with foil and bake for 1 hour more, until a meat thermometer inserted in the pork registers 155°F.

Pour the reserved marinade into a small saucepan and bring to a boil over high heat. Cook for 10 minutes, until reduced to about ¼ cup. Strain the marinade and reserve.

Transfer the pork loin to a platter, cover with foil, and let stand for 15 minutes before carving (the meat's temperature will rise 5 degrees while standing). Discard any excess fat in the roasting pan. Add the red wine to deglaze the pan, loosening any browned bits on the bottom of the pan with a wooden spoon. Add the reduced marinade and cook for about 10 minutes, until the liquid is reduced by half. Add the mushrooms, demi-glace, and cream. Reduce the heat and simmer for about 5 minutes, until the mushrooms are soft. Season with salt and pepper to taste.

To serve, remove the string and slice the roast. Serve the sauce with the meat and garnish with the scallions.

John Adams, while known for disapproving of culinary excess, was a man who enjoyed his Madeira. While attending one of many feasts associated with the first Continental Congress, he wrote, "I drank Madeira at a great rate and found no inconvenience in it."

Beef & Morels

⬥•⬥•⬥

Regular domestic mushrooms, or "mushrumps" as Martha Washington called them, were most commonly dried, pickled, cooked in cream to make a "ragoo," or combined with garlic and cloves to make mushroom "catsup." Occasionally, they would be added directly to other dishes in their raw, wild form. Specialty mushrooms, such as porcini, cèpes, or morels would have arrived dried on ships from Europe, the same way we most frequently find them today. The morel is one of the best mushrooms to preserve in this fashion, as the drying process doesn't compromise the mushroom's subtle, earthy flavor. This typical French recipe is one Thomas Jefferson would have enjoyed during his stay in Paris as Minister Plenipotentiary.

Overnight preparation recommended.

SERVES 6

Place the beef in a medium-sized shallow dish. Add 1 cup of the wine, half the shallots, and half the garlic. Cover with plastic wrap and marinate in the refrigerator for at least 4 hours or overnight.

Remove the beef from the marinade and discard the marinade. Pat the beef dry with paper towels.

Melt the butter in a large skillet over medium heat, add the remaining shallots and garlic, and sauté for 3 minutes, until golden brown. Add the beef strips in batches to avoid overcrowding the pan, and sauté for 5 minutes, until brown.

Add the remaining 1½ cups wine to deglaze the pan, loosening any browned bits on the bottom of the pan with a wooden spoon. Stir in the sour cream and mustard. Stir in the mushrooms, parsley, and thyme. Reduce the heat and simmer for 2 to 3 minutes, until the sauce is velvety. Stir in the demiglace and simmer for 5 minutes, until the demi-glace comes to a boil. Add the beef and season with salt and pepper to taste.

3 pounds beef tenderloin, fat trimmed, sliced, and cut into 1-inch strips

2½ cups red Burgundy wine

5 medium shallots, chopped

2 garlic cloves, chopped

1 tablespoon unsalted butter

¼ cup sour cream

¼ cup Dijon mustard

½ cup whole fresh morel mushrooms or ¼ cup dried morel mushrooms

½ bunch fresh parsley, chopped (about 3 tablespoons)

4 sprigs fresh thyme, leaves pulled

2 cups Demi-Glace (page 367)

Salt and freshly ground black pepper

Roasted Turkey
with Giblet Gravy

1 (18- to 20-pound) turkey, with giblets

Salt and freshly ground black pepper

1 medium yellow onion, quartered

¼ cup chopped fresh parsley

2 tablespoons chopped fresh thyme

2 tablespoons dried rubbed sage

2 medium shallots, finely chopped

1½ tablespoons olive oil

1 cup imported Madeira

1 medium yellow onion, coarsely chopped

2 large carrots, peeled and chopped

2 celery ribs, chopped

¼ cup dry white wine,
such as Sauvignon Blanc

3 cups Chicken Stock (page 364)

1½ tablespoons cornstarch

Turkeys were plentiful in England before 1550, having made their way to Europe on Spanish ships transporting them from Mexico. Therefore, British colonists were already in possession of recipes for turkey before they landed in the New World, where they would find flocks of up to 5,000 wild turkeys gathered by certain rivers, making a veritable feast for starving émigrés. In addition to boiling, frying, and baking them, roasting was one of the most common means of preparing turkey in colonial times. Amelia Simmons' recipe in *American Cookery* calls for stuffing the bird with bread stuffing, roasting, and basting it. In what may have set the precedent for the modern Thanksgiving, she instructs the cook to serve the turkey with "cramberry-sauce" and mashed potatoes.

SERVES 8 TO 10

Preheat the oven to 325°F. Place an oven rack on the bottom level. Place a wire roasting rack in a large roasting pan and spray it with vegetable cooking spray.

Remove the giblets and neck and any visible fat from the turkey cavity and reserve for the giblet stock. Discard the liver and fat. Rinse the turkey inside and out with cold water and pat dry with paper towels.

Sprinkle the turkey cavity with salt and pepper. Place the quartered onion in the cavity.

In a small bowl, combine the parsley, thyme, sage, shallots, and 1 tablespoon of the oil. Sprinkle with salt and a generous grinding of pepper.

With your fingers, separate the turkey skin from the breast meat, taking care not to tear the skin or pierce the meat. Rub the herb mixture on the meat under the skin on each side of the breastbone. Tie the drumsticks together with kitchen string and twist the wing tips behind the back. Place the turkey, breast side up, in the prepared roasting pan.

Roast the turkey for about 2 hours, until the breast is browned. Cover the turkey with aluminum foil and roast for 3 to 4 hours, until a meat thermometer inserted in a thigh muscle registers 185°F. Add ½ cup of the Madeira, and baste the turkey every 15 minutes.

While the turkey roasts, heat the remaining ½ tablespoon oil in a large saucepan over medium heat, add the coarsely chopped onion, the carrots, celery, and reserved giblets and neck, and cook, stirring frequently, for about 15 minutes, until the giblets, onion, carrots, and celery are well browned.

(continued)

Add the white wine to deglaze the pan, scraping up the browned bits on the bottom of the pan with a wooden spoon. Cook for about 1 minute, until it comes to a boil. Add the stock and bring back to a boil over high heat. Reduce the heat to low, partially cover the pan, and simmer for 30 minutes.

Strain the giblet stock through a fine sieve into a medium bowl (you should have about 2 cups). Chop the giblets and add them back into the stock. Bring to room temperature, then cover and refrigerate until ready to use.

When the turkey is done, transfer it to a carving board, loosely cover it with aluminum foil, and let it rest for 15 to 20 minutes before carving.

While the turkey rests, pour the drippings from the roasting pan through a fine sieve into a small bowl. Place the bowl in the freezer for about 20 minutes to solidify the fat.

Meanwhile, set the roasting pan back on the stovetop over medium heat. Add the rest of the Madeira to deglaze the pan, scraping up any browned bits on the bottom of the pan with a wooden spoon. Cook for about 1 minute, until it comes to boil. Strain the liquid through a fine sieve into a medium saucepan.

Skim the fat from the chilled drippings and discard. Add the drippings to the Madeira mixture in the saucepan. Add the reserved giblet stock and giblets. Bring to a simmer over medium heat.

In a small bowl, dissolve the cornstarch in 2 tablespoons cold water. Slowly add to the simmering Madeira mixture, whisking until the gravy thickens slightly. Season with salt and pepper to taste.

Remove the string from the turkey and carve (see directions below). Serve with the warm Madeira gravy.

CHEF'S NOTE

CARVING A TURKEY

Using a carving knife and fork, cut between the lower part of the breast and the thigh, pushing down until the leg joint separates. Wiggle each leg to find the joint between the thigh and the drumstick and slice downward through the joint. Slice the meat off the bones. Bend each wing to find the joint, then cut straight downward to remove the wing. Make a long cut along one side of the breastbone. Carve the meat from the breast, working toward the first cut in smooth, even slices.

Eighteenth-century cooking utensils

Roasted Prime Rib
on Yorkshire Pancakes

———•◦•———

In colonial days, a beef roast would have been served with Yorkshire pudding, which was made from the same batter recipe below, but cooked in a pan placed under the roasting spit to catch the beef juices. Depending on where it was grown, horseradish would have been introduced to the colonies by either Germans or the British, as both cultures made extensive use of this quick-growing root in their home countries. Abigail Adams left behind her version of the typical English recipe for horseradish sauce, in which the cream is whipped before adding the horseradish and a touch of dry mustard.

Overnight preparation required.

Makes 8 pancakes; Serves 6 to 8

PREPARE THE ROAST: Combine the parsley, thyme, rosemary, shallots, and olive oil in a small mixing bowl.

Place the roast in a deep dish and rub the herb mixture all over it. Let the roast marinate in the refrigerator overnight.

Preheat the oven to 500°F.

Place a rack in a roasting pan and place the roast, fat side up, on the rack. Roast for 15 minutes.

Reduce the oven temperature to 350°F. and roast for 1½ to 2 hours more, until a meat thermometer inserted in the center of the roast registers 140°F for rare (160°F for medium).

PREPARE THE PANCAKES: Heat a large nonstick sauté pan over medium heat. Combine all of the pancake ingredients in a large bowl and mix until smooth. Ladle ½ cup of the batter into the hot pan and cook for about 1 minute, until bubbles start to form. Flip the pancake and cook on the second side for another 1 minute, until cooked through. Turn the pancake out onto a plate, cover loosely with a towel to keep warm, and continue with the remaining batter.

Remove the beef from the oven and let rest for 15 minutes. Cut the beef into 1½-inch-thick slices.

Place the beef slices on the pancakes, garnish with the watercress, and serve with Horseradish Sauce.

ROAST

2 tablespoons chopped fresh parsley

2 tablespoons chopped fresh thyme

2 tablespoons chopped fresh rosemary

2 medium shallots, finely chopped

1½ tablespoons olive oil

1 bone-in beef rib eye roast
(6 to 8 pounds)

Fresh watercress, for garnish

1 cup Horseradish Sauce (page 371)

PANCAKES

2¼ cups all-purpose flour

3 eggs, beaten

2¼ cups whole milk

1½ tablespoons clarified butter or olive oil
(see Chef's Note, page 54)

1 tablespoon finely chopped fresh basil

1 tablespoon finely chopped fresh parsley

1 tablespoon stemmed
and finely chopped fresh thyme

1 tablespoon finely chopped fresh chives

Pinch of freshly grated nutmeg

Pinch of teaspoon salt

Pinch of freshly ground white pepper

Brook Trout
with Black Walnuts

---

4 (8- to 10-ounce) whole fresh trout, heads, tails, and fins removed

¼ cup Worcestershire sauce

Juice of 1 lemon

1 cup all-purpose flour

½ cup vegetable oil

2 tablespoons unsalted butter

2 medium shallots, finely chopped

½ cup dry white wine, such as Sauvignon Blanc

½ cup fresh lemon juice (about 2 large lemons)

¼ pound (1 stick) unsalted butter, cut into ½-inch pats

Salt and freshly ground black pepper

Fresh parsley, chopped, for garnish

¾ cup chopped black walnuts, for garnish (See Chef's Note)

1 recipe Herbed Barley (page 226), for serving

This dish combines two of the most common foods available to eighteenth-century cooks, trout and black walnuts. Brook trout ran in the cool, rocky streams of the Northeast and were easily fished for a quick dinner. Black walnut trees, also called American walnut trees, were a native species of tree that grew in the Northeast as well. Colonists tended mainly to pickle walnuts, make walnut "catsup," and all seem to have shared the same recipe for a dense, delicious black walnut cake. Occasionally, though, the distinctive flavor of black walnuts could be used to bolster the flavor of a mild savory ingredient, such as trout.

Serves 4

Preheat the oven to 350°F.

Place the trout on their backs, with the open cavities facing up, and remove any excess bones. Wash the fish thoroughly in cold running water and pat dry with paper towels.

Combine the trout, Worcestershire sauce, and lemon juice in a mixing bowl and toss together. Marinate at room temperature for 5 minutes, then remove the trout and pat dry with paper towels.

Place the flour in a medium-sized shallow bowl. Dip both sides of the trout into the flour.

Heat the oil in a large skillet over high heat, add the trout, and cook for 2 minutes on each side, until golden brown. Transfer the trout to a baking sheet and bake for 3 to 4 minutes, until crisp. Transfer to a serving platter and keep warm.

Melt the 2 tablespoons butter in the same skillet over medium heat, add the shallots, and sauté for 3 minutes, until golden brown. Add the wine to deglaze the pan, loosening any browned bits on the bottom of the pan with a wooden spoon. Add the lemon juice and bring to a boil over high heat. Add the butter pats one at a time, whisking with a wire whisk, until all of the butter is incorporated into the sauce. Season with salt and pepper to taste.

To serve, place the trout on a bed of Herbed Barley, and spoon the sauce over it. Garnish with the parsley and walnuts.

CHEF'S NOTE

Black walnuts can be difficult to find, so feel free to substitute regular walnuts or pecans.

Salmon Corn Cakes

⬥

Salmon was abundant on the East Coast in the early colonies, so much so that it was often used as fertilizer. By the beginning of the nineteenth century, overfishing and dams that blocked spawning migrations brought about a significant decline in the salmon population, so it became a dear commodity. These savory fish cakes would have enabled the colonial cook to utilize every last morsel of the fish's expensive pink flesh.

Serves 4

Fill a small saucepan with salted water and bring to a boil. Add the corn kernels and cook for 5 to 8 minutes, until tender. Do not overcook. Drain and let cool.

In a medium saucepan over high heat, bring the bouillon to a boil. Add the salmon and sprigs of dill. Reduce the heat and simmer for 5 to 8 minutes, until the salmon is cooked and appears thoroughly light pink, not dark or translucent. Drain the salmon, transfer it to a medium mixing bowl and set aside to cool.

Melt 2 tablespoons of the butter in a small skillet over medium heat. Add the onion and bell peppers and cook for 5 to 8 minutes, until the onion is translucent and the liquid released by the peppers has evaporated. Set aside to cool completely.

Break up the salmon into ¼-inch pieces. Add the corn, onion and pepper mixture, eggs, bread crumbs, lemon juice, half the chopped dill, Worcestershire sauce, and hot sauce. Mix well.

Using your hands, form the salmon mixture into 8 patties and place them on a baking sheet. Refrigerate for 30 minutes.

Preheat the oven to 350°F.

Melt the remaining 4 tablespoons butter in a large skillet over medium heat and add the salmon patties in batches, to avoid crowding the pan. Cook for 2 minutes on each side, until brown. Place the patties back on the baking sheet and bake for about 10 minutes, until golden brown.

To serve, place the salmon cakes on individual plates and garnish with the remaining dill. Serve with the Herb Rémoulade.

2 ears fresh white corn, kernels cut from cobs

6 cups Court Bouillon (page 365), or dry white wine, such as Sauvignon Blanc

1½ pounds fresh salmon fillets or trimmings, skinned and boned, ¾-inch thick

2 sprigs fresh dill

6 tablespoons unsalted butter

1 small yellow onion, finely chopped

1 large red bell pepper, finely chopped

1 large green bell pepper, finely chopped

2 eggs

¼ cup dry fine bread crumbs

¼ cup fresh lemon juice (about 1 large lemon)

½ bunch fresh dill, finely chopped (about 1 tablespoon)

Dash Worcestershire sauce

Dash hot sauce

1 cup Herb Rémoulade (page 44)

Baked Turbot
with Sorrel

—•••—

8 (8- to 10-ounce) turbot fillets,
1-inch thick

2 bay leaves

4 tablespoons unsalted butter

Salt and freshly ground white pepper

½ cup dry sherry

1 cup heavy cream

1 cup shredded fresh sorrel or spinach

In *The Art of Cookery Made Plain and Easy*, Hannah Glasse included a recipe for baked turbot, which is very heavily perfumed with nutmeg. In this traditional French preparation, the delicate flavor of sorrel allows the flavor of the turbot to shine through. Sorrel, which can refer to any of several varieties of perennial herbs belonging to the buckwheat family, has grown wild for centuries in North America. Looking very much like spinach, fresh sorrel is at its peak in the spring. Notes in his *Garden Book* show that Thomas Jefferson planted sorrel several times between 1774 and 1813.

SERVES 8

Preheat the oven to 375°F.

Place the fish in a large baking dish and place the bay leaves on top. Dot with 2 tablespoons of the butter.

Bake for about 10 minutes, until a white film, like the texture of cooked egg white, appears on the fish. Remove from the oven. Remove and discard the bay leaves and sprinkle the fish with salt and pepper. Keep warm.

Pour the sherry into a medium saucepan and heat over high heat until the sherry comes to a boil. Add the cream, lower the heat to medium, and cook, stirring frequently, for about 5 minutes, until the sauce thickens and coats the back of a spoon. Remove from the heat and whisk in the remaining 2 tablespoons of butter. Stir in the sorrel and bring the sauce to a boil over medium heat. Remove from the heat.

To serve, spoon the sauce over the fish.

Citrus-Marinated Salmon

8 (8- to 10-ounce) skinless salmon fillets

Juice of 2 oranges

Juice of 2 lemons

Juice of 1 lime

Salt and freshly ground white pepper

3 tablespoons unsalted butter

1 cup all-purpose flour

3 large eggs, lightly beaten

Herbed Barley (page 226), for serving

1 cup Béarnaise Sauce

The incorporation of any kind of citrus in a colonial dish would have indicated that the cook came from, or was in the employ of, a wealthy household. When Thomas Jefferson was president, his maître d'hotel paid eighty-five cents per dozen for oranges. In comparison, the most expensive meat at the time was venison, at thirteen cents per pound. Consequently, cooks would ensure that not a drop of the fruit was wasted, incorporating the juice, pulp and rind into as many dishes as possible. Until the citrus fruits were used, servants would painstakingly polish the fruit and display them in blue and white china bowls on a table in the entryway of the household.

Advance preparation required.

SERVES 8

Place the salmon in a shallow baking dish and add the orange, lemon, and lime juices. Cover and refrigerate for 4 to 6 hours.

Remove the salmon from the dish, discard the marinade, and pat the salmon dry with paper towels. Season with salt and pepper.

Melt the butter in a large skillet over medium heat.

Dip the salmon fillets in the flour and shake off any excess. Dip them in the eggs, and add them to the pan, cooking for about 2 minutes per side, until golden brown.

Serve on a bed of Herbed Barley and top with the Béarnaise Sauce.

> Philadelphia's two main rivers, the Delaware and the Schuylkill, teemed with fish in the eighteenth-century, including shad, salmon, perch, rockfish, catfish, as well as terrapins, the small, diamond-back turtles for which the city was known.

Roasted Squab

S quab is a four-week-old domesticated pigeon weighing no more than one pound, which has never flown, giving its meat unparalleled tenderness. Squab would have been roasted and "dressed" in the same manner of the plethora of other game birds that colonials hunted and prepared. In her *Booke of Cookery*, Martha Washington recommends using her recipe "to make sause for foule" for "turkeys, Capons, partridge, phesants, woodcock, tele, duck, plover, curlues, & quailes." Susannah Carter's *The Frugal Colonial Housewife* includes preparations for all of the aforementioned game birds, as well as larks, ortolans, pigeons, ruffs, reeves, snipes, and widgeons.

Overnight preparation required.

SERVES 4

Cut the squab in half along the breastbone and remove the breastbones. Make a slice down the inside of each thigh and leg.

Combine the squab, wine, peppercorns, bay leaf, sprig of thyme, and sprig of sage in a roasting pan. Cover and refrigerate overnight, turning periodically.

Remove the squab from the marinade and discard the marinade. Pat the squab dry with paper towels.

Preheat the oven to 425°F.

Season the squab with the sage, thyme, salt and pepper. Place them skin-up in a baking dish and roast for 15 minutes, until the squab become brown, then baste with the pan drippings and cover with foil. Lower the oven temperature to 350°F and continue to roast for an additional 20 minutes, until the thigh bones can be wiggled easily.

Combine the demi-glace and Madeira in a small saucepan and cook over medium heat for 5 to 8 minutes, until completely warmed through. Remove from the heat and whisk in the butter.

Place the squab on a large serving platter or carve. Divide among individual plates and top with the Madeira demi-glace.

4 (1-pound) squab

1 (750ml) bottle dry red wine, such as Burgundy

6 whole peppercorns

1 bay leaf

1 sprig fresh thyme

1 sprig fresh sage

2 tablespoons dried sage

2 tablespoons dried thyme

Salt and freshly ground black pepper

1½ cups Demi-Glace (page 367)

¼ cup imported Madeira

2 tablespoons unsalted butter

Ale-Braised Sausage

Early American housewives made their own sausages, usually with ground pork and beef suet or ground pork and veal. Hannah Glasse seems to have been an expert in sausage-making, having mastered the Oxford, Bologna, Hamburg, and other versions of German sausages. Most colonial cooks would simply fry their sausages in butter and serve over toast, but German settlers would have occasionally prepared this special recipe by incorporating two of their most favorite ingredients: ale and mustard.

SERVES 4

Preheat the oven to 350°F.

With a small paring knife, make shallow, diagonal cuts in the sausages. Place them in a shallow baking pan and bake for about 5 minutes, until brown. Remove from the oven and reserve.

Heat the butter in a large skillet over high heat, add the onions, shallots, and garlic, and cook for 3 minutes, until golden. Add the sausages. Add the ale to deglaze the pan, loosening any browned bits on the bottom of the pan with a wooden spoon. Cook over medium heat for about 10 minutes, until the ale is reduced so it just coats the bottom of the pan. Transfer the sausage to a serving platter and keep warm.

Increase the heat to high and stir the demi-glace and mustard. Cook for 5 to 8 minutes, until the mixture is reduced by half. Season with salt and pepper to taste.

To serve, spoon the onion mixture over the sausages. Serve with sauerkraut and mashed potatoes. Garnish with the sprig of watercress.

8 purchased pork sausages (about 2 pounds), cooked

2 tablespoons unsalted butter

2 large yellow onions, thinly sliced

2 medium shallots, chopped

2 garlic cloves, chopped

4 cups dark ale

1 cup Demi-Glace (page 367)

2 teaspoons Dijon mustard

Salt and freshly ground black pepper

Sauerkraut (page 211), for serving

Mashed Potatoes (page 219), for serving

1 sprig watercress, for garnish

STEWS, RAGOÛTS, AND SAVORY PIES

As with soups, the cooking equipment available to eighteenth-century chefs, such as large cauldrons and braising pots, lent itself better to the preparation of certain types of foods, like stews, ragoûts, and the fillings for savory pies, which cooked slowly in liquid with vegetables, herbs, and spices. These preparations required little attention, so the cook could add the ingredients to the pot and let the stew simmer unattended for hours while he or she attended to other domestic chores, like gardening and cleaning. Another benefit of this cooking method was that the long, slow cooking process allowed the relatively flavorless and tough meats from grass-fed animals to be infused with flavor and rendered tender enough to chew.

Tenderness was an important quality in food because many colonials had very poor dental hygiene, especially the upper class, whose richer diets and love of sweets contributed greatly to the deterioration, and often complete lack, of their teeth. Consequently, stews and ragoûts graced colonial tables with amazing frequency. These dishes crossed cultural and economic borders. Teamed with a slice of homemade bread, "spoonfood," a term which colonists used to describe such hearty stews and casseroles, made a meal fit for a peasant or a president. In wealthier households, these would have joined a whole litany of other foods on an elegant dinner table. For poor families, any of these would have served as a complete meal on its own.

Ragoût is simply the French word for a thick stew and does not differ from stew in its methodology. Colonial housewives stewed and "ragooed" everything from fish and seafood, to beef, pork, and poultry, to vegetables of all types.

Savory pies served many different purposes. In summer months it was obviously difficult to keep meats and vegetables for long periods of time, so this cooking method acted as a life-saving means of making sure that all bacteria were eliminated. First, the meats would be roasted, then cooked again with a "good gravy" and whatever vegetables or herbs the cook wished to add, and cooked for a third time when placed in *pâte brisée* (plain pastry dough) and baked in a beehive oven. The savory pie also appealed to housewives' sense of frugality, as it served as a means of recycling leftover meats, and concealed vegetables that were not perfect enough to send up on their own.

Because City Tavern was the finest establishment of the era, the stews, ragoûts, and pies it offered were a step up in sophistication from the versions made at humbler inns or in home kitchens.

Pork Ragoût

Since pigs were relatively inexpensive to raise—even poor colonial families could manage to fatten a pig with a meager ration of daily scraps—pork was a very popular meat. The slaughter of pigs was a very important, and often communal, event as it took a great deal of work to make sure that no part of the pig was wasted. Certain cuts were pickled, others salted, and any leftover cuts or scraps were used to make one-pot meals, a welcome respite after a day of serious butchering.

SERVES 8

Heat the oil and butter in a medium-size stockpot over high heat, add the pork, and cook, stirring frequently, for about 5 minutes, until brown. Reduce the heat to medium, then add the onions, bacon, and garlic, and sauté, stirring frequently, for about 10 minutes more, until the juices are reduced. Remove the mixture from the pan and drain excess fat from the pan.

Add 2¾ cups of the wine to deglaze the pan, loosening any browned bits on the bottom of the pan with a wooden spoon. Add the pork mixture, the sage, paprika, thyme, and bay leaves. Bring to a boil over high heat.

Reduce the heat to low, cover, and simmer for about 1 hour, until thickened. Remove from the heat and discard the bay leaves.

In a small mixing bowl, whisk together the remaining ¼ cup wine and the arrowroot until velvety smooth. Slowly stir the mixture into the ragout and simmer for about 5 minutes more, until the ragoût thickens. Season with salt and pepper to taste.

Serve in a deep platter or large serving bowl. Garnish with the chives.

3 tablespoons olive oil

2 tablespoons unsalted butter

5 pounds boneless pork shoulder,
cut into 2-inch cubes

5 large white onions, chopped

9 slices lean bacon, chopped

3 garlic cloves, finely chopped

3 cups dry red wine, such as Burgundy

1 teaspoon dried rubbed sage

1 teaspoon Hungarian paprika

2 sprigs fresh thyme

2 bay leaves

1 tablespoon arrowroot
or 2¼ teaspoons cornstarch
(see Chef's Note)

Salt and freshly ground black pepper

Fresh chives, finely chopped, for garnish

CHEF'S NOTE

This ragoût is even more flavorful when made with mushrooms, such as chanterelles or cèpes. Simply sauté the mushrooms and add them to the stew prior to stirring in the arrowroot mixture.

Arrowroot, a thickener commonly used by colonial cooks, is a delicate starch obtained from the West Indian plant of the same name. Cornstarch makes an ideal substitute.

Note: 2¼ teaspoons of cornstarch is equivalent to 1 tablespoon of arrowroot.

West Indies Curried Lamb

"Curry powder is used as a fine flavoured seasoning for fish, fowls steaks, chops, veal cutlets, hashes, minces, alamodes, turtle soup, and in all rich dishes, gravies, sauce, &c., &c." So wrote Mary Randolph, whose cookbook *The Virginia Housewife* includes recipes for curried fish, chicken, and rice. One normally wouldn't imagine curry being a part of the colonial culinary repertoire, but cooks in seaport towns were very familiar with this pungent blend of spices, as ships returning from the West Indies counted curry among the many commodities in their holds.

Overnight preparation recommended.

SERVES 8

In a large bowl or casserole dish, combine the lamb, curry, thyme, habañero pepper, onions, scallions, garlic, ginger, and salt and pepper to taste. Pour the wine over the mixture, cover with plastic wrap, and let marinate in the refrigerator, stirring occasionally, for at least 6 hours or overnight.

Remove the lamb from the marinade, reserving the marinade. Pat the lamb dry with paper towels.

Melt the butter in a large Dutch oven over high heat, add the lamb and sauté for 8 to 10 minutes, until the lamb is brown and the juices are reduced. Add the marinade and bring the mixture to a boil over high heat. Reduce the heat to low, cover, and cook, stirring frequently, for 1½ hours. Add the carrots, tomatoes, potatoes, and stock, and continue to cook for 25 to 30 minutes, until the potatoes are al dente and the lamb no longer appears pink.

Before serving, discard the thyme and season with salt and pepper to taste.

Serve in a large serving bowl or deep platter. Garnish with the chopped parsley.

5 pounds boneless lamb shoulder, cut into 2-inch cubes

1 cup curry powder

3 large fresh thyme sprigs

½ habañero pepper, finely chopped (see Chef's Note, page 58)

2 onions, diced

1 bunch scallions, diced

½ cup chopped garlic

½ cup peeled and minced ginger

Salt and freshly ground black pepper

1 cup dry red wine, such as Burgundy

4 tablespoons unsalted butter

1 carrot, peeled and diced

2 tomatoes, diced

1 pound red skinned potatoes, peeled and diced

3 quarts Chicken Stock (page 364)

1 bunch fresh parsley, chopped

VEAL

5 pounds boneless veal shoulder, cut into 2-inch cubes

8 cups dry white wine, such as Sauvignon Blanc

4 leeks (white parts only), trimmed, rinsed well, chopped

2 celery ribs, chopped

2 large yellow onions, chopped

2 cloves garlic, chopped

1 Bouquet Garni (page 366)

3 tablespoons salt

1½ teaspoons freshly ground white pepper

MEATBALLS

3 tablespoons unsalted butter

1 yellow onion, finely chopped

1 pound ground veal

2 eggs

1 egg yolk

1 scallion, trimmed and finely chopped

½ cup soaked bread (see Chef's Note)

1 tablespoon chopped fresh parsley

Salt and freshly ground black pepper

SAUCE

6 tablespoons unsalted butter, softened

1 cup all-purpose flour

½ cup heavy cream

4 egg yolks, lightly beaten

Juice of 2 large lemons (about ¼ cup), strained

Salt and freshly ground black pepper

OYSTERS

2 cups dry white wine, such as Sauvignon Blanc

2 medium shallots, chopped

24 Bluepoint oysters, shucked (see Chef's Note, page 45)

Chopped fresh parsley, for garnish

Veal Fricassée
with Veal Meatballs & Oysters

The *fricassée* technique originated in France around 1300, and referred originally to chicken that was broken into pieces (*cassé*), fried (*frit*), then stewed in a thick sauce laced with vinegar and bound with either egg yolks or flour and butter (*beurre manié*). Depending on the whim of the cook, cream could be added to make a velvety white *fricassée*, or left out to make a rich brown version.

Recognizing the tenderizing value of slow cooking any kind of meat, enterprising cooks began to use this method for virtually every type of fowl, meat, or game, and even loosened the definition to include poaching the meat first. Toward that end, colonial housewives left rather general recipes for the preparation of a fricassée, such as Martha Washington's recipe, "To Make A Frykacy Of Chickin Lamb Veale Or Rabbits." The recipe below, however, more closely resembles her recipe "To Stew A Breast Of Veale," which calls for the addition of lemon and oysters.

SERVES 8

PREPARE THE VEAL: In a large saucepan, bring the veal, wine, and 8 cups of water to a boil over high heat, skimming and discarding any foam that rises to the surface. Add the leeks, celery, onions, garlic, bouquet garni, salt, and pepper, and return to a boil. Reduce the heat to medium-low, and simmer for 1 hour.

PREPARE THE MEATBALLS: Heat 1 tablespoon of the butter in a small sauté pan over medium heat, add the onion and sauté until translucent. Remove from heat, and set aside to cool completely.

In a medium-size bowl, mix together the onion, the veal, eggs, egg yolk, scallion, bread, parsley, and salt and pepper. Using a teaspoon-size measuring spoon, scoop up portions of the mixture and roll into balls.

Heat the remaining butter in a large skillet over medium heat, and add the meatballs. Cook for 5 to 8 minutes, until they are firm and cooked completely through. Set aside and keep warm.

PREPARE THE SAUCE: Remove the veal from the saucepan with a slotted spoon. Strain the stock through a fine mesh strainer or cheesecloth into a large bowl, and discard the vegetables and bouquet garni. Return the stock to the saucepan, and bring to a boil over high heat. Reduce the heat to

(continued)

medium, and simmer until the stock is reduced by half, about 15 minutes.

In a small bowl, knead together the butter and flour to form a smooth paste (*beurre manié*). Whisk the *beurre manié*, a little at a time, into the stock, and continue to simmer, stirring frequently, until the sauce is thickened and smooth, about 15 minutes. Strain the sauce again, and return it to the saucepan, maintaining it at a low simmer over low heat.

In a small bowl, whisk together the cream and egg yolks. Gradually stir this mixture into the sauce and fold in the reserved veal, simmering gently until just heated. Do not bring to a boil. Stir in the lemon juice, and season to taste with salt and pepper. Gently stir the meatballs into the sauce.

PREPARE THE OYSTERS: In a medium-size sauté pan over low heat, combine the wine and shallots and bring to a simmer. Gently drop in the oysters and poach until the edges begin to curl, about 1 to 2 minutes.

Transfer the fricassée to a large serving tureen or platter. Gently remove the oysters with a slotted spoon and place on top of the fricassée. Garnish with the parsley.

CHEF'S NOTE

Soak about 1½ cups of large slices or chunks of bread (do not use bread cubes, as they will absorb too much liquid) in about ⅔ cup of water until they have absorbed most of the liquid. Squeeze the pieces to remove as much water as possible, and they are ready to use. You should have ½ cup of soaked bread after squeezing out the water.

One month before City Tavern opened for business, Moses Cox advertised his new grocery store, located two blocks west of the Tavern at Second and Spruce Streets, in the Pennsylvania Gazette. Like many shops in Philadelphia at that time, Cox sold a variety of merchandise, from foodstuffs to household goods. Among the items he was offering in November 1773 *"at the lowest prices" were "cinnamon…melasses…raisins, currants…[and] ginger" (November 17, 1773).*

Chicken
with Fines Herbes

The world-renowned French dish Coq au Vin is prepared with red wine, resulting in a rich brown sauce; however, in the French province of Alsace, the same dish is made with Riesling and served in a velvety white sauce. Both preparations are technically *fricassées*. The recipe below is the white version. However unknown this white Coq au Vin may be to us today, it was a preparation with which the colonial cook was very familiar. In *The Art of Cookery Made Plain and Easy*, Hannah Glasse gives a choice of three different versions of her recipe "To make a White Fricassee."

SERVES 6

In a large pot over high heat, combine the chickens, pierced onion, and enough cold water to cover, and bring to a boil. Reduce the heat to low, and simmer until the chickens are fully cooked, about 25 to 30 minutes.

Discard the onion, remove the chickens from the pan, and set aside, covered. Bring the stock to a gentle boil over medium-high heat, and reduce the stock by about three-quarters, about 30 to 45 minutes. (Make sure you end up with at least 3 cups of reduced stock.) Strain and set aside.

Heat 3 tablespoons of the butter in a large saucepan over medium-high heat, add the shallots and onion and sauté until translucent and softened, about 2 minutes. Whisk in the flour to make a roux, add the Riesling and 3 cups of the reduced stock, and bring to a boil. Reduce the heat to medium-low, and simmer the sauce until it is thickened, stirring occasionally, about 3 to 5 minutes.

Meanwhile, heat the remaining 2 tablespoons of butter in a large sauté pan over medium-high heat, add the pearl onions and mushrooms and sauté for 5 to 8 minutes, until the onions are slightly translucent and the mushrooms are slightly softened.

Remove the kitchen twine from the chickens and carve them, removing the breast meat, separating the legs and thighs, and reserving the wings for another use. Arrange the chicken pieces on a serving platter, sprinkle them with salt and pepper, and spoon the pearl onions and mushrooms overtop.

Stir the cream into the thickened sauce and season with salt and pepper.

To serve, pour the sauce over the chicken and garnish with the parsley.

2 whole chickens (2½ to 3 pounds each), legs tied together with kitchen twine

1 yellow onion, pierced with 6 whole cloves

5 tablespoons unsalted butter

2 shallots, finely chopped (about 3 tablespoons)

½ small white onion, finely chopped (about 3 tablespoons)

3 tablespoons all-purpose flour

3 cups Riesling, or other delicate fruity white wine

1 cup pearl onions, peeled

2 cups quartered white button mushrooms

Salt and freshly ground black pepper

1 cup heavy cream

Chopped fresh parsley, for garnish

Braised Rabbit Legs

In the eighteenth century, the Pennsylvania woods were rich with all kinds of small game, including rabbits and hare. The mild flavor of rabbit—it does indeed taste like chicken—allows it to embrace the flavor of any sauce in which it is prepared, so most eighteenth-century rabbit recipes recommend slow cooking the rabbit in a stew of red wine and aromatic herbs and vegetables.

Overnight preparation recommended.

SERVES 8

At least 4 hours or the day before serving the dish, cut each rabbit leg in half at the joint (or ask your butcher to do so). Place the pieces in a medium bowl and add 2 cups of the wine, the rosemary, sage, and peppercorns. Cover with plastic wrap and marinate in the refrigerator for at least 4 hours or overnight.

When you are ready to proceed, remove the rabbit from the wine, discard the wine, and pat the rabbit dry with paper towels.

Heat the oil and 2 tablespoons of the butter in a large skillet, add the rabbit and cook on all sides for about 3 minutes, until brown. Reduce the heat to medium. Add the celery, carrots, onion, and garlic, and sauté until the vegetables are softened, about 5 to 8 minutes.

Stir in the remaining 1 cup of wine, the bay leaf, demi-glace, parsley, and thyme. Bring to a boil over high heat, reduce the heat to medium-low, and simmer until the rabbit is still tender but no longer pink, about 20 minutes. Remove from the heat and set aside.

Heat the remaining 2 tablespoons of butter in a large skillet over medium heat, add the zucchini, squash, and cabbage, and sauté for 5 minutes, until al dente. Add the mushrooms and tomatoes and cook until the mushrooms are just softened, about 5 minutes more.

Return the rabbit to medium heat, stir in the sautéed vegetables, and simmer for about 5 to 7 minutes.

Season with salt and pepper and serve on a large platter over Homemade Egg Noodles.

5 pounds rabbit legs, skinned
(see Resources, page 378)

3 cups full-bodied red wine,
such as Burgundy

1 sprig fresh rosemary

1 sprig fresh sage

6 whole peppercorns

½ cup vegetable oil

4 tablespoons unsalted butter

4 celery ribs, chopped

2 carrots, peeled and chopped

1 large onion, chopped

3 cloves garlic, chopped

1 bay leaf

6 cups Demi-Glace (page 367)
or prepared brown sauce

3 tablespoons chopped fresh parsley

1 sprig fresh thyme,
stemmed and chopped

2 medium zucchini,
trimmed and chopped

2 medium yellow squash,
trimmed and chopped

½ small red cabbage, chopped
(about 1 cup)

1 cup sliced white button mushrooms

2 large plum tomatoes,
seeded and chopped

Salt and freshly ground black pepper

Homemade Egg Noodles (page 212),
for serving

CHEF'S NOTE

The legs are the only meaty cut of the rabbit, but you can roast the whole rabbit if you wish. Whole rabbits and rabbit legs are available at any specialty butcher shop or by mail order (see Resources, page 378).

Goose & Turnips

⟨⟩

1 domestic goose (10 to 12 pounds)

Salt and freshly ground black pepper

1 teaspoon dried thyme

1 Granny Smith apple, quartered

1 yellow onion, quartered

1 celery root, quartered

1 small bunch fresh parsley stems

3 tablespoons unsalted butter

4 tablespoon vegetable oil

3 large white onions, sliced

9 slices lean bacon, chopped

3 garlic cloves, chopped

2 tablespoons all-purpose flour

2 quarts Chicken Stock (page 364)

1 cup dry white wine,
such as Sauvignon Blanc

2 bunches scallions, green and
white parts chopped separately,
greens reserved for garnish

1 bunch fresh parsley, chopped
(about 6 tablespoons)

2 bay leaves

10 small turnips (about 2 pounds),
peeled and quartered (see Chef's Note)

Wild geese were plentiful in the colonies and were prized for their hearty flavor and copious layer of fat. Since goose would typically have been prepared in the winter months, it was often paired with root vegetables, such as turnips, parsnips, and carrots. This recipe is inspired by Hannah Glasse's recipe, "To Dress a Goose in Ragoo," but here we roast the goose first to render most of the fat from it, for a far less greasy dish. Use the fat in other recipes to add flavor (see page 203).

SERVES 8

Preheat the oven to 325°F.

Rinse the goose thoroughly in cold water and pat dry. Rub the cavity with salt, pepper, and thyme. Stuff the cavity with the apple, yellow onion, celery root, and parsley stems, and tie the legs together with kitchen twine. Place the goose on a rack in a large roasting pan and bake for 1 hour 15 minutes.

Remove the goose from the oven and let it rest for 30 minutes.

Remove the kitchen twine from the legs and the vegetables from the cavity, and discard both. Cut the goose into 16 pieces. Reserve.

Melt the butter and 1 tablespoon of the oil in a Dutch oven over medium heat, add the white onions, bacon, and garlic, and sauté for about 5 minutes, until golden brown. Sprinkle the flour over the bacon mixture, and cook for 3 to 5 minutes more. Add the stock, wine, chopped scallion whites, parsley, and bay leaves. Bring to a boil over high heat, then reduce the heat, cover, and simmer for 8 to 10 minutes.

Heat the remaining 3 tablespoons of oil in a large skillet medium heat, add the goose and cook on all sides for 10 minutes, until the skin is crisp.

Add the turnips and goose to the Dutch oven, and simmer, covered, about 10 to 15 minutes more, until the vegetables are fork-tender. Season with salt and pepper to taste. Remove and discard the bay leaves.

To serve, place the goose on a large platter and arrange the turnip mixture around the goose. Garnish with the reserved chopped scallion greens.

CHEF'S NOTE

**All varieties of turnips do not cook at the same rate,
test them often with a fork to avoid overcooking.**

Turkey Stew
with Fried Oysters

————◆————

In *The Art of Cookery Made Plain and Easy*, Hannah Glasse opines that "The best sauce for a boiled turkey is good oyster and celery sauce." Susannah Carter also includes recipes for boiled turkey and oyster sauce in *The Frugal Colonial Housewife*, as does Mary Randolph in *The Virginia Housewife*. All three women had recipes for fried oysters as well, which impart the same flavor, but add a more interesting texture to the finished dish. However, this was not the only consideration in adding oysters to meat dishes, as the relatively low cost of oysters allowed colonial cooks to stretch dishes inexpensively.

Overnight preparation required.

Serves 4 to 6

In a large mixing bowl, combine the turkey, shallots, garlic, basil, parsley, thyme, and 2 tablespoons of the oil. Cover with plastic wrap and marinate overnight in the refrigerator, stirring occasionally.

Remove the turkey from the marinade and discard the marinade. Pat the turkey dry with paper towels and place in a medium-size mixing bowl. Sprinkle the flour over the turkey and toss to coat thoroughly.

In a large skillet, cook the turkey in 2 tablespoons of the oil over high heat for 5 minutes, until brown. Add the onions, celery, and carrots, and sauté for 5 to 8 minutes, until the vegetables are crisp-tender. Add the sherry to deglaze the pan, loosening any browned bits on the bottom of the pan with a wooden spoon. Reduce the heat to medium and cook, until the liquid is reduced by half, about 30 minutes. Add the stock and bring to a boil over high heat.

Add the bay leaf. Reduce the heat and simmer, until the liquid is reduced by half. Add the demi-glace and bring to a boil over high heat. Remove from the heat.

Melt the butter and remaining oil in another large skillet over medium heat, add the red cabbage, zucchini, and yellow squash, and sauté for 5 minutes, until the vegetables are soft.

Add the tomato and sauté for 2 minutes more, until the tomato is soft. Gently stir the vegetable mixture into the turkey mixture.

Serve the stew over Homemade Egg Noodles and garnish with Cornmeal Fried Oysters and Fried Leek Garnish.

3 pounds skinless boneless turkey thighs, cut into 2-inch cubes

4 medium shallots, chopped

4 garlic cloves, chopped

½ bunch fresh basil, chopped (about ¼ cup)

½ bunch fresh parsley, chopped (about 3 tablespoons)

1 sprig fresh thyme, chopped (about 1 teaspoon)

½ cup olive oil

½ cup all-purpose flour

3 medium yellow onions, diced

4 celery ribs, diced

3 large carrots, peeled and diced

½ cup dry sherry

1 quart Chicken Stock (page 364)

1 bay leaf

2 cups Demi-Glace (page 367)

½ pound (2 sticks) unsalted butter

2 cups shredded red cabbage

2 medium zucchini, halved lengthwise and sliced

2 medium yellow squash, halved lengthwise and sliced

½ cup chopped tomato

Salt and freshly ground black pepper

Homemade Egg Noodles (page 212), for serving

Cornmeal Fried Oysters (page 45), for serving

Fried Leek Garnish, optional (page 89), for garnish

Traditional Beef Stew

————◆————

Since cows were more valuable to colonials for their milk, they were not typically used as a food source until they were old and their meat was lean and tough. But even the toughest beef could be rendered tender by stewing for hours over the colonial hearth. Depending on the time of year, this recipe was varied by adding whatever was in season—spring vegetables, mushrooms, pearl onions—or whatever people had stored in their root cellars, like potatoes or celery root.

The addition of paprika would indicate that this recipe originated with the many German settlers whose culinary traditions included paprika-laced dishes, such as Goulash and Shashlik.

Overnight preparation required.

SERVES 8 TO 10

In a medium-size bowl, combine the beef, wine, the quartered onion, 1 tablespoon olive oil, bay leaves, peppercorns, and thyme. Cover with plastic wrap and marinate in the refrigerator overnight.

Remove the beef from the marinade and reserve the marinade. Pat the meat dry with paper towels. Strain the marinade through a fine sieve or cheesecloth into a large bowl and reserve.

In a Dutch oven, sauté the bacon in the remaining 2 tablespoons olive oil over high heat for 3 minutes, until crisp. Remove the bacon from the pan and reserve. Add the beef to the pan and cook over high heat for about 10 minutes, until brown. Add the chopped onions and garlic, and sauté for 3 minutes, until the onions are golden. Stir in the flour and reserve.

In a large saucepan, bring the marinade to a boil over high heat. Remove from the heat. Pour 3 cups of the marinade into the pan with the meat mixture. Bring to a boil over high heat, then reduce the heat to medium and cook, stirring frequently, for about 30 minutes, until the sauce thickens.

Add the reserved bacon, the carrots, pearl onions, paprika, allspice, and the remaining marinade. Cook over high heat for 3 minutes.

Reduce the heat to low, cover, and cook about 1 hour, until the meat is done.

Melt the butter in a large skillet over medium heat, add the mushrooms, and sauté for 5 minutes, until browned. Add the mushrooms to the stew and simmer for 5 minutes more. Season with salt and pepper to taste.

To serve, place in a large serving bowl or platter and garnish with the chopped parsley.

---

5 pounds boneless beef chuck, cut into 2-inch cubes

1½ quarts red Burgundy wine

1 medium yellow onion, quartered

3 tablespoons olive oil

2 bay leaves

1 teaspoon black peppercorns, crushed

1 sprig fresh thyme

9 slices slab bacon or fat back, cut into small cubes

4 medium yellow onions, chopped

3 garlic cloves, chopped

2 tablespoons all-purpose flour

3 large carrots, peeled and sliced

20 pearl onions, peeled

1 tablespoon sweet paprika

1 teaspoon freshly ground allspice

2 tablespoons unsalted butter

2½ cups button mushrooms (about 8 ounces)

Salt and freshly ground black pepper

Fresh parsley, chopped, for garnish

Venison Stew

In Europe, venison was enjoyed principally by European royalty who had the unique rights to hunt game that roamed noble parks and woodlands. Only the occasional poacher would have enjoyed this "royal prerogative." In America, no such laws or customs existed, so colonials were free to help themselves to any food source they could readily hunt. As a result, venison played a great role in the colonial culinary repertoire.

Long before the advent of farm raising, venison would have been grass-fed and would have lacked the rich, refined flavor that modern grain-fed venison has. To make the meat tender and disguise its gamey flavor, colonial cooks would either marinate or stew the cuts, often incorporating bold flavors like red wine and paprika.

SERVES 8

Heat the oil and butter in a large saucepan over high heat, add the venison, and sauté, stirring occasionally, until well browned, about 5 minutes.

Reduce the heat to medium, add the onions, bacon, garlic, and all the mushrooms, and sauté, stirring frequently, about 10 minutes more, until the vegetables and bacon have begun to brown lightly and any liquid they release has evaporated.

Transfer the venison, vegetables, and bacon to a bowl, drain the fat from the pan, and return it to medium heat. Add 2¾ cups of the wine to deglaze, stirring with a wooden spoon to loosen any browned bits on the bottom of the pan. Return the venison, vegetables, and bacon to the pan, add the sage, paprika, thyme, and bay leaves, and bring to a boil over high heat. Reduce the heat to low, cover, and simmer for about 1 hour, or until the venison is fully cooked and tender, and the juices have reduced and thickened slightly.

In a small bowl, whisk together the remaining ¼ cup of wine and the arrowroot until velvety smooth.

Remove the thyme sprigs and bay leaves from the pan and stir the wine mixture into the ragoût in a steady stream. Simmer for about 5 minutes more until the ragoût has thickened, and season with salt and pepper.

To serve, ladle the ragoût into a deep serving platter or bowl, and garnish with chives.

---

3 tablespoons olive oil

2 tablespoons unsalted butter

5 pounds venison leg,
cut into 2-inch cubes (make sure silver
skin and tendons are removed)

5 large white onions, chopped

9 slices lean bacon, chopped

3 cloves garlic, finely chopped

½ cup sliced porcini mushrooms

½ cup sliced portobello mushrooms

½ cup sliced white button mushrooms
(see Chef's Note)

3 cups full-bodied red wine,
such as Burgundy

1 teaspoon dried sage

1 teaspoon Hungarian paprika

2 sprigs fresh thyme

2 dried bay leaves

1 tablespoon arrowroot,
or 2¼ teaspoons cornstarch

Salt and freshly ground black pepper

Chopped fresh chives, for garnish

CHEF'S NOTE

For a more interesting presentation, sauté half of the mushrooms in butter at the last moment. Season with salt and pepper and place over the ragoût after it's plated.

Lobster Pie

¾ pound (2½ sticks) unsalted butter

2 tablespoons chopped shallots

1 cup dry sherry

1 quart Lobster Stock (page 365)

1 quart heavy cream

2 tablespoons tomato paste

2 cups all-purpose flour

1 tablespoon chopped fresh parsley,
for serving

Pinch of fresh thyme

Pinch of cayenne pepper

Salt and freshly ground white pepper

3 pounds lobster tail meat

18 jumbo shrimp (about 1¼ pounds),
peeled and deveined

1 cup sliced button mushrooms

½ cup dry sherry

Salt and freshly ground black pepper

3 pounds Quick Puff Pastry (page 60)
or purchased puff pastry

1 egg, lightly beaten
with 1 teaspoon water

Hannah Glasse offers six recipes for lobster in *The Art of Cookery Made Plain and Easy*, including the recipe for lobster pie that inspired the recipe below. However, her example is the exception rather than the rule, as lobster dishes are remarkably scarce in colonial cookbooks. This is mainly because colonials had a low opinion of lobster and generally considered it so undesirable that it was used as fertilizer and fish bait. When it was cooked and served, it was given only to children, prisoners, and indentured servants. In fact, so many servants were sick of eating lobster, they often specified in their contracts that they couldn't be served lobster more than three times per week.

SERVES 6

Heat 1 cup (2 sticks) of the butter in a 4-quart saucepan over medium heat. Add the shallots and sauté for 2 to 3 minutes, until translucent. Add the sherry and bring to a boil. Continue cooking until the liquid is reduced by half, about 8 to 10 minutes. Stir in the stock and bring back to a boil. Stir in the cream and bring back to a boil. Reduce the heat to let simmer.

Heat 1 cup of the butter in a medium-size saucepan over medium heat, add the tomato paste, and slowly stir in the flour to form a smooth paste (or roux). Cook until the roux bubbles. Remove from the heat and slowly whisk into the sherry-stock mixture. Return to medium heat and cook until the sauce starts to thicken, about 2 minutes. Add the parsley, thyme, and cayenne pepper, and season to taste with salt and pepper. Reserve.

Preheat the oven to 450°F.

Heat 3 tablespoons of the butter in a large skillet over medium heat, add the lobster, shrimp, and mushrooms, and sauté for 5 minutes, until the mushrooms are soft, the lobster is white and the shrimp are pink. Add the sherry to deglaze the pan, loosening any browned bits on the bottom of the pan with a wooden spoon. Divide the mixture among six 16- to 18-ounces ovenproof au gratin or casserole dishes. Divide the reserved sauce among the six dishes. (The sauce should cover the filling.)

On a lightly-floured surface, roll out the Quick Puff Pastry to ⅛-inch thickness. Cut out 6 circles allowing 1-inch overhang and place on top of the au gratin dishes. Crimp the pastry to the edge of the dishes, prick the dough with a fork to allow steam to escape, and brush with the egg-water wash.

Bake for 12 minutes, until the edges of the pastry are brown and the centers are golden brown.

Ham & Veal Pie

Meat pies like this one were common on sixteenth- and seventeenth-century tables. If the average colonial housewife were to make this dish, she would most likely have doubled the amount of ham and omitted the veal—a rare commodity in those days, given that cows were more valuable as producers of milk rather than meat. Savory pies were popular because they could be prepared ahead and they offered the cook another way to use leftover meat. This recipe works as well cold as it does straight from the oven.

Overnight preparation recommended.

Serves 8

In a shallow, medium-size bowl, combine the ham, veal, onions, wine, brandy, garlic, thyme, and bay leaves. Cover and marinate in the refrigerator for at least 6 hours, or overnight.

Preheat the oven to 400°F.

Divide the Pâte Brisée in half. On a lightly-floured surface, roll out half of the dough as thinly as possible (⅛-inch thick) and drape over the bottom and sides of a buttered 9-inch pie pan.

Strain the ham mixture through a fine wire sieve or cheesecloth into another container. Transfer the meat and onions to a medium-size bowl and reserve. Discard the bay leaves and reserve the marinade.

Coarsely chop the meat and onions in a food processor or by hand. Return the chopped meat and onions to the bowl. Add the parsley, salt, and pepper, and mix well. Add the meat mixture to the dough-lined pan.

Roll out the remaining dough and cover the top of the pie. Crimp the edges of the pastry with moistened fingers. Cut a 2-inch hole in the center of the top pastry. Roll a 6 x 2-inch piece of parchment paper into a cylinder about 2 inches in diameter. Insert the cylinder into the hole at least ¼-inch deep to form a "chimney."

Brush the top and edges of the pastry with the egg yolk mixture and bake for about 12 minutes, until golden brown.

(continued)

1 pound country-style ham, chopped

1 pound boneless veal shoulder roast, chopped

4 medium white onions, sliced

1 cup dry white wine, such as Sauvignon Blanc

½ cup brandy

4 garlic cloves, chopped

3 sprigs fresh thyme

2 bay leaves

12 ounces Pâte Brisée (page 372)

2 bunches fresh parsley, finely chopped (about ¾ cup)

1 tablespoon salt

1½ teaspoon freshly ground black pepper

1 egg yolk, lightly beaten with 1 tablespoon water

Meanwhile, bring the reserved marinade to a boil in a medium-size skillet over high heat and cook until it's reduced to about ¼ cup, about 8 to 10 minutes. Reserve.

Reduce the oven temperature to 300°F and bake for about 20 minutes, until the meat mixture reaches 190°F. Remove the pie from the oven and pour the reduced wine into the pie through the chimney. Return the pie to the oven and bake for about 10 minutes more, until the wine mixture has been absorbed.

To serve, remove the chimney and let the pie cool on a wire cooling rack for 10 to 15 minutes, until it's warm but not hot.

CHEF'S NOTE

If you want to serve this meat pie cold, perhaps for a summer supper or picnic, do not remove the chimney after the pie has been cooked. Instead, add one packet of unflavored gelatin to a ¼ cup of the cooled wine mixture and stir to dissolve. While the pie is still warm—but not hot—pour the gelatin-wine mixture into the chimney and refrigerate for 2 hours before cutting.

SERVER IN THE LONG ROOM

The main difference between dining at City Tavern today, and dining there in the 1770s, is that women and children are now allowed to dine in public. In the eighteenth century, the very idea of a woman eating in public was scandalous. Although women did attend the balls held in the Long Room, the second largest ballroom in the nation (the largest was in Independence Hall, just blocks away), they were confined to the two or three upstairs guest rooms, should they ever want to eat.

Beef & Pork Pie

Making meat pies was actually a safety measure in colonial times. Since refrigeration was nonexistent back then, cooking leftover meat a second time in a pie eliminated any bacteria which might have developed since the first roasting. Since no piece of valuable meat was wasted—even the tougher scraps left over from the slaughter—the process of roasting, then cooking, and finally baking was a great way to ensure that the meat was as tender and flavorful as possible.

Overnight preparation required.

MAKES 8 LARGE OR 24 SMALL TRIANGLES;
SERVES 8

TO ROAST THE MEATS: Preheat the oven to 350°F.

In a small bowl, mix together the oil, salt, and pepper. Rub the oil mixture over the meats.

Roast the pork shoulder for about 1 hour; roast the beef chuck for about 1½ hours, until a meat thermometer registers 170°F for each meat.

Remove the meats from the oven and let cool for 20 minutes. Cut the meats into ½-inch cubes and reserve.

Melt the butter in a large skillet over high heat, add the beef and pork cubes, onions, and garlic, and sauté for 5 minutes, until the onions are golden brown.

Add the wine to deglaze the pan, loosening any browned bits on the bottom of the pan with a wooden spoon. Add the mushrooms, basil, parsley, thyme, salt, and pepper, and cook until the liquid has evaporated.

Stir in the demi-glace and cook for about 5 minutes more, until all liquid has evaporated again.

Remove from the heat. Spread the mixture out onto a baking sheet and let it cool for 10 minutes. Refrigerate for about 1 hour to cool completely.

(continued)

ROAST MEATS

¼ cup vegetable oil

2 teaspoons salt

1 teaspoon freshly ground
black pepper

2¼ pounds boneless pork
shoulder roast

2¼ pounds boneless
beef chuck roast

PIE

3 tablespoons unsalted butter

1 cup chopped yellow onions

4 garlic cloves, chopped

1 cup red Burgundy wine

1 cup chopped button mushrooms

1 small bunch fresh basil, chopped
(about ¼ cup)

½ small bunch fresh parsley, chopped
(about 3 tablespoons)

1 sprig fresh thyme

2 teaspoons salt

1 teaspoon freshly ground black pepper

1 cup Demi-Glace (page 367)

3 pounds Quick Puff Pastry
(page 60) or purchased puff pastry

1 egg, lightly beaten
with 1 tablespoon water

TO PREPARE PIE: Preheat the oven to 450°F.

On a lightly-floured surface, roll out the Quick Puff Pastry to ⅛-inch thickness. Cut out six 6- to 8-inch squares and brush the edges with the egg mixture.

Place 1 cup of the meat mixture in the center of each square. Fold each square over diagonally to form a triangle and press the edges firmly to seal. Using a fork, gently prick the center of each triangle to allow steam to escape. Lightly brush the edges again with the egg mixture.

Arrange the triangles 2 inches apart on a greased baking sheet.

Bake for 8 to 10 minutes, until golden brown.

CHEF'S NOTE

This recipe can be easily adapted into a tasty appetizer, by making individual pastry triangles—perfect finger food for a party.

Turkey Pot Pie

——— •◦•◦• ———

Turkey was a prized bird in the colonies. Wild turkeys "of incredible Bigness" weighing up to forty pounds, were mentioned by naturalist and writer Robert Beverley in his writings of 1705. Turkeys that roamed the dense forests surrounding Philadelphia were a free and easy source of food for colonials, so recipes for turkey abound in most colonial cookbooks. Benjamin Franklin was such a fan of the turkey that he recommended this "unique American Creature" as our national symbol because it was "humble," and "minds his own Business, respecting the Rights of others."

Overnight preparation recommended.

SERVES 8

TO PREPARE THE TURKEY: In a small bowl, mix together the oil and 1½ teaspoons each of the thyme, parsley, shallot, and garlic. Reserve the remaining herbs. Rub the oil-seasoning mixture all over the turkey. Place the turkey on a tray, cover with plastic wrap, and refrigerate overnight.

Preheat the oven to 450°F.

Place the turkey on a rack in a large roasting pan. Reduce the oven to 350°F and roast the turkey for about 2½ hours or until a meat thermometer inserted into the thigh reads 185°F.

Remove the turkey from the oven and let cool thoroughly. Remove the skin and the meat from the bones. Cut the turkey meat into 1-inch pieces and reserve. Discard the skin and bones.

Preheat the oven to 350°F.

Discard the pan drippings in the roasting pan and place the pan on the stove top over medium heat. Add the onion, celery, and carrots, and sauté for 3 minutes, until tender. Add the wine to deglaze the pan, loosening any browned bits on the bottom of the pan with a wooden spoon. Add the stock, peas, mushrooms, and potatoes. Bring to a boil over high heat. Add the cream and the reserved thyme, parsley, shallot, and garlic. Season with salt and pepper to taste. Bring to a boil over high heat and add the turkey meat. Bring back to a boil. Reduce the heat and simmer for about 5 minutes, until the ingredients are fully cooked.

——— *(continued)* ———

TURKEY

½ cup vegetable oil

3 sprigs fresh thyme, chopped
(about 1 tablespoon)

½ bunch fresh parsley, chopped
(about 3 tablespoons)

1 medium shallot, chopped

4 garlic cloves, chopped

1 whole turkey (8 to 10 pounds)

1 large white onion, diced

4 celery ribs, diced

2 large carrots, peeled and diced

1 cup dry white wine,
such as Sauvignon Blanc

1 quart Chicken Stock (page 364)

1 cup shelled fresh peas

1 cup sliced button mushrooms

1 cup chopped red skinned potatoes

2 cups heavy cream

Salt and freshly ground black pepper

PIE

¼ pound (1 stick) unsalted butter,
softened

½ cup all-purpose flour

3 pounds Quick Puff Pastry (page 60)
or purchased puff pastry

1 egg, lightly beaten
with 1 teaspoon water

TO PREPARE THE PIE: In a small bowl, combine the butter and flour into a paste. Slowly stir the butter-flour mixture into the turkey mixture until it is combined and the mixture is thickened.

Ladle the turkey mixture into a large ovenproof dish or eight 14- to 16-ounce individual casserole dishes.

On a lightly-floured surface, roll out the Quick Puff Pastry to ⅛-inch thickness. Cut the dough into a circle (or 8 circles) allowing 1-inch overhang and place on top of the casserole dish(es). Crimp the pastry to the edge of the dish(es), prick the dough with fork to allow steam to escape, and brush with the egg-water wash. Bake for 12 to 15 minutes, until the pastry edges are brown.

On November 9, 1785, just two blocks from City Tavern "in Second street, eight doors below Arch street," Joseph Walker was selling "A Neat And General Assortment Of Groceries." Among the English wares he offered, including "best London pewter, tin plates in boxes, glass and queens ware," Mr. Walker also sold exotic foodstuffs from Europe and the Orient. On his shelves, one could find such goods as "Fine and coarse salt," "Coffee in barrels and bags," "Hyson, souchong & bohea teas," and "Cocoa," as well as "Raisins in barrels and kegs" and "Ginger."

SIDE DISHES

Hearty side dishes were served in copious amounts at City Tavern feasts. It wasn't uncommon to have as many as ten served in one meal, including vegetables of all types, barley, rice, potatoes, and stuffing. Although meat was on the Tavern menu daily, it was very precious and served in small portions, so the sides made up a significant portion of the meal. In fact, the average cook in colonial times considered vegetables and starches as main dishes and only rarely flavored them with meat, fowl, or fish. Even our greatest gastronome, Thomas Jefferson, ate meat in conservative portions "as a condiment to the vegetables which constitute my principal diet."

In summer months, side dishes consisted mainly of a seasonal bounty of fresh vegetables. Colonial cooks poached or sautéed them in butter, adding only a bit of salt and pepper to permit the natural flavors of the vegetables to shine through. In Jefferson's case, he enjoyed vegetables "Dressed in the French Manner," meaning tossed in a simple vinaigrette of olive oil and red wine vinegar.

As winter approached and the availability of quality fresh vegetables began to wane, cooks would hide inferior vegetables in casseroles, stews, ragoûts and puddings, or cover them with thick sauces, like brown gravy, onion sauce and butter sauce. Any vegetables that would have been pickled or made into relishes, preserves, and catsups made their debut as side dishes at that time. In winter, side dishes also included all sorts of root vegetables, either boiled, "ragooed," fried, or mashed. Rice grown in the Carolinas was dressed up with dried herbs or spiced with curry. Germans, or Pennsylvania Dutch, grew an abundance of wheat on their farms and ground it into flour in their mills, making homemade noodles, pasta, and dumplings a regular accompaniment to the hearty stews and ragoûts they favored. Legumes, such as lentils and dried peas, and a dizzying array of beans were stewed and "sent up" to complete the first or second plate side dish offering.

Salsify Gratin

———————

Believed to have originated in Spain, spread throughout Europe by the seventeenth century, and brought to America by Europeans, salsify became a favorite of colonials because it wintered well in root cellars. Its subtle, oyster-like flavor lent itself to many different preparations and paired well with almost any meat, fowl, or fish. In *The Virginia House-wife*, Mary Randolph penned three recipes for salsify: one in which the salsify is simply boiled in water, a second recipe for salsify cakes, and the third a gratin similar to the recipe below. Hinting at additional preparations not committed to paper she adds, "they are delicious in any way they can be dressed."

SERVES 6 TO 8

2½ pounds salsify, stemmed, peeled, and cut on the diagonal into 2-inch pieces

Juice of 1 lemon

3 tablespoons unsalted butter

3 medium shallots, finely chopped

3 heaping tablespoons all-purpose flour

1 cup dry white wine, such as Sauvignon Blanc

1 cup heavy cream

⅛ teaspoon freshly grated nutmeg

Salt and freshly ground white pepper

½ cup grated Parmesan cheese

To make the salsify, prepare a steamer. Butter a 9-inch gratin dish or six to eight 6-ounce ramekins.

Toss together the salsify and lemon juice in a large bowl, place the salsify in the steamer, and cook until just tender, about 3 minutes. Set aside while preparing the sauce.

To make the sauce, melt the butter in a large saucepan over medium heat, add the shallots, and sauté until softened and translucent, about 1 minute.

Whisk in the flour to form a roux, stir in the wine and cream, and simmer until the sauce is thickened and slightly reduced, about 3 to 5 minutes.

Stir in the nutmeg and season to taste with salt and white pepper.

To assemble the dish, preheat the broiler. Add the salsify to the sauce, gently mixing to coat, and pour into the prepared gratin dish or individual ramekins. Sprinkle with Parmesan cheese, set under the broiler until golden and bubbly, and serve hot.

Red Cabbage
with Apples

Red cabbage was most likely brought to America by the Germans who settled in Pennsylvania from 1683 on. German farmers brought wagons loaded with produce into Philadelphia to sell in the markets, and red cabbage was surely among their wares. Cabbage would normally have been preserved in vinegar before storing in root cellars for the winter, so the apples would have been added to balance the flavor with their natural sweetness.

For a truly inspiring presentation of this dish, slice an additional apple thinly and sauté it in butter until just slightly browned. Arrange the apple slices on top of the cabbage before serving.

SERVES 8

Melt the butter in a large sauté pan over medium heat, add the shallot and garlic, and sauté until golden, about 1 minute.

Add the cabbage and apples, tossing several times, and pour in the wine to deglaze the pan, stirring with a wooden spoon to loosen any browned bits on the bottom of the pan. Stir in the sugar and season to taste with salt and pepper.

Bring to a boil over high heat, stirring constantly to prevent the sugar from burning, reduce the heat to medium-low, and simmer until the liquid is reduced by three-fourths, about 10 minutes. (The reduction will be concentrated and have a light syrup consistency.)

2 tablespoons unsalted butter

1 medium shallot, chopped

1 clove garlic, chopped

2 ½ to 3 pounds red cabbage, cored and shredded (about 10 cups)

5 large Red Delicious apples, peeled, cored, and thinly sliced

½ cup red wine, such as Burgundy

½ cup sugar

Salt and freshly ground black pepper

CHEF'S NOTE

Colonial cooks always kept on hand a variety of animal fats, or schmaltzes, to add rich flavor to recipes, especially vegetable dishes like this one. You can use the goose fat from the Goose & Turnips recipe on page 186 in place of the butter here. Just strain the hot fat through a fine mesh sieve lined with cheesecloth first.

Creamed Savoy Cabbage

—•◦•◦•—

2½ to 3 pounds Savoy cabbage
(1 large or 2 small cabbages)

3 tablespoons unsalted butter

¼ pound slab bacon, sliced into 2-inch by
¼-inch strips

1 clove garlic, finely chopped

1 small yellow onion, finely chopped

3 cups heavy cream

1 cup Demi-Glace (page 367)

Salt and freshly ground white pepper

Savoy cabbage is distinguished from regular cabbage by its bright green, crinkled leaves, which cling more loosely to the core. Though relatively unknown to modern cooks, it appeared regularly in eighteenth-century gardens. Thomas Jefferson's Garden Book indicates a planting of Savoy cabbage on March 15, 1774, followed by another later that spring on May 2. Here, it is prepared in the typical eighteenth-century manner of a vegetable "Ragoo."

SERVES 8

Slice the cabbages into quarters and remove the cores. Slice into 1½-inch-square pieces.

Bring a large pot of lightly salted water to a boil and add the cabbage. Cook until just al dente, about 2 minutes. Transfer to a colander and allow to drain.

Melt the butter in a large sauté pan over medium heat, add the bacon and cook until crisp. Remove the bacon and drain on paper towels. Reserve and keep hot.

Add the garlic to the bacon drippings and sauté for 2 to 3 minutes, until golden. Add the onion and sauté for 3 to 5 minutes, until translucent.

Add the cream and cook until reduced by half, about 15 minutes. Stir in the demi-glace and cook for another 5 minutes.

Toss in the cabbage, reduce the heat to low, and cook for 2 to 3 minutes, until warmed through. Season with salt and pepper.

Transfer the cabbage to a large serving bowl and top with the bacon.

Braised Artichokes

⁘———⁘

Artichokes are the flower of a thistle, the consumption of which dates back to Roman times when they were enjoyed mainly by the nobility. Called "hartychoak" or "hardychoak" by colonial housewives, they were most frequently used to flavor meat and fish pies, but were occasionally served up as the main ingredient in a pie of their own. Both Martha Washington and Hannah Glasse include them in many recipes, but Washington uses them mainly as an ingredient in other dishes. Glasse, on the other hand, was much more inventive, making them fricasseed, fried, pickled, preserved, and stewed in the "Spanish Way" with oil, vinegar, and egg yolks.

Serves 8

Fill a large mixing bowl halfway with water and add the lemon juice.

Using a pair of kitchen scissors, trim off the stems and tough outer leaves of the artichokes, then snip off the tips of the remaining leaves. Gently fold back the leaves and remove the thistle in the center. Cut into quarters and place in the water.

Bring a large saucepan filled with lightly salted water to a boil and drop in the artichokes. Cook until they just begin to soften, about 2 to 3 minutes. Remove the artichokes with a slotted spoon and place on a towel to drain.

Melt the butter in a large skillet over medium heat. Add the artichokes and bell pepper, and cook for 5 to 8 minutes, until al dente. Add the parsley and season with salt and pepper.

Juice of 1 lemon

8 large fresh artichokes

2 tablespoons unsalted butter

1 small red bell pepper, finely julienned

1 tablespoon finely chopped fresh parsley

Salt and freshly ground white pepper

Brussels Sprouts

‹—•••—›

Said to have been cultivated as far back as the thirteenth century in Belgium, these hardy members of the cabbage family were a favorite of Thomas Jefferson, who grew them in his garden. Though his Garden Book shows no entries of Brussels sprouts before 1812, it is hard to imagine that he didn't plant them before that.

Brussels sprouts were popular with colonial cooks because they wintered well right on the stalk. When a touch of green was needed to liven up a winter dish, colonial cooks would simply walk out to the garden, shake the ice and snow off the stalk and pick the perfectly preserved sprouts. Fennel seeds, long known for their digestive properties, were generally added to the recipe to prevent "windiness."

SERVES 6

1½ pounds fresh Brussels sprouts, trimmed

2 slices lean bacon, finely chopped

1 teaspoon olive oil

1 medium yellow onion, finely chopped

¾ cup Chicken Stock (page 364)

1 teaspoon fennel seeds, lightly crushed in a mortar and pestle (or with the bottom of a pan)

Salt and freshly ground black pepper

With a small paring knife, cut a small cross ⅛-inch deep into the stem end of each Brussels sprout.

Bring a large saucepan of salted water to a boil over high heat. Add the Brussels sprouts and cook for 6 to 8 minutes (depending on their size), until just tender. Drain, then add enough cold water to cover the Brussels sprouts. Let stand for about 5 minutes, until cool. Drain again.

In a large skillet, cook the bacon over medium heat, stirring occasionally, about 5 minutes, until crisp and brown. Remove from the skillet and drain on a paper towels.

Wipe out the skillet with paper towels. Add the oil and onion and cook over medium heat, stirring occasionally, about 5 minutes until soft.

Stir in the stock, fennel seeds, Brussels sprouts, and bacon, and cook over medium heat, stirring frequently, about 3 minutes, until most of the liquid is evaporated.

Season with salt and pepper to taste. Serve hot.

CHEF'S NOTE

To make this a vegetarian dish, omit the bacon and use vegetable stock instead of chicken stock.

Fennel Purée

Fennel seems to be one of the most underrated vegetables in America. Long appreciated in Italy and France for its delicate anise flavor and toothsome texture, it was among the many crops in Thomas Jefferson's garden. Introduced to fennel by his neighbor, Philip Mazzei, a Florentine émigré and fellow plant enthusiast, Jefferson soon elevated fennel above all favorites: "The fennel is beyond every other vegetable, delicious. It greatly resembles in appearance the largest size celery, perfectly white, and there is no vegetable equals it in flavour. It is eaten at dessert, crude, and with, or without dry salt, indeed I preferred it to every other vegetable, or to any fruit." This recipe prepares fennel in a manner that is traditional both in France and Italy, so Jefferson could have discovered this preparation from Mazzei or from any one of his cooks in France.

SERVES 8

Cut off the bases, tops, and any bruised or tough outer layers of the fennel. Cut each fennel bulb into 6 pieces and remove the core.

Bring a large saucepan of lightly salted water to a boil over high heat. Add the fennel and potatoes and cook for 15 to 20 minutes, until the vegetables are fork-tender. Drain the vegetables and let them cool slightly.

Transfer the vegetables to a blender or food processor and purée until smooth. Add the cream and process until combined. Season with salt and pepper to taste.

Transfer to a serving bowl.

Sprinkle with the Parmesan cheese and paprika. Garnish with 1 tablespoon of the chopped fennel leaves. Serve hot.

---

5 large fresh fennel bulbs, leaves chopped and reserved for garnish

2 medium Yukon gold potatoes (about 4 ounces), peeled and sliced

3 tablespoons heavy cream

Salt and freshly ground black pepper

½ cup grated Parmesan cheese, for serving

1 tablespoon sweet paprika, for serving

Creamed Green Beans

—◆—

3 pounds fresh tender green beans,
such as haricot verts

2 tablespoons unsalted butter

2 medium onions, finely chopped

2 garlic cloves, chopped

1 cup Béchamel Sauce (page 369)

½ cup heavy cream

⅛ teaspoon cayenne pepper

Salt and freshly ground white pepper

Fresh parsley, chopped, for garnish

Green beans, brought to Europe in the sixteenth century by returning Portuguese and Spanish explorers, are native to Mexico and Central America. Europeans, in turn, brought the beans back across the Atlantic to North America in colonial days. A great many colonial households grew green beans because they could be preserved in salt and used to add color to their dishes in winter, a time when green vegetables were sorely missed.

Amazingly, not one single recipe for green beans can be found in Martha Washington's *Booke of Cookery*. However, both Hannah Glasse and Elizabeth Taylor, who penned *The Lady's, Housewife's and Cookmaid's Assistant: Or the Art of Cookery Explained and Adapted to the Meanest Capacity*, include the same recipe "to ragoo French Beans," which is the inspiration for the recipe below.

SERVES 8

Bring a large saucepan of lightly salted water to a boil over high heat. Add the green beans and cook for 3 to 5 minutes, until crisp-tender. Drain and reserve.

Melt the butter in a medium-size saucepan over medium heat, add the onions and garlic and sauté for 3 minutes, until translucent.

Slowly stir in the Béchamel Sauce, cream, and cayenne pepper. Gently stir in the green beans and cook for about 3 minutes until the Béchamel Sauce is heated through.

Season with salt and pepper to taste. Transfer to serving bowl. Garnish with the chopped parsley. Serve immediately.

Creamed Spinach

◆━◆━◆

1 pound fresh spinach,
well rinsed, stems removed,
and roughly chopped

1 teaspoon salt

1 cup Béchamel Sauce (page 369)

½ cup heavy cream

¼ teaspoon freshly grated nutmeg

2 tablespoons unsalted butter

Salt and freshly ground black pepper

First documented in two separate works in 1390, *The Forme of Cury* and *Le Ménagier*, spinach is presumed to have originated in Arabic Spain, a fact supported by the Old French term for spinach, *Herbe d'Espaigne* (Spanish grass). A version of creamed spinach appears in many colonial cookbooks, but it is typically served with poached eggs, bread and a "boat" of melted butter, similar to what we now know as eggs Florentine. Here, we serve up the creamed spinach by itself, in the English tradition.

SERVES 4

Place the spinach and salt in a large saucepan and cook over low heat for about 5 minutes, stirring occasionally, until it is wilted. Let cool for 3 to 5 minutes.

Drain and squeeze out the excess water from the spinach. Transfer the spinach to a cutting board, and finely chop it; reserve.

In a medium-size saucepan, combine the Béchamel Sauce, cream, and nutmeg. Cook the mixture over medium heat, stirring occasionally, about 3 minutes, until thoroughly heated. Stir in the chopped spinach and the butter. Season with salt and pepper to taste.

Pennsylvania Dutch–Style
Sauerkraut

Although *sauerkraut* is the German word for sour cabbage, this dish is actually Chinese in origin, where it was served fermented in rice wine. It eventually found its way to Europe, where Germans and Alsatians adopted it as their own, later bringing it to the New World. In fact, Captain Cook provisioned his ships with sauerkraut because the vitamin C that remained, even after fermentation, prevented the dreaded disease scurvy.

Hanna Glasse called it "a dish much made use of amongst the Germans, and in the North Countries, there the frost kills all the cabbages." In Pennsylvania, with its large number of German settlers, sauerkraut was a popular side dish, mainly because it offered the best way to preserve this particular vegetable for use in the winter months.

SERVES 6

Melt the butter in a large saucepan over medium heat, add the bacon, and cook for 3 minutes, until crisp. Add the onions and garlic and sauté for about 5 minutes, until golden brown.

Stir in the sauerkraut, stock, wine, and caraway seeds. Bring to a boil over high heat. Reduce the heat to medium and cook for about 30 minutes, until the stock is reduced by three-fourths.

Stir in the apples and potato and cook about 30 minutes more, until the apples and potato are dissolved. Season with salt and pepper to taste.

3 tablespoons unsalted butter

9 slices lean bacon, diced

2 medium onions, chopped

1 garlic clove, chopped

4 cups (32 ounces) refrigerated or canned sauerkraut (see Chef's Note), rinsed and drained

1½ cups Chicken Stock (page 364)

1 cup sweet white wine, such as Riesling

½ teaspoon caraway seeds

2 large apples, peeled, cored, and thinly sliced

1 large red skinned potato (about 3 ounces), peeled and grated

Salt and freshly ground white pepper

CHEF'S NOTE

I prefer refrigerated-style sauerkraut because it tends to be cooked less than the canned variety. Use any of the different types of commercially prepared sauerkraut available, but be sure to rinse it several times to remove the salt. Then, drain it thoroughly in a colander.

Homemade
Egg Noodles

2 cups all-purpose flour

2 eggs, lightly beaten

2 egg yolks, lightly beaten

2 teaspoons vegetable oil

2 tablespoons water

2 tablespoons unsalted butter

Salt

Noodles are another example of the German contribution to early American cuisine, especially in and around Philadelphia where the concentration of German settlers was heaviest. Many colonials experienced noodles prepared in the French or Italian traditions, which came to America via the English, so the general colonial term for any kind of pasta became "maccaroni." Amazingly, the most common preparation of "macca-roni" was baked with cheese, which Thomas Jefferson even served at the White House while he was president!

SERVES 8

Combine the flour, eggs, egg yolks, oil, and water in the bowl of an electric mixer fitted with the paddle attachment. Mix on medium speed until the dough comes together and forms a stiff ball. Remove the dough, wrap it in plastic wrap, and reserve to rest at room temperature for 1 hour.

On a lightly-floured surface, flatten the ball to about ¼-inch thick and roll with a rolling pin until very thin, about ¹⁄₁₆-inch thick. Cut the dough into strips of noodles about 1-inch wide and 4 inches long.

Bring 2 quarts of salted water to a boil in a large saucepan, add the noodles, and cook until al dente, about 2 minutes.

To serve, drain and pour the noodles into a large serving bowl. Add the butter, tossing to coat, and season with salt.

CHEF'S NOTE

If you plan to dry this pasta and store it for later use, replace about ¼ cup of the all-purpose flour with semolina flour. This will make the dough a bit more durable. Arrange the freshly cut strips of dough on a parchment-lined baking sheet and set aside to dry completely, about 2 hours. Seal the dried pasta in an airtight container and it will keep for several weeks.

The first pasta machine, or extruder, in America
was shipped to Thomas Jefferson from Naples, Italy.

Pumpkin Gratin

Although edible gourds were used in soups as early as the sixteenth century, it was the Native Americans who introduced the colonists to pumpkin. Never ones to ignore a good food source, colonists quickly set about learning and inventing ways to cook this new vegetable. However, with most foods native only to America, colonial cooks typically relied upon what they already knew. This dish is a perfect example of the seamless, and delicious, melding of Native American foods with European culinary savior faire.

SERVES 8

Preheat the oven to 350°F.

Bring a Dutch oven of salted water to a boil over high heat. Add the pumpkin and cook for about 20 minutes, until fork-tender. Drain.

In a medium-size skillet, cook the bacon over medium heat, stirring occasionally, about 5 minutes, until crisp and brown. Remove from the skillet and drain on paper towels. Reserve.

In the same skillet with the bacon drippings, sauté the onions over medium heat for about 5 minutes, until golden brown. Reserve.

Place the pumpkin on a baking sheet and bake for 3 to 5 minutes, until dry.

Purée the pumpkin in a food processor until smooth. (Or press it through a sieve or food mill.) Transfer the purée to a large bowl. Stir in the eggs, reserved onions, reserved bacon, nutmeg, and cinnamon. Sprinkle with salt and pepper.

Increase the oven temperature to 375°F.

Pour the mixture into a 2-quart au gratin dish or medium-size baking dish. Sprinkle with the Parmesan cheese, dot with the butter, and bake for 20 to 30 minutes, until golden brown.

1 small pumpkin (about 3 pounds), seeded, peeled, and cut into large pieces

9 slices lean bacon, cut into pieces

4 medium onions, chopped

4 eggs, lightly beaten

¼ teaspoon freshly grated nutmeg

⅛ teaspoon ground cinnamon

Salt and freshly ground black pepper

1 cup grated Parmesan cheese

2 tablespoons unsalted butter, softened

Sweet Potatoes & Apples

Sweet potato is generally associated with southern foodways; the cultivation of the tuber in Virginia dates to the early 1700s, if not before then, and for nearly three hundred years it has continued to appear in a wide variety of southern dishes. It originated in the tropical New World and, thanks to Christopher Columbus, was being cultivated in Spain by the end of the fifteenth century and in England by the mid-sixteenth century. The tuber, therefore, was familiar to colonial Americans before they ever arrived in the New World, and dishes like sweet potatoes and apples refer directly to traditional British foodways.

6 medium sweet potatoes
(about 3 pounds)

4 medium Granny Smith apples, peeled, cored, and sliced

1 cup packed light brown sugar

4 tablespoons unsalted butter

1 teaspoon ground mace

Salt and freshly ground black pepper

Serves 8

Preheat the oven to 325°F.

Fill a Dutch oven with lightly salted water and bring to a boil over high heat. Add the sweet potatoes and cook for 15 to 20 minutes, until just fork-tender. Do not overcook. Drain the potatoes and set them aside until they are cool enough to handle.

Peel and cut the potatoes into ¼-inch-thick slices.

Butter a large baking dish and place half of the potato slices in the bottom of the dish. Top with half of the apple slices. Sprinkle with half of the brown sugar, butter, and mace. Season to taste with salt and pepper. Repeat with alternate layers of the remaining potato slices, apple slices, sugar, butter, and mace.

Bake for about 1 hour, until the top is brown and the liquid has evaporated.

Although called a potato, the sweet potato is actually a root vegetable in the morning glory family.

Candied Sweet Potatoes

T his recipe combines two colonial favorites: sweet potatoes and citrus fruits. Lemons and oranges were symbols of wealth and afflu-
ence among the Philadelphia elite, who prominently displayed the
treasures in elaborate bowls in their homes. The fruits were imported from
Spain because, at that time, no lemons or oranges grew in the Caribbean or
North America. With only Europe as a source, the fruits were quite expensive in the colonies; in turn, serving anything prepared with citrus fruits was
considered a coup and a status symbol. Both lemons and oranges were featured items on the trendy City Tavern menu. Every bit of the fruits, from the
juice to the pulp to the peel (in the case of this recipe, all three), was used in
recipes of every type.

SERVES 6 TO 8

Preheat the oven to 350°F.

Arrange the sweet potatoes in a large baking dish.

In a medium-size mixing bowl, combine 1¼ cups water, the brown sugar,
orange, lemon, butter, and salt. Pour over the sweet potatoes, cover with aluminum foil, and bake for 30 minutes.

Uncover the potatoes and continue to bake them, basting frequently, for
about 30 minutes more, until they are tender and golden brown.

6 medium sweet potatoes
(about 3 pounds), peeled and
cut into julienne strips

1 cup packed light brown sugar

1 large orange, peeled and chopped

1 large lemon, peeled and chopped

2 tablespoons unsalted butter

¼ teaspoon salt

Turnip, Potato, &
Parsnip Mash

½ pound white turnips,
peeled and cut into 1-inch cubes

½ pound russet potatoes,
peeled and cut into 1-inch cubes

½ pound parsnips,
peeled and cut into 1-inch cubes

1½ quarts Chicken Stock (page 364)

4 tablespoons unsalted butter

1 small onion, finely chopped

¼ cup heavy cream

1 small bunch fresh parsley,
chopped (about ¼ cup)

½ teaspoon freshly grated nutmeg

Salt and freshly ground black pepper

Turnips and parsnips were brought to America as early as the 1600s by Europeans who understood the need for a vegetable that wintered well in a root cellar. Colonial cooks embraced them and included them in many winter recipes. Martha Washington made a "Tart Of Parsneps & Scyrrets (carrots)" in which she boiled and mashed them, then "bedew(ed)" them with rose water. The result was similar to pumpkin pie, but cloyingly sweet.

In *Thomas Jefferson's Cookbook*, he notes that "Parsnips may be cooked, mashed and fried in cakes like salsify." Hanna Glasse agreed, and treated parsnips and turnips as we would potatoes. In her recipe, "To dress Turnips," she instructs the reader to "mash them with butter, a little cream, and a little salt, and send them to table."

SERVES 6 TO 8

In a large saucepan, combine the turnips, potatoes, parsnips, and stock and bring to a boil over high heat. Reduce the heat and simmer for 15 to 20 minutes, until the vegetables are fork-tender. Drain the vegetables and return them to the saucepan.

Melt 1 tablespoon of the butter in a small saucepan over medium heat, add the onion, and sauté for 3 minutes, until golden brown. Add the onions, cream, the remaining 3 tablespoons butter, the parsley, and nutmeg to the vegetables and mash with a potato masher until smooth. Season with salt and pepper to taste. Serve hot.

Smashed Red Potatoes

———◆———

Ancient Inca were cultivating the potato high in the Andes Mountains as early as 3000 B.C. After the Spanish Conquistadores brought the tuber to Europe in the sixteenth century, the potato eventually made its way to England via established trade routes. The English transported the new vegetable to their colonies in the West Indies and began cultivation there. In 1621, the Governor of Bermuda included potatoes in a cargo of unique plants and vegetables he shipped to Governor Francis Wyatt of Virginia. Potatoes soon became a staple in the colonial diet, and were much prized for their ability to survive long winters in a root cellar.

SERVES 8

Bring a large saucepan of salted water to a boil over high heat. Add the potatoes and cook for 10 to 15 minutes, until fork-tender.

In a small bowl, combine the sour cream, shallots, and chives. Stir until smooth and reserve.

Drain the potatoes and smash them with a potato masher or the back of a large spoon. Do not completely mash the potatoes. Stir in the sour cream mixture and season with salt and pepper to taste. Serve hot.

2 pounds red skinned potatoes,
halved (quartered if large)

½ cup sour cream

¼ cup finely chopped shallots

1 bunch fresh chives, chopped
(about ¼ cup)

Salt and freshly ground black pepper

Potato, Mushroom, & Onion Casserole

7 tablespoons unsalted butter

2 tablespoons vegetable oil

6 cups sliced button mushrooms
(about 1½ pounds)

2 large onions, sliced

2 garlic cloves, chopped

8 medium red skinned potatoes
(about 1½ pounds), peeled and
very thinly sliced

Salt and freshly ground white pepper

2 bunches fresh parsley,
finely chopped (about ½ cup)

1 cup heavy cream

½ cup grated Parmesan cheese

This dish combines two great recipes from two famous colonial cooks. In *The Virginia Housewife*, Mary Randolph's straightforward recipe for mashed potatoes and onions makes for a delicious side dish. Martha Washington penned a recipe for mushroom and onion casserole entitled, "To Dress A Dish Of Mushrumps," which is also a delicious recipe, but complicated somewhat by the addition of egg yolks as a thickening agent. In combining the two, the result is a much simplified recipe that offers all the flavor, and a bit more panache, of the originals. Exotic mushrooms, such as porcini, chanterelles, or morels can be substituted for an even more impressive dish.

SERVES 8

Preheat the oven to 375°F.

Heat 4 tablespoons of the butter and the oil in a large skillet over high heat, add the mushrooms, and sauté for 5 minutes, until light brown and tender. Remove from the skillet and reserve.

In the same skillet, sauté the onions and garlic for 3 minutes, until golden brown. Reserve.

Pat the sliced potatoes dry with paper towels. Place half of the potato slices in the bottom of a large baking dish and sprinkle with salt and pepper. Add the parsley, the reserved mushroom and onion mixtures, and the remaining potato slices. Sprinkle again with salt and pepper and dot with the remaining 3 tablespoons butter.

Bake for 15 minutes.

Pour the cream evenly over the potato mixture, top with the Parmesan cheese, and bake about 10 minutes more, until the potatoes are fork-tender and the mixture is bubbly. Serve hot.

Mashed Potatoes

Since it is a member of the lethal nightshade family, the potato was long considered by Europeans to be poisonous—and the leaves are indeed poisonous, but the potato itself, lacking exposure to the sun, never has the chance to activate its latent poisonous quality. As with the tomato, which was thought to be unfit for human consumption until Thomas Jefferson became its champion and forced his friends to eat it, the potato initially encountered a great deal of resistance. In the sixteenth century, Sir Walter Raleigh effectively made the case for potatoes in England by planting them on lands he owned in Ireland. Two centuries later, in the 1780s, people on the Continent still weren't convinced, until Antoine Auguste Parmentier brought potatoes into vogue in France by convincing King Louis XVI and Marie Antoinette to try them and serve them at Court. Various forms of this most basic recipe for potatoes have existed since that time.

1½ pounds Yukon Gold potatoes, peeled and cut into 1-inch cubes

4 tablespoons unsalted butter

¼ cup heavy cream

½ teaspoon freshly grated nutmeg (see Chef's Note)

Salt and freshly ground black pepper

SERVES 6 TO 8

In a large saucepan, combine the potatoes with just enough lightly salted water to cover, and bring to a boil over high heat. Reduce the heat and simmer for 15 to 20 minutes, until fork-tender.

Drain the potatoes and return them to the saucepan, allowing the steam to escape so the potatoes dry.

Add the butter and cream, and mash with a potato masher until smooth.

Season with the nutmeg and salt and pepper to taste. Serve hot.

CHEF'S NOTE

Every spice begins to lose its flavor as soon as it is ground, so I don't recommend using pre-ground spices at all. Nothing can compare to the flavor that freshly ground nutmeg imparts to a dish. Whole nutmeg is available in virtually every supermarket and spice store nowadays.

Crisp Potato Cakes

Potato cakes were often made to conceal potatoes that were less than perfect. In *The Virginia Housewife*, Mary Randolph suggests "when the potatos are getting old and speckled, and in frosty weather, this is the best way of dressing them—you may put them into shapes, touch them over with yolk of egg, and brown them very slightly before a slow fire." The classical way of preparing any potato dish, especially one that includes cream, calls for the addition of a touch of nutmeg, a very common spice in colonial times.

SERVES 8

Preheat the oven to 350°F.

Place the potatoes in a large saucepan filled with lightly salted water, bring to a boil over high heat, and boil until the potatoes are just tender, about 15 minutes. Drain the potatoes, place on a baking sheet, and set in the oven to dry further, about 5 minutes. Set the potatoes aside to cool slightly.

Push the potatoes through a potato ricer or food mill into a large bowl, add the egg yolks, salt, pepper, nutmeg, bacon, and chives, and mix thoroughly to combine.

Using slightly wet hands shape the potatoes into cakes about 3 inches in diameter and ½ inch thick. Arrange the cakes on a parchment-lined baking sheet coated with vegetable spray and bake until golden brown, about 15 minutes.

8 large Yukon gold potatoes, peeled

4 egg yolks

1 teaspoon salt

½ teaspoon freshly ground white pepper

⅛ teaspoon freshly grated nutmeg

4 slices bacon, cooked and finely chopped

1 tablespoon finely chopped chives

Thomas Jefferson's culinary tastes were forever influenced by his stint as the American ambassador to France in 1789. One of the dishes he learned to love was French fried potatoes—when he became president a few years later, he instructed the White House chef to prepare this tasty side dish frequently for dinner guests.

Potato & Bread Dumplings

Every culture, European and otherwise, has some kind of dumpling in its culinary repertoire. In colonial times, dumplings were made in a variety of ways—some with potatoes, some with flour and water, and some with bread. For colonial cooks, bread dumplings offered the best way to make use of leftover bread. Hannah Glasse's most prominent dumpling recipe, "To make Dumplings when you have White Bread," taught cooks how to avoid wasting the fruits of a very labor-intense process. The recipe below, which also includes potatoes, is an updated version of the original dumpling recipes brought to America by the wave of German immigrants that first arrived in the 1680s.

SERVES 8

In a large mixing bowl, soak the bread in the milk for 2 to 3 minutes, until soggy. Using your hands, squeeze out and discard the milk.

Place the bread in a large mixing bowl. Stir in the potatoes, onions, parsley, salt, pepper, nutmeg and marjoram. Add the eggs and mix well.

Shape the mixture into 24 (1½-inch) round dumplings and dip them in the flour to coat generously.

Bring a large saucepan of lightly salted water to a boil over high heat.

With a slotted spoon, gently add the dumplings to the water. Bring back to a boil.

Reduce the heat to medium. Cover and cook for about 15 minutes, until the dumplings expand and float to the surface.

Remove with a slotted spoon and serve.

---

15 slices day-old white sandwich bread, crusts removed

1 cup whole milk

7 large red-skinned potatoes, peeled and grated (about 2 cups)

2 medium yellow onions, grated (about 1 cup)

About ⅓ cup chopped fresh parsley

1 tablespoon salt

¼ teaspoon freshly ground white pepper

⅛ teaspoon freshly grated nutmeg

⅛ teaspoon dried marjoram

3 large eggs, beaten well

All-purpose flour, for dredging

Molasses Baked Beans

———— •◆•• ————

Baked beans actually had their roots as a Native American dish—beans mixed with maple sugar and bear fat and cooked in "bean holes," holes in the ground that were lined with hot rocks. The colonists substituted molasses or sugar for the maple syrup and bacon or ham for the bear fat. They simmered their beans for hours in pots over the fire, instead of in underground bean holes, but the savory results were the same.

Overnight preparation recommended.

Serves 8

To pre-soak the beans, place them in a colander and rinse thoroughly with water to clean. Place the beans in a large bowl and cover with water. Let stand at room temperature for at least 8 hours or overnight.

Drain and thoroughly rinse the beans; reserve.

Preheat the oven to 300°F.

In a large saucepan, cover the beans with water and bring to a boil over high heat. Reduce the heat to medium and cook, covered, for 30 minutes.

Drain the beans. Stir in the bacon, brown sugar, molasses, and mustard.

Transfer the bean mixture to a medium-size bean pot or casserole dish and bake, covered, for about 7 hours, until tender.

Check the consistency several times during baking. If the beans become overly dry, add the stock. Season with salt and pepper to taste.

1 pound dried navy beans

9 slices lean bacon, chopped

¼ cup packed dark brown sugar

½ cup molasses

1½ teaspoons dry mustard

½ cup Chicken Stock (page 364), optional

Salt and freshly ground black pepper

Because Pilgrims were not allowed to do any work on the Sabbath, they started cooking their beans the night before, thereby beginning the tradition of Boston baked beans.

White Bean & Shallot Purée

———•◦◦•———

2 pounds dried white beans,
such as great Northern

1 tablespoon salt,
plus more as needed

1 teaspoon freshly ground
black pepper, plus more as needed

1 Bouquet Garni (page 366)

4 medium red skinned potatoes,
peeled and coarsely chopped

6 tablespoons unsalted butter,
softened

2 medium onions, chopped

3 garlic cloves, chopped

¼ cup heavy cream

5 medium shallots, finely chopped

Dried beans are rich in protein, calcium, phosphorus, and iron, so they were a staple in the colonial larder. White beans were, and still are, used heavily in French and Italian cooking, which is most likely where Thomas Jefferson received his first introduction to them. Although his Garden Book shows no reference to white beans, there is a curiously vague entry stating that he "sowed Mazzei's beans, snap beans, & parsley." Philip Mazzei, the Florentine émigré who introduced him to fennel, could very well have given him white beans from Italy, but this is only conjecture. However, it is certain that Jefferson found them somewhere in America because the notes he kept on dishes served at the President's House (now the White House) list a recipe for "White Beans, Brown Onion Sauce," similar to the recipe below.

Overnight preparation required.

SERVES 8 TO 10

To pre-soak the beans, place them in a colander and rinse thoroughly with water to clean. Place the beans in a large bowl and cover with water. Let stand at room temperature for at least 8 hours or overnight.

Drain and thoroughly rinse the beans, then place them in a Dutch oven, cover them with water, and add the salt and pepper. Bring to a boil over high heat. Reduce the heat to medium and add the Bouquet Garni. Cover and cook for 1½ hours, until the beans are tender.

Stir the potatoes into the beans and cook for an additional 30 minutes.

Melt 1 tablespoon of the butter in a medium-size saucepan over medium heat, add the onions and garlic and sauté for 3 minutes, until golden brown. Stir into the beans.

Remove the Bouquet Garni. Drain the beans in a colander.

Transfer the bean mixture to a food processor and purée until smooth. Stir in the cream and 4 tablespoons of the butter; season with salt and pepper to taste. Transfer to a casserole dish and keep warm.

In a small saucepan, sauté the shallots in the remaining 1 tablespoon butter over medium heat for 2 minutes, until golden brown.

To serve, spoon the shallots over the bean mixture.

Red Beans & Wine

———⟨·•·⟩———

Thomas Jefferson once said, "the greatest service which can be rendered any country is to add a useful plant to its culture." Ever practicing what he preached, at least in all things horticultural, Jefferson grew thirty-six varieties of kidney beans in his garden at Monticello. During his whirlwind tour of France's most famous winemaking provinces in 1787, Jefferson lingered in the picturesque hills of Burgundy before continuing on through the Rhône Valley, Northern Italy, and Bordeaux. He is sure to have enjoyed this typical Burgundian preparation of red beans, and after having imported several cases of red Burgundies to stock his wine cellars, he is sure to have asked his cooks to reproduce this dish at Monticello.

Overnight preparation required.

SERVES 8

To pre-soak the beans, place them in a colander and rinse thoroughly with water to clean. Place the beans in a large bowl and cover with water. Let stand at room temperature for at least 8 hours or overnight.

Drain and thoroughly rinse the beans. Place the beans in a large saucepan and cover them with water. Add the Bouquet Garni, salt, and pepper, and bring to a boil over high heat. Reduce the heat and simmer for 1½ to 2 hours, until the beans are tender.

Remove the Bouquet Garni. Drain the beans in a colander and reserve.

In the same saucepan, cook the bacon over high heat for 3 minutes. Remove the bacon and reserve.

Sauté the onions and garlic in the bacon drippings over medium heat for 3 minutes, until golden brown. Add the carrots and sauté for 5 to 10 minutes, until soft. Add the beans, bacon, wine, and sage and bring to a boil over high heat. Reduce the heat to medium and, stirring frequently, cook about 10 minutes, until the wine is absorbed by the beans.

Season with salt and pepper to taste.

1½ pounds dried red beans
or red kidney beans

1 Bouquet Garni (page 366)

1 tablespoon salt, plus more as needed

1 teaspoon freshly ground black pepper,
plus more as needed

4 slices lean bacon

2 medium onions, chopped

1 garlic clove, chopped

2 large carrots,
peeled and finely chopped

1 quart red Burgundy wine

1 teaspoon dried rubbed sage

Herbed Barley

2 cups regular pearl barley

1 teaspoon salt, plus more as needed

2 tablespoons unsalted butter

1 medium shallot, finely chopped

1 garlic clove, chopped

1½ tablespoons chopped fresh parsley

⅛ teaspoon curry powder

Freshly ground black pepper

arley, in existence since the Stone Age, has long been prized both for its nutritional value and its healthfulness. Once realized that barley was even filling and hearty enough to act as a main course for the average family, it became a staple crop in the colonies. Among the copious notes George Washington took on his farming operation at Mount Vernon, he notes, "Sowd abt. One Bushl. of Barley in a piece of Ground near the Tobo. House in the 12 Acre Field." Some of his barley crop was used to make whiskey in his distillery, but recipes for creamed barley and barley water in Martha Washington's *Booke of Cookery* indicate that even the upper classes enjoyed this most basic grain as well as their poorer compatriots.

SERVES 4

In a large saucepan, combine 6 cups of water, the barley, and salt and bring to a boil over high heat. Cook for about 25 minutes, until al dente. Drain the barley in a colander and reserve.

Melt the butter in the same saucepan over medium heat, add the shallot and garlic, and sauté for 2 minutes, until golden. Stir in the barley, parsley, and curry. Season with salt and pepper to taste.

Transfer to a serving dish and serve hot.

Starch played a dominant role in the colonial diet, whether in the form of potatoes, German spätzle or egg noodles, grains such as barley and rice, or freshly baked bread. Meat was an expensive commodity, not consumed by the average family except on special occasions. What the City Tavern served as hearty side dishes were main dishes to the common folk.

Rice Pilaf

In colonial times, rice was an export crop grown in the wetlands of South Carolina and Georgia, and sold in the European markets through English brokers. While Minister to France, Jefferson pondered the tepid sales of American rice, believing that it didn't sell well because of inferior quality. When he embarked on his tour of the major wine-producing regions in France, he made a side trip to Italy to smuggle, under penalty of death, some rice grains out of Piedmont, recounting that "I could only bring off as much as my coat and surtout pockets could hold." He hoped that sowing this strain of rice in America would boost sales in France. However, not long after this harrowing exercise, he learned that poor sales were the result of high prices, rather than poor quality, so upon his return to America, he arranged to take the English middlemen out of the equation and sell rice directly to France.

SERVES 6 TO 8

2 tablespoons unsalted butter

1 medium onion, finely diced

2 celery ribs, finely diced

1 carrot, peeled and diced

4 button mushrooms, sliced

1 quart Chicken Stock (page 364)

2 cups long-grain white rice

1 bay leaf

1 tablespoon chopped fresh parsley

Preheat the oven to 400°F.

Melt 1 tablespoon of the butter in large sauté pan over medium heat, add the onion, celery, carrot, and mushrooms, and cook for 3 to 5 minutes, until the onions are translucent.

In a deep ovenproof dish, combine the sautéed vegetables, the remaining 1 tablespoon butter, the stock, rice, bay leaf, and parsley. Cover with aluminum foil or a lid and bake for 40 minutes.

Wild Rice Stuffing

———◆-◆-◆———

Native to North America, wild rice looks like rice, and is used in the same way, but it's actually a water grass. It was a familiar food to the eighteenth-century colonists. Julian Niemcewicz, a Polish visitor to America, writes in his book, *Under Their Vine and Fig Tree* (1797–1799), about an encounter he had with wild rice, at a dinner with Thomas Jefferson and a Dr. Scandella in Philadelphia: "The Dr. showed us a bag of Wilde Rize . . . grains which grow wild in marshy places in all of America up to the Hudson Bay. Cattle are extremely fond of it. It even provides good nourishment for people."

This dish can also be used to stuff any type of poultry.

MAKES 6 CUPS; SERVES 6

4 tablespoons unsalted butter

1 small yellow onion, finely chopped

1 cup finely chopped celery root

3½ cups Chicken Stock (page 364)

2 cups wild rice

1 cup dry white wine,
such as Sauvignon Blanc

½ bunch fresh parsley, chopped
(about 3 tablespoons)

1 bay leaf

1 sprig fresh thyme

1 tablespoon salt

1 teaspoon freshly ground black pepper

½ cup fine dry bread crumbs

2 eggs, lightly beaten

Melt the butter in a medium-size saucepan over medium heat, add the onion and celery, and sauté for 5 minutes, until tender. Add the stock, wild rice, wine, parsley, bay leaf, thyme, salt, and pepper.

Bring to a boil over high heat. Reduce the heat, cover, and simmer about 40 minutes, until most of the stock is absorbed. Set aside to cool.

Preheat the oven to375°F.

Remove and discard the bay leaf and the sprig of thyme. Stir in the bread crumbs and eggs.

Transfer the mixture to a greased medium-size baking dish and bake for about 30 minutes, until heated through.

Sage & Marjoram Stuffing

◦—◦•◦—◦

Sage and marjoram were grown widely in colonial America, having made the voyage from Europe where they featured prominently in many flavorful dishes, and were prized for their medicinal qualities. In Thomas Jefferson's notes on "Objects for the garden this year" in 1794, sage and marjoram are listed, and correspondence shows that he requested sweet marjoram from his neighbor, George Divers, in 1820.

In *American Cookery*, Amelia Simmons uses these herbs, among others, extensively in her recipes. The recipe below replicates almost exactly her instructions for making stuffing "To stuff a turkey," which included copious amounts of both sage and marjoram.

MAKES 8 TO 10 CUPS; SERVES 8

Preheat the oven to 350°F.

Spread the bread cubes in a single layer in a shallow baking pan and bake for 15 to 25 minutes, until crisp, dry and golden. Transfer the bread cubes to a large bowl.

In a large skillet, sauté the onions in ½ tablespoon of the oil over medium-low heat for 10 to 15 minutes, until golden.

Add the celery, garlic, thyme, marjoram, sage salt, and pepper, and sauté for 5 minutes, until the celery is soft.

Add the wine and cook about 5 minutes, until the liquid is evaporated. Add the vegetable mixture to the bread cubes in the bowl.

In the same skillet over high heat, sauté the mushrooms in the remaining ½ tablespoon oil for 5 to 8 minutes, until browned and the liquid is evaporated. Add the mushrooms and parsley to the bread cubes and mix well. Add enough of the chicken stock to moisten the mixture, but be careful not to make it soggy.

Transfer the mixture to a lightly greased 3-quart baking dish and cover with aluminum foil. Bake for 45 minutes. Uncover and bake about 15 minutes more, until crisp. Serve hot.

1 loaf firm white bread (about 1 pound), crust trimmed and cut into ½-inch cubes

2 onions, chopped

1 tablespoon olive oil

2 celery ribs, chopped

3 garlic cloves, chopped

1 tablespoon fresh thyme leaves

1 teaspoon dried marjoram

1 teaspoon dried sage

1 tablespoon salt

1 tablespoon freshly ground black pepper

½ cup dry white wine, such as Sauvignon Blanc

4 cups sliced mushrooms (about 12 ounces)

½ cup chopped fresh parsley

¾ cup Chicken Stock (page 364)

CHEF'S NOTE

You can refrigerate the stuffing for up to 24 hours before baking, but if you do, you'll need to increase the baking time by 15 minutes.

Chestnut Stuffing

In his *History of the Present State of Virginia* (1705), Robert Beverly mentions "Wild Turkeys of incredible Bigness" weighing up to forty pounds. Stuffing a bird that size would take some volume, which is why stuffings made of bread, rice, or cornmeal and embellished with nuts, vegetables, and other savories were common choices.

Chestnut trees dotted the eastern seaboard, dropping their fruit for anyone who could brave the spiny outer coating and hard inner shell to get to the delectable nut meat inside. It was believed that the American chestnut was "sweeter and generally superior" to European chestnuts.

MAKES 8 TO 10 CUPS: SERVES 8

1 pound fresh unshelled chestnuts (18 medium chestnuts)

1 loaf firm white bread (about 1 pound), crust trimmed and cut into ½-inch cubes

2 onions, chopped

1 tablespoon olive oil

2 celery ribs, chopped

3 garlic cloves, chopped

1 tablespoon fresh thyme leaves

1 tablespoon salt

1 tablespoon freshly ground black pepper

½ cup dry white wine, such as Sauvignon Blanc

4 cups sliced mushrooms (about 12 ounces)

½ cup chopped fresh parsley

½ cup dried currants

¾ cup Chicken Stock (page 364)

Preheat the oven to 325°F.

With the point of a small paring knife, make a crisscross cut through the shell in the flat side of each chestnut shell. Place the chestnuts on a baking sheet and bake for about 25 minutes, until the shells break. Allow them to cool slightly (if the chestnuts cool too much, they won't peel easily). Peel and discard the shells. Using a paper towel, rub off the thin layer of the inner brown skins.

Return the peeled chestnuts to the saucepan and add enough water to cover. Bring to a boil over high heat. Reduce the heat and simmer for 30 to 45 minutes, until tender.

Drain and rinse with cold water. When cool enough to handle, cut each chestnut into quarters and reserve.

Preheat the oven to 350°F. Spread the bread cubes in a single layer in a shallow baking pan and bake for 15 to 25 minutes, until crisp, dry, and golden. Transfer the bread cubes to a large bowl.

In a large skillet, sauté the onions in ½ tablespoon of the oil over medium-low heat for 10 to 15 minutes, until golden.

Add the celery, garlic, thyme, salt, and pepper, and sauté for 5 minutes, until the celery is soft. Add the wine and cook about 5 minutes, until the liquid is evaporated. Add the vegetable mixture to the bread cubes in the bowl.

In the same skillet, sauté the mushrooms in the remaining ½ tablespoon oil over high heat, until browned and the liquid is evaporated. Add to the bread cubes. Add the quartered chestnuts, parsley, and currants. Mix well. Add enough of the stock to moisten the mixture, but be careful not to make it soggy. Transfer the mixture to a lightly greased 3-quart baking dish and cover with aluminum foil. You can refrigerate the stuffing for up to 24 hours before baking, but if you do, you'll need to increase the baking time by 15 minutes. Bake for 45 minutes. Uncover and bake about 15 minutes more, until crisp. Serve hot.

CHEF'S NOTE

If you wish to use the stuffing to stuff a turkey, allow the mixture to cool after you add the stock to the bread mixture. Rinse the cavity of the turkey with cold running water, drain, and then sprinkle salt and pepper into the clean cavity. Place the cooled stuffing into the turkey, loosely packing the mixture until it reaches the cavity opening. Transfer the turkey to a roasting pan and roast until a meat thermometer inserted in a thigh muscle registers 185°F.

Employees of the City Tavern are required by the National Park Service to be trained in the historic high points of the era. They must be well versed in the locations and significance of everything from the Liberty Bell to Independence Hall to the Betsy Ross House, which are all located within walking distance from City Tavern.

Cakes

CAKES WERE AMONG the most popular of eighteenth-century confections. Not only did Philadelphians prepare them in home kitchens, but they were also able to purchase many varieties in local bakeries. Period cookbooks and advertisements in the *Pennsylvania Gazette* reveal that city residents enjoyed the simplest of sponge and pound cakes, as well as more elaborate and costly spice cakes, fruit- and cream-filled trifles, and rich cheesecakes.

Like today's finest baking instructors, those of the eighteenth century emphasized that understanding basic baking methods was essential to preparing successful cakes. Some, like Elizabeth Raffald, author of *The Experienced English Housekeeper*, opened her chapter on cakes with clear instructions that applied to the recipes that followed. Today's bakers would benefit as much from these suggestions that are more than two hundred years old as they would from any other:

OBSERVATIONS UPON CAKES

When you make any kind of cakes be sure that you get your things ready before you begin. Then beat your eggs well, and don't leave them till you have finished the cakes, or else they will go back again and your cakes will not be light. If your cakes have butter in, take care you beat it to a fine cream before you put in your sugar, for if you beat it twice the time it will not answer so well. . . . Bake all kinds of cake in a good oven according to the size of the cake, and follow the directions of your receipt, for though care hath been taken to weigh and measure every article belonging to every kind of cake, yet the management and the oven must be left to the maker's care.

Sour Cream Coffee Cake

TOPPING

½ cup sugar

½ cup chopped walnuts

¼ cup all-purpose flour

2 tablespoons unsalted butter, melted

1 teaspoon ground cinnamon

CAKE

2 cups sifted all-purpose flour

1½ teaspoons baking powder

½ teaspoon baking soda

½ teaspoon salt

1 cup sugar

¼ pound (1 stick) unsalted butter, softened

2 large eggs

1 teaspoon vanilla

1 cup sour cream

By the mid to late 1600s, coffee was being enjoyed in the French court and in London. Ever interested in imitating European fashion, colonists soon began drinking this beverage that had been introduced into their homes and taverns by the Dutch by 1670. Whether taken in the morning, afternoon, or evening, coffee was commonly enjoyed with a variety of cakes. This one, with its streusel topping, reflects the German foodways that were so prevalent in colonial America.

MAKES ONE 9-INCH CAKE;
SERVES 10 TO 12

Preheat the oven to 350°F. Grease one 9-inch round cake pan with butter, and coat lightly with flour.

PREPARE THE TOPPING: In a small bowl, combine the sugar, walnuts, flour, melted butter, and cinnamon. Reserve.

PREPARE THE CAKE: In a large bowl, sift together the flour, baking powder, baking soda, and salt.

In the bowl of an electric mixer fitted with the paddle attachment, beat the sugar and butter together on medium to high speed until light and fluffy, scraping down the sides of the bowl often. Add the eggs and vanilla slowly and beat well, scraping down the sides of the bowl often.

With the electric mixer on low speed, slowly add the dry ingredients, alternating with the sour cream, and mix until just combined.

Pour the batter into the prepared pan. Sprinkle the topping on top of the batter. Bake for 45 to 50 minutes, or until golden brown and a toothpick inserted in the center comes out clean.

Cool the cake in the pan on a wire rack for 10 minutes. Remove from the pan. Cut into slices and serve.

Pound Cake

Nearly every recipe book available in colonial America included a recipe for pound cake. Because they were ever interested in incorporating exotic spices into their baked goods, it is hardly surprising that most eighteenth-century recipe writers suggested adding caraway seeds to the batter. Named for each pound of its ingredients—flour, butter, sugar, and eggs—it was a rich, dense cake that remained moist for a number of days and complemented the coffee, tea, or spirited beverages that often accompanied it. This recipe, like most contemporary interpretations of the traditional favorite, alters the original ratio of ingredients to produce a somewhat lighter, easier-to-prepare cake.

MAKES TWO 8-INCH LOAVES

Preheat the oven to 325°F. Grease two 8½ x 4½ x 2½-inch loaf pans with butter.

In the bowl of an electric mixer fitted with the paddle attachment, beat the sugar and butter together on medium to high speed until light and fluffy, scraping down the sides of the bowl often. Add the eggs and vanilla slowly and beat well, scraping down the sides of the bowl often. Add the sour cream and beat well.

In a separate bowl, sift together the flour, baking powder, baking soda, and salt. With the electric mixer on low speed, slowly add the dry ingredients, and mix until just combined.

Divide the batter between the two prepared pans. Bake for about 1 hour, or until the cakes are golden brown and pull away from the sides of the pans.

Cool the cakes in the pans on wire racks for 10 minutes. Remove the cakes from the pans, and cool completely before serving. To store for later use, wrap the cakes well in plastic wrap and freeze for up to 4 weeks.

4 cups sugar

¼ pound (1 stick) unsalted butter, softened

6 large eggs

½ tablespoon vanilla

½ cup sour cream

2½ cups plus 2 tablespoons sifted all-purpose flour

½ teaspoon baking powder

½ teaspoon baking soda

¼ teaspoon salt

Gingerbread

Although gingerbread is commonly associated with early American comfort food, its popularity dates back many centuries. Chinese recipes for this spicy sweet emerged in the tenth century, and by the Middle Ages Europeans had developed versions of their own. Through more than three millennia of trade, ginger, an Asian spice, made its way to such far-reaching places as the Middle East and Africa; after the Spanish introduced it to the West Indies, Jamaican ginger was one of a variety of exotic spices available in European shops.

Ever popular in England, gingerbread naturally maintained its fashion in colonial America. Recipes commonly appear in eighteenth- and early-nineteenth-century American receipt (recipe) books. Quite a few, like M. E. Rundell's *A New System of Domestic Cookery*, list more than one variety; among the four this author included in her book were "A good plain sort" and "A good sort without butter."

MAKES ONE 10-INCH CAKE; SERVES 10

2½ cups dark brown sugar

3 large eggs

1⅓ cups bread flour

1 tablespoon baking powder

½ teaspoon baking soda

2 tablespoons ground cinnamon

1 teaspoon ground ginger

1 teaspoon ground cardamom

½ teaspoon ground cloves

½ teaspoon salt

12 tablespoons (1½ sticks) unsalted butter, melted

¾ cup whole milk, at room temperature

Chantilly Cream (page 375), for serving (optional)

Preheat the oven to 350°F. Grease one 10-inch round cake pan with butter, and coat lightly with flour.

In the bowl of an electric mixer fitted with the paddle attachment, beat together the brown sugar and eggs on medium to high speed until light and foamy, scraping down the sides of the bowl often.

In another bowl, sift together the bread flour, baking powder, baking soda, cinnamon, ginger, cardamom, cloves, and salt. Add the dry ingredients to the sugar and egg mixture in two increments, mixing on low speed between additions until just combined.

In a separate bowl, combine the butter and the milk and add to the batter slowly, scraping down the sides of the bowl.

Pour the batter into the prepared pan. Bake for 45 minutes, or until golden brown and a toothpick inserted in the center comes out clean.

Cool the cake in the pan on a wire rack for 10 minutes. Remove from the pan, and cool completely before serving. Serve with Chantilly Cream,

Martha Washington's
Chocolate Mousse Cake

The sweet chocolate beverages and confections that came to be enjoyed in colonial America had their roots in ancient Aztec culinary traditions. Columbus might have introduced cocoa beans to Spain, but it was Hernando Cortés who, having drunk chocolate with Montezuma, showed his countrymen how to utilize the beans. The bitter, spicy beverage enjoyed by the Aztecs did not appeal to the Spanish, however. It wasn't until they added sugar to it that Europeans developed a passion for this exotic drink. The enthusiasm that led a Frenchman to open the first "cocoa house" in London in 1657 spread to the colonies, where drinking chocolate became increasingly fashionable throughout the eighteenth century. Like many of the fashionable Europeans with whom Thomas Jefferson mingled, Jefferson's particular fondness for chocolate was based on his belief that it was healthier than coffee or tea. George Washington, too, was keen on the confection, and it is likely that Martha Washington kept a recipe for a cake like this one in her cookery books.

MAKES TWO 9-INCH CAKES; SERVES 10 TO 12

PREPARE THE CAKE: Preheat the oven to 350°F. Grease two 9-inch round cake pans with butter, and line the bottoms with parchment paper circles. Place the bowl and whip attachment of an electric mixer in the freezer to chill for later use.

In the bowl of an electric mixer fitted with the paddle attachment on medium to high speed, beat the sugar and butter until light and fluffy, scraping down the sides of the bowl often. Add the eggs slowly, scraping down the sides of the bowl often.

In a separate bowl, sift together the cake flour, cocoa powder, baking soda, and salt. With the mixer on low speed, add the dry ingredients to the butter-sugar mixture, alternating with the milk, scraping down the sides of the bowl as necessary. Mix until just combined.

Divide the batter between the two prepared pans. Bake for 30 to 35 minutes, or until firm to the touch or until a toothpick inserted in the center comes out clean. Cool the cakes in the pans on wire racks for 10 minutes. Remove the cakes from the pans and cool completely before assembling.

PREPARE THE MOUSSE: Fill the bottom pan of a double boiler with water to ½ inch below the upper pan and place over low heat. (The water in the

CAKE

2 cups sugar

½ pound (2 sticks) unsalted butter

4 large eggs

5 cups sifted cake flour

¼ cup sifted unsweetened Dutch cocoa powder

2 teaspoons baking soda

½ teaspoon salt

1 cup whole milk

MOUSSE

4 ounces semisweet chocolate

4 large eggs, separated

½ cup heavy cream

GANACHE

1 pint (2 cups) heavy cream

24 ounces semisweet chocolate

Candied flowers or chopped nuts, for garnish (optional)

(continued)

bottom of the double boiler should not come to a boil.) Place the chocolate in the upper pan, and stir constantly until it is melted.

Remove the melted chocolate from the heat, and let cool for a minute. Add the egg yolks and beat well with a whisk. Set aside to cool.

In the chilled bowl of an electric mixer fitted with the chilled whip attachment, beat the cream on medium speed until soft peaks form. Cover with plastic wrap and refrigerate until chilled.

In a separate bowl of an electric mixer fitted with the whip attachment, whip the egg whites on medium speed until soft peaks form. Reserve.

With a rubber spatula, gently fold the chilled whipped cream into the chocolate mixture until the cream is just combined into the mixture. Do not over fold. Gently fold the reserved whites into the chocolate until just combined. Cover the mixture with plastic wrap, and refrigerate for at least 1 hour before using.

PREPARE THE GANACHE: In a heavy 1-quart saucepan, bring the cream just to a boil over low heat, stirring frequently. Remove the saucepan from the heat.

Place the chocolate in a large bowl. Pour the hot cream over the chocolate and let it sit for 1 minute. Whisk to thoroughly combine ingredients. (The chocolate should have melted from the heat of the cream.) Let cool. When the mixture is room temperature, cover with plastic wrap and refrigerate. Remove 1 hour before ready to use.

When the cake has cooled completely, use a serrated knife to carefully cut each cake in half horizontally into 2 layers, for a total of 4 layers.

To assemble, place the first cake layer on a large serving plate. Alternate the cake layers and mousse filling, spreading the mousse evenly onto each cake layer.

Frost the outside of the cake with the ganache. Refrigerate the cake until ready to serve. Garnish with candied flowers or chopped nuts, if desired.

CHEF'S NOTE

This recipe calls for eggs that are only partially cooked, which may present a health concern for the young, the elderly, or those whose immune systems are compromised.

Like Thomas Jefferson, George Washington had a fondness for chocolate. Records at Mount Vernon reveal that he first ordered chocolate from England in 1757 and that he received twenty pounds one year later. Correspondences between the general and his guests reflect that he served chocolate as a special beverage to them during his presidency.

Yule Log

FILLING

9 ounces semisweet chocolate

1 cup whole milk

4 large egg yolks

1 pound (2 sticks) unsalted butter,
softened

1 cup sifted confectioners' sugar

CAKE

4 large eggs

½ cup sugar

¾ cup sifted all-purpose flour

¼ cup sifted unsweetened
Dutch cocoa powder

Confectioners' sugar, for dusting

Candies and chocolates,
for garnish (optional)

The Yule log, as it was called in England, was based on the French *bûche de Noël*, a decorative, rolled sponge cake filled with buttercream. Although this cake doesn't appear in American cookbooks until later in the nineteenth century, the French who emigrated to colonial America certainly brought such confectionery traditions with them and influenced American cooks and cookbook authors. The sponge cake upon which the Yule log is based appears in Martha Washington's recipe book, as well as those written by such noted eighteenth- and nineteenth-century authors as Eliza Leslie, Lydia Maria Child, and Susannah Carter. Be sure to have a clean kitchen towel ready that is as long as your jelly-roll pan. You will need it for rolling up the sponge cake layer after it's baked.

MAKES ONE JELLY ROLL;
SERVES 8 TO 10

PREPARE THE FILLING: Fill the bottom pan of a double boiler with water to ½ inch below the upper pan and place over low heat. (The water in the bottom of the double boiler should not come to a boil.) Place the chocolate in the upper pan, and stir constantly until it is melted. Transfer the chocolate to a bowl and set aside to cool slightly.

Wash and dry the upper pan of the double boiler. Add the milk and egg yolks, stir to combine, and heat until just warm. Add the melted chocolate, stirring until combined. Transfer to a bowl. Cover with plastic wrap and refrigerate for 30 minutes.

In the bowl of an electric mixer fitted with the paddle attachment, beat the butter and confectioners' sugar on medium to high speed until light and fluffy, scraping down the sides of the bowl often. Add the cooled chocolate-milk mixture and mix until combined. Refrigerate.

PREPARE THE CAKE: Preheat the oven to 400°F. Grease a 15 x 10 x 1-inch jelly-roll pan with butter and line the bottom with parchment paper.

In the bowl of an electric mixer fitted with the whip attachment, beat the eggs and sugar on high speed for 5 minutes, or until pale yellow and thick. With a rubber spatula, gently fold in the flour and cocoa. Pour the batter into the prepared pan.

Bake for 12 to 15 minutes, or until a toothpick inserted in the center comes out clean.

While the cake is still warm, immediately turn it out onto a towel sprinkled with confectioners' sugar. Carefully peel off the parchment paper. With the towel under the cake, gently roll up the long side of the cake into a jelly-roll shape so that the towel is both rolled up inside and covers the outside of the cake. Let the cake cool completely.

To assemble the cake, unroll the cake. Spread with a third of the filling, reserving the rest for coating the outside. Roll the cake back up into a log shape, with the seam side down. To make the roll look like a log, cut a ½-inch diagonal piece from each end of the roll. Form "branches" by placing these wedge-shaped pieces of the cake on either side of the log's "trunk," and secure with toothpicks.

Spread the remaining filling evenly on the outside of the log and around each of the branches to secure them in place. To give the log a realistic look, carefully score the frosting with the tines of a fork, so that it resembles the irregular texture of bark. Dust the "bark" with cocoa powder and then some confectioners' sugar to create "snow." If desired, decorate with candies and chocolates. Refrigerate until ready to serve. To serve, cut the roll into slices and serve on dessert plates.

Marmaduke Cooper's writing desk at Pomona Hall

Vanilla Cheesecake

1½ cups Graham Cracker Crust
(page 371)

1 vanilla bean

2 (8-ounce) packages
cream cheese, softened

1 cup sugar

3 large eggs

2 cups sour cream

¼ teaspoon salt

Eighteenth- and nineteenth-century recipe books commonly included cheesecake—a practice that dates to the fifteenth century. Today we are most familiar with cheesecakes made from either cream cheese or ricotta cheese. In the eighteenth century, however, all of these cakes called for a cheese the consistency of ricotta or cottage cheese, which was beaten smooth and often pushed through a fine sieve to create an even silkier texture. Although cheese was available for purchase, period recipes detail the cheese-making process, suggesting that many women did, in fact, prepare their own.

Unlike cheesecakes today, eighteenth-century varieties nearly always called for the additional textures and flavors of crushed macaroons, almonds, Naples biscuits (similar to ladyfingers), and nutmeg. This recipe relies exclusively on the scent and flavor of vanilla, which was not only very expensive in the period, but also seemingly somewhat of a novelty, even in cosmopolitan Philadelphia.

MAKES ONE 9-INCH CHEESECAKE;
SERVES 12 TO 14

Preheat the oven to 350°F. Grease a 9-inch springform pan with butter. Wrap the bottom of the pan with aluminum foil to prevent water from seeping in around the sides of the springform pan during the water bath. Press the Graham Cracker Crust mixture onto the bottom and about 2 inches up the sides of the pan. Reserve.

With a paring knife, cut the vanilla bean in half lengthwise, and scrape out the seeds with the back of the knife. Reserve.

In the bowl of an electric mixer fitted with the paddle attachment, beat the cream cheese sugar, and vanilla seeds on medium to high speed until combined, scraping down the sides of the bowl often.

With the mixer on low speed, add the eggs. Mix until just incorporated.

Add in the sour cream and salt, and mix on medium speed until incorporated, scraping the sides of the bowl down often.

Pour the batter into the prepared pan. Place the pan into a larger high-sided roasting pan, and carefully pour boiling water into the roasting pan around the springform pan to a depth of 1½ inches. (This step reduces cracking on the top of the cheesecake.)

Bake for 40 to 45 minutes, or until the center of the cheesecake is nearly set when shaken and slightly puffy. Remove from the oven and let cool completely on a wire rack before serving. Wrap and store the cake in a refrigerator for up to 5 days.

Cheesecake has been popular for centuries, long before New York cheesecake became a staple on American menus— long before New York even existed, for that matter. The first mention in print of a dessert made with cream cheese or ricotta dates back to 1440. Flavoring cheesecake with a vanilla bean was a natural in early Philadelphia—vanilla beans were one of the many spices and seeds imported to American shores from the West Indies.

Parmesan Cheesecake

FILLING

1 cup freshly grated Parmesan cheese

8 ounces cream cheese, softened

2 eggs, separated

1 cup sugar

1 tablespoon lemon juice

1 teaspoon lemon zest

CRUST

2 cups graham cracker crumbs

½ cup finely chopped walnuts

¼ cup sugar

6 tablespoons unsalted butter, melted

TOPPING

½ pint heavy cream

½ pint sour cream

2 tablespoons sugar

At some point in his early travels, it is uncertain exactly when, Benjamin Franklin discovered Parmesan cheese. In 1769, he wrote his friend John Bartram, "And for one I confess that if I could find in any Italian Travels a Receipt for making Parmesan Cheese, it would give me more Satisfaction than a Transcript of any Inscription from any Stone whatever." Four years later, Dr. Leith, a Scottish Physician and Fellow of the Royal Society, communicated the recipe to Franklin by way of an article that appeared December 20-23, 1773, in *Lloyd's Evening Post*.

Franklin made good use of the recipe, distributing it to several friends and incorporating it into recipes of his own, namely, cheese soufflé and this recipe for cheesecake.

MAKES ONE 9-INCH CAKE

Preheat the oven to 350°F. Grease a 9-inch springform cake pan with butter. Wrap the bottom of the pan with aluminum foil to prevent water from seeping in around the sides of the springform pan during the water bath.

PREPARE THE FILLING: In the bowl of an electric mixer fitted with the paddle attachment, beat together the Parmesan cheese, cream cheese, egg yolks, and sugar on medium speed, scraping down the sides of the bowl often. Add the lemon juice and zest and mix until just incorporated.

In a separate bowl of an electric mixer fitted with the whip attachment, beat the egg whites to stiff peaks (meringue) on medium to high speed. Gently fold the meringue into the cheese mixture. Reserve.

Prepare the crust: In a mixing bowl, blend together the graham cracker crumbs, walnuts, sugar and butter. Press the crust onto the bottom and about 2 inches up the sides of the pan. Bake for 15 minutes, then remove from the oven.

Pour the batter into the prepared pan and return to the oven for another 25 to 30 minutes, or until the center of the cheesecake is nearly set when shaken and slightly puffy. Remove from the oven and cool completely on a wire rack. Refrigerate for at least 4 hours before serving.

PREPARE THE TOPPING: Just before serving, in a mixing bowl whisk together the cream, sour cream and sugar until stiff, and serve on the side with the cake.

Apple-Walnut Cakes

These cakes utilize two of the most popular ingredients in Early America: apples and walnuts. Many wealthy Philadelphians kept country houses complete with a variety of gardens and orchards. It was common for travelers from abroad to remark on them. "The country . . . [around] the great and noble city of Philadelphia is extremely pleasant, well inhabited, fruitful, and full of orchards," Lord Adam Gordon wrote in his journal of 1765. Walnuts were abundant as well. George Washington was particularly fond of eating a variety of nuts after dinner. Recalling the meals he enjoyed, Eleanor Parke Custis Lewis wrote in 1823, "After dinner he drank three glasses of Madeira. Late a small plate of Indian [Native American] walnuts."

These cakes, reminiscent of quick bread, are easy to prepare, aromatic, and flavorful due to the generous amounts of cinnamon and nutmeg.

Advance preparation required.

MAKES EIGHT 3 x 1½-INCH (½-CUP) RAMEKINS; SERVES 8

2 medium McIntosh or
Granny Smith apples, peeled, cored, and chopped (about 2 cups)

½ cup B&B liqueur

1 cup packed light brown sugar

¾ cup vegetable oil

2 large eggs

1 cup sifted all-purpose flour

1 tablespoon ground cinnamon

1 teaspoon baking soda

1 teaspoon ground nutmeg

¾ cup walnuts, toasted
(see Chef's Note),
ground and chopped

In a medium-size bowl, combine the apples and liqueur, adding more liqueur if necessary to make sure the apples are covered so they don't turn brown. Let marinate for 8 hours or overnight in the refrigerator.

When ready to bake the cake, preheat the oven to 350°F. Grease eight 3 x 1½-inch (½-cup) ramekins with butter, and coat lightly with flour.

In the bowl of an electric mixer fitted with the paddle attachment, beat the brown sugar, oil, and eggs on medium speed until just combined, scraping down the sides of the bowl often.

In a separate bowl, sift together the flour, cinnamon, baking soda, and nutmeg. With the electric mixer on low, add the dry ingredients to the sugar-and-oil mixture and mix until combined. With a rubber spatula, gently fold in the marinated apples and walnuts.

Divide the batter among the prepared ramekins and place them on a baking pan. Bake for 20 to 25 minutes, or until slightly puffed and golden brown and a toothpick inserted in the center comes out clean. Remove from the oven and let cool completely on a wire rack before serving.

CHEF'S NOTE

TO TOAST NUTS: Bake the nuts in a single layer on a sheet pan at 350°F. for about 20 minutes, or until golden brown. Let cool. Sliced, slivered, or chopped nuts require less time to toast—watch carefully.

Almond Cake

ALMOND PASTE

1 cup sugar

10 ounces (3 cups) dry, blanched almonds

2¼ cups confectioners' sugar

CAKE

1⅓ cups Almond Paste, or use purchased

¾ pound (3 sticks) plus 2 tablespoons unsalted butter, softened

1¾ cups sugar

¼ cup sifted cake flour

9 large eggs

BUTTERCREAM

5½ cups plus 2 tablespoons sifted confectioners' sugar

8 large egg whites

1¼ pounds (5 sticks) unsalted butter, cubed and softened

½ cup very strong cold coffee

1 cup purchased chocolate sauce

Recipe books of the eighteenth and nineteenth centuries commonly referred to *frangipane* as "almond cake" or "French almond cake." It was baked in a variety of pans, including large and small tins and decorative molds, and it was served tender and moist, as well as fairly firm and crisp. Naturally, almond cake is based on almond paste. This slightly sweet and crumbly paste is a traditional component of many European pastries. In the eighteenth century, almond paste was most commonly used as the main ingredient in "marchpane"—an early term for marzipan—and marchpane cakes (candy-coated marzipan).

America, like England, imported almonds from Spain, and these almonds are often referred to as Jordan almonds in recipe books of the eighteenth and nineteenth centuries. Bitter almonds, considered poisonous and now illegal in the United States, were also frequently used in almond cake, although peach kernels (the meaty center of the pit) were considered an acceptable substitute.

Almond cakes were served either plain or, like Eliza Leslie's version, iced with a lemon-flavored meringue. This variation is finished a bit more luxuriously with a coffee buttercream and a garnish of chocolate sauce, although it is equally delicious simply served with fruit.

MAKES ONE 15 x 10-INCH CAKE, ABOUT 3 CUPS BUTTERCREAM; SERVES 8 TO 10

PREPARE THE ALMOND PASTE: In a small saucepan, combine the sugar and 1 cup water and bring to a boil over medium-high heat. Cook, stirring often, until the sugar dissolves. Remove from the heat and let cool. Reserve.

In a food processor bowl, grind the almonds to a fine, powder-like consistency. Stop the processor and scrape down the sides of the bowl. Add the confectioners' sugar and process with on/off pulses for 30 seconds. Scrape down the sides of the bowl.

With the processor running, add the cooled sugar syrup through the feed tube and mix until the mixture forms a paste. (The amount of syrup needed will vary depending on how dry the almonds are.)

Remove the almond paste from the bowl. If not using immediately, wrap the almond paste tightly in plastic wrap and refrigerate until ready to use. Almond paste will keep in the refrigerator for up to 4 weeks if well sealed.

PREPARE THE CAKE: Preheat the oven to 400°F. Grease two 15 x 10 x 1-inch jelly-roll pans with butter, and line the bottoms with parchment paper.

In the bowl of an electric mixer fitted with the paddle attachment, begin creaming the almond paste on medium speed. Add the butter in chunks gradually, until combined. Add the sugar and beat well, scraping down the sides of the bowl often. With the mixer on medium-low speed, add the flour, a little at a time, until just combined. Add the eggs three at a time, mixing well to incorporate after each addition.

Evenly divide the mixture into the two prepared pans. Bake for 12 to 15 minutes, or until golden and the cakes pull away from the sides of the pans.

Turn the cakes out of the pans onto cooling racks. Let cool for 10 minutes, then peel off the parchment paper and let the cakes cool completely. Trim ½ inch off the edges of the cake on all sides.

PREPARE THE BUTTERCREAM: In a 1-quart saucepan, bring 1 inch of water to a boil. In a large bowl, combine the confectioners' sugar and the egg whites. Place the bowl over the saucepan of boiling water, and whisk the mixture until hot (about 160°F on a candy thermometer).

Remove the bowl from the heat, and transfer the mixture to the bowl of an electric mixer fitted with the whip attachment. Beat on high speed until the whites become stiff (meringue) and the bowl is cool to the touch.

When the meringue is cool completely, add the butter a little at a time. Beat until the mixture becomes slightly thick and fluffy. Add the coffee a little at a time to desired taste.

To assemble the cake, place the first layer of the cake on a large serving plate. Spread evenly with 1 to 1½ cups of the coffee buttercream. Top with the second cake layer. Frost the top and then the sides of the cake with the remaining buttercream. If desired, use any extra buttercream to pipe a decorative border.

To serve, cut the cake into 3-inch squares and transfer to dessert plates. Garnish each square with about 1 tablespoon of the prepared Chocolate Sauce.

Almond cake was one of the simplest of confections, consisting usually of four or five ingredients: almonds, flour, eggs, sugar, and rose water or lemon essence. But in eighteenth-century America, baking was a time-consuming and labor-intensive task. Imported almond paste was very expensive, so cooks often processed almonds themselves. Martha Washington explained this procedure clearly; one of her almond cakes called for "a quarter of a pound of almonds, blanched in well water, & beaten in rose water." The other ingredients required refining as well. Sugar was mostly available in hard lumps or cones, so these recipes often called for "loaf-sugar, powdered and sifted" and "fine flower, well dryed against ye fire." In addition, it would have taken quite a few hours to heat an oven and usually another hour or so to bake the cake.

Raspberry Trifle

The British trifle required little translation in the American colonies. Recipe books reveal that this simple but often highly decorative dessert required a few select ingredients: pieces of cake or biscuit; custard; sack (wine); syllabub (a mixture of wine or cider, fresh milk, and cream); and decoration, such as jelly, flowers, small candies, or additional biscuits.

Unlike the traditional version, in which the soaked biscuits or cake were simply covered with one layer of custard and jelly, this trifle is built in colorful, multiple layers, with the final layer consisting of custard rather than of strongly flavored syllabub.

MAKES ONE 3-QUART (12-CUP) TRIFLE;
SERVES 12

PREPARE THE CAKE: Preheat the oven to 350°F. Grease one 9-inch cake pan with butter. Line the bottom of the pan with parchment paper, and grease the top of the paper with butter.

Fill the bottom pan of a double boiler with water to ½ inch below the upper pan and place over low heat. (The water in the bottom of the double boiler should not come to a boil.) Place the eggs and sugar in the upper pan, and whisk constantly until warm. Do not allow the eggs to curdle. Remove from the heat, and whisk in the vanilla and almond extracts.

Transfer the warmed egg mixture to the bowl of an electric mixer fitted with the whip attachment. Beat on high speed until the mixture is pale yellow and has thickened and tripled in volume.

Remove the bowl from the mixer and sift ⅓ cup of the flour over top of the eggs. Gently fold the flour into the mixture with a rubber spatula. Repeat sifting and folding with the remaining ⅓ cup of flour. Fold in the melted butter, scraping down the sides of the bowl often.

Pour the mixture into the prepared cake pan and bake for 20 to 25 minutes, or until golden and a toothpick inserted in the center comes out clean. Cool the cakes on a wire rack for 10 minutes before removing from the pan.

Using a serrated knife, cut the cake layer horizontally into four layers.

CAKE

4 large eggs

½ cup sugar

½ teaspoon vanilla

¼ teaspoon almond extract

⅔ cup sifted all-purpose flour

3 tablespoons butter, melted and cooled

FILLING

2½ cups heavy cream

½ cup sifted confectioners' sugar

4 cups Pastry Cream (page 375)

1 cup brandy

1 cup purchased raspberry preserves

4 pints (8 cups) fresh raspberries

(continued)

PREPARE THE FILLING: In the chilled bowl of an electric mixer fitted with the whip attachment, beat the cream on medium to high speed until soft peaks form. Add the confectioners' sugar and beat a few seconds more. Using a rubber spatula, gently fold the Pastry Cream into the whipped cream. Cover with plastic wrap and refrigerate until ready to use.

ASSEMBLE THE TRIFLE: Place one cake layer into the bottom of a 10-inch glass trifle bowl. Using a pastry brush, brush the cake with the brandy. Spread ⅓ cup of the preserves over the cake layer. Spread one quarter of the filling over the preserves and cover with 1 pint of the raspberries. Repeat the layering process two more times and top with a cake layer.

Transfer the remaining filling into a pastry bag fitted with the star tip, leaving enough room to close and twist the top of the bag. Pipe the filling around the edges of the bowl. Fill the center with the remaining raspberries. Refrigerate for 2 hours before serving.

In *The Art of Cookery Made Plain and Easy*, Hannah Glasse's recipe for trifle called for three types of biscuit and cake: "Naples biscuits [ladyfingers] broke in pieces, mackeroons broke in halves, and ratafia cakes [crisp almond cookies]." Her version was particularly decorative among those of the period, for she suggested, "You may garnish it with ratafia cakes, currant jelly, and flowers, and stew different coloured nonpareils over it." It was clear, however, that she was attempting to make the decorating task as simple as possible for the busy cooks creating this dessert, as she added at the end, "Note, these are bought at the confectioners."

This colorful dessert was inspired not only by the availability of raspberries in eighteenth-century Philadelphia but also by the elegant, molded desserts based on cream and cake that were stylish during the period. Philadelphians enjoyed raspberries fresh in the summer and preserved during the fall and winter months, when they would consume jam and whole berries cooked in sugar syrup.

Fruitcake

Eighteenth-century cookbooks are filled with recipes for rich butter cakes flavored with dried and candied fruit, spices, and wine or liquor. Fruitcake, however, referred to a specific type of cake—one dense with fruit and nuts and flavored liberally with spices and brandy. According to British tradition, this cake was commonly served at weddings and so became known as "Bride Cake," recipes for which most often appear in English cookery books of the period. Surely the practice of serving fruitcake at weddings continued in colonial America. The celebratory connotations of this cake seem to have led further to its frequent appearance on holiday tables, much as rich plum puddings and fruit-filled yeast breads had for centuries in Europe.

Overnight preparation required.

MAKES ONE 10-INCH CAKE;
SERVES 10 TO 12

In a medium-size mixing bowl, combine the carrots, almonds, coconut, Candied Citrus Peel, currants, raisins, pineapple, and Candied Ginger. Add the rum and soak overnight.

Preheat the oven to 375°F. Grease two 10-inch round cake pans with butter, and coat lightly with flour.

In a mixing bowl, sift together the flour, baking powder, baking soda, nutmeg, ginger, allspice, cloves, cardamom, mace, and salt.

In a large bowl, whisk together the brown sugar and olive oil until light in color. Add the eggs one at a time, whisking after each addition. Whisk in the honey, vanilla and almond extracts, and rose water.

Whisk the dry ingredients into the wet ingredients in three additions. Using a spatula, fold in the apricot preserves and fresh ginger, followed by the presoaked dried fruit and nut mixture.

Divide the batter between the 2 prepared cake pans. Bake for 30 minutes, or until set and a toothpick inserted in the center of each comes out clean. Allow the cake to cool in the pan, then unmold and dust with confectioners' sugar. Serve with Chantilly Cream.

½ cup shredded carrots

½ cup slivered almonds

¼ cup sweetened flaked coconut

¼ cup finely chopped
Candied Citrus (page 346)

2 tablespoons dried currants

2 tablespoons golden raisins

2 tablespoons finely chopped
dried pineapple

2 tablespoons finely chopped
Candied Ginger (page 348)

1 cup dark rum

2¼ cups sifted bread flour

1 tablespoon baking powder

2 teaspoons baking soda

1 teaspoon ground nutmeg

1 teaspoon ground ginger

1 teaspoon ground allspice

1 teaspoon ground cloves

Pinch of ground cardamom

Pinch of ground mace

1 teaspoon salt

2 cups brown sugar

2 cups olive oil

9 large eggs

¼ cup honey

1 tablespoon vanilla

1 teaspoon almond extract

2 teaspoons rose water

2 cups purchased apricot preserves

1 tablespoon peeled and
finely chopped fresh ginger

Confectioners' sugar, for dusting

Chantilly Cream (page 375),
for serving

Cobblers & Crisps

THE MOST PRACTICAL eighteenth-century desserts were those that relied on seasonal, fresh ingredients or on preserved foodstuffs requiring little preparation. Cobblers and crisps, inspired by English and German food traditions, were thus not only practical but also easy to make and subject to much delicious variation. Nearly any kind of fruit—fresh, cooked, or preserved—was, and still is, suitable for these desserts. Baked in pans or individual dishes, the sweetened fruit becomes comfortingly soft and juicy, while the cloak of butter, flour, sugar, spices, and/or oats and nuts transforms into a crisp, complementary topping.

In the eighteenth century, desserts were not served individually.
Rather, they were displayed in abundance on elegant tables or sideboards like
this one in the dining room at Pomona Hall

Blueberry Cobbler

————•‑•‑•————

This cobbler was as simple to prepare in the eighteenth century as it is today. Sweetened fresh berries are topped with a basic streusel made with sugar, flour, butter, and spices, and baked until the fruit is soft and juicy and the topping is golden.

MAKES EIGHT 3 x 1½-INCH (½-CUP) RAMEKINS
OR ONE 1½-QUART BAKING DISH: SERVES 8

Preheat the oven to 350°F. Grease eight 3 x 1½-inch ramekins or one 1½-quart shallow baking dish with butter.

In a large bowl, gently toss together the blueberries, sugar, cornstarch, cinnamon, and lemon juice.

Divide the mixture evenly among the prepared ramekins (or place in the baking dish).

Top each ramekin with ½ cup of the Streusel topping (or spread all of the topping over the baking dish).

Place the ramekins (or baking dish) on a baking sheet. Bake for 25 to 30 minutes, or until the tops are golden brown and the filling starts to bubble. Serve warm.

4 pints (8 cups) fresh blueberries

1 cup sugar

¼ cup cornstarch

½ teaspoon ground cinnamon

2 tablespoons freshly squeezed lemon juice

4 cups Streusel topping (page 376)

Apple & Cranberry Cobbler

———◆———

6 Granny Smith apples,
peeled, cored, and cut into 8 slices each

2 cups whole fresh cranberries

½ cup sugar

2 tablespoons cornstarch

½ teaspoon ground cinnamon

2 cups Oat Topping (page 377)

Colonial Americans found native cranberries similar in flavor to the lingonberries with which they had been familiar in Europe, although they quickly learned that the cranberry required quite a bit of sweetening. In the eighteenth century, cranberries were most often preserved or stewed to sweeten them for use in pies.

This cobbler relies upon the apples and the oat topping to add sweetness to the cranberries and to create a light dessert that is pleasantly tart.

MAKES EIGHT 3 X 1½-INCH (½-CUP) RAMEKINS
OR ONE 1½-QUART BAKING DISH: SERVES 8

Preheat the oven to 375°F. Grease eight 3 x 1½-inch ramekins or one 1½-quart shallow baking dish with butter.

In a large bowl, combine the apples, cranberries, sugar, cornstarch, and cinnamon.

Divide the mixture evenly among the prepared ramekins (or place in the baking dish). Top each ramekin with ¼ cup of the Oat Topping (or spread all of the topping over the baking dish).

Place the ramekins (or baking dish) on a baking pan. Bake for 25 to 30 minutes, or until the tops are golden brown and the filling starts to bubble. Serve warm.

This cobbler is an updated version of the sort that appeared in late-eighteenth-century cookbooks like Amelia Simmons's *American Cookery*. Her recipe for cranberry tart called for "Cranberries. Stewed, strained, and sweetened, put in paste No. 9 [a sweet, butter pastry, add spices till grateful, and baked gently."

Pear & Sour Cherry Cobbler

1½ cups dried tart red cherries

½ cup brandy

8 pears, peeled, cored, and sliced

1 cup sugar

3 tablespoons cornstarch

½ teaspoon ground cinnamon

4 cups Streusel topping (page 376)

In the eighteenth century, cherries were frequently preserved, made into wine, dried, and used in baked goods. The puddings (baked or boiled in pastry) and cherry pies that were also common inspired this cobbler, which marries the soft and tart fruit with a crisp, German streusel.

Advance preparation required.

MAKES EIGHT 3 X 1½-INCH (½-CUP) RAMEKINS
OR ONE 1½-QUART BAKING DISH; SERVES 8

In a small bowl, combine the cherries and brandy and soak for 2 hours, or until softened. Drain the cherries and discard the soaking liquid.

Preheat the oven to 350°F. Grease eight 3 x 1½-inch ramekins or one 1½-quart shallow baking dish with butter.

In a large bowl, combine the pears, sugar, cornstarch, and cinnamon. Add the softened cherries, and gently toss together. Divide the mixture evenly among the prepared ramekins (or place in the baking dish). Top each ramekin with ½ cup of the Streusel topping (or spread all of the topping over the baking dish).

Place the ramekins (or baking dish) on a baking pan. Bake for 25 to 30 minutes, or until the tops are golden brown and the filling starts to bubble. Serve warm.

Apple & Fig Crumble

⊷━◆━⊶

The Spanish introduced figs to the Americas in the early 1500s. Since then, figs have thrived on these shores. Throughout the eighteenth century, Philadelphians purchased imported figs and grew them locally as the climate permitted. George Washington, in fact, is known to have had a fondness for the fruit. Records show that in 1772 he sent an order to the West Indies for "A Pot of good dryed Figs" and desired them only if they were reasonably priced. By 1797, he was growing the fruit at Mount Vernon as well, possibly for enjoying them both fresh and dried.

This richly flavored crumble relies not only on the concentrated sweetness of dried figs, but also on the intense flavor achieved by precooking the fruit with Madeira, sugar, cinnamon, and vanilla—ingredients that were popular in the eighteenth century as well.

MAKES EIGHT 3 X 1½-INCH (½-CUP) RAMEKINS
OR ONE 1½-QUART BAKING DISH; SERVES 8

1 bottle (750 ml) imported Madeira

1½ cups sugar

15 dried figs, stemmed and cubed

3 cinnamon sticks

1 vanilla bean, split lengthwise

8 Granny Smith apples,
peeled, cored, and sliced

4 cups Streusel topping (page 376)

1½ cups Crème Anglaise (page 376)

Preheat the oven to 350°F. Grease eight 3 x 1½-inch ramekins or one 1½-quart shallow baking dish with butter.

In a medium-size saucepan, bring the Madeira, sugar, figs, cinnamon sticks, and vanilla bean to a boil. Reduce the heat to medium and cook for 20 to 30 minutes, or until thickened and reduced by half.

Place the apples in a medium, ovenproof bowl. Remove the saucepan from the heat and pour the mixture over the apples. Stir until well combined. Discard the vanilla bean and cinnamon sticks. Divide the mixture evenly among the prepared ramekins (or place in the baking dish).

Top each ramekin with ½ cup of the Streusel topping (or spread all of the topping over the baking dish).

Place the ramekins (or baking dish) on a baking pan. Bake for 25 to 30 minutes, or until the tops are golden brown and the filling starts to bubble.

Serve warm with Crème Anglaise or, if desired, a high-quality purchased vanilla ice cream.

Rhubarb & Strawberry Crisp

1½ pounds fresh rhubarb, leaves removed and diced

1 pint (2 cups) fresh strawberries, stems removed and halved

¼ cup sugar

¼ cup packed light brown sugar

2 tablespoons cornstarch

1 teaspoon freshly squeezed lemon juice

4 cups Streusel topping (page 376)

In the eighteenth century, desserts and savory dishes reflected the use of seasonal ingredients. Fruit, like other foods, was certainly preserved, and nearly every period cookbook included recipes for a wide variety of sweetmeats, including fruit jellies. When prepared in season, however, baked goods like this crisp were based on fresh fruit, which Philadelphians obtained from local markets or, in the case of wealthier families, from country houses outside of the city.

Here, the tart flavor of rhubarb is combined with ripe strawberries and streusel to create a simple dish of varied textures and complementary flavors.

MAKES EIGHT 3 x 1½-INCH (½-CUP) RAMEKINS
OR ONE 1½-QUART BAKING DISH; SERVES 8

Preheat the oven to 350°F. Grease eight 3 x 1½-inch ramekins or one 1½-quart shallow baking dish with butter.

In a large bowl, combine the rhubarb and strawberries.

In a separate bowl, stir together the sugar, brown sugar, cornstarch, 2 tablespoons water, and the lemon juice. Pour the sugar mixture over the fruit and gently toss together.

Divide the mixture evenly among the prepared ramekins (or place in the baking dish).

Top each ramekin with ½ cup of the Streusel (or spread all of the topping over the baking dish).

Place the ramekins (or baking dish) on a baking pan. Bake for 25 to 30 minutes, or until the tops are golden brown and the filling starts to bubble. Serve warm.

Peach & Raspberry Crisp

—◦◦◦—

Eighteenth-century Philadelphians enjoyed preserved peaches and raspberries year-round, but they would have prepared a crisp such as this one to take advantage of the summer's bounty of fresh fruit. The walnuts in the oat topping are the perfect complement to the soft texture of the cooked peaches and raspberries.

MAKES EIGHT 3 x 1½-INCH (½-CUP) RAMEKINS
OR ONE 2-QUART BAKING DISH; SERVES 8

Preheat the oven to 375°F. Grease eight 3 x 1½-inch ramekins or one 2-quart baking dish with butter.

In a large bowl, combine the sugar, sour cream, egg, flour, cornstarch, and vanilla. Gently fold in the peaches and raspberries.

Evenly divide the fruit mixture among the prepared ramekins (or place in the baking dish). Top each ramekin with ¼ cup of the Oat Topping (or spread all of the topping over the baking dish).

Place the ramekins (or baking dish) on a baking pan. Bake for 15 to 20 minutes, or until the tops are golden and the filling starts to bubble.

½ cup sugar

⅓ cup sour cream

1 large egg

2 tablespoons all-purpose flour

2 tablespoons cornstarch

1 teaspoon vanilla

5 ripe peaches, sliced, skin on

1 pint (2 cups) fresh raspberries

2 cups Oat Topping (page 377)

In eighteenth-century Philadelphia, crisps of this sort were prepared from fresh and preserved fruit. During the summer, Elizabeth Drinker most likely took advantage of the ripe peaches she obtained from her garden and local markets, but it is possible that she used preserved fruit during warm months as well. In April 1779, she wrote that "all our Fruit in the Yard and Garden spoild with the Frost." Perhaps it was due to this devastating event that in May of the same year she thought it important to mention in her journal that a relative "brought over some dry'd peaches this afternoon." Once re-hydrated in water or brandy, these peaches would have added a deliciously concentrated flavor to any fresh fruit–based dessert.

Pies and Tarts

PIES AND TARTS, these seemingly ordinary, uncomplicated dishes, were among the most important baked items of the eighteenth century. In Philadelphia, as in other early American cities and towns, they were made in confectioneries, in taverns, and in home kitchens. Some were elegant and expensive, prepared with puff pastry and imported spices and citrus, while others were modest and frugal, consisting of a short dough and custard. The two terms were often used interchangeably and referred to a wide variety of dishes. They were sweet or savory; they were filled with fresh fruit, dried fruit, preserves, custards, or puddings; they had top crusts, bottom crusts, or both; they were prepared in deep dishes or shallow tins; and they were baked in ovens as well as in bake kettles—lidded pans that stood in hot coals in the fireplace, covered with additional embers.

As they are today, pies and tarts of the eighteenth century were considered pastries, for they were based on "pastes," or doughs—a term derived from the French word for pastry, *pâte*. Despite the many varieties available in the period, all pies and tarts were assembled and baked in pans. They differ, therefore, from the pastries discussed in the Pastries chapter (page 322), the components of which were, and still are, most often prepared separately before being assembled.

Eighteenth-century cookbook authors included numerous recipes for pies and tarts in their books, a testament to the significance of these dishes during the period. Elizabeth Raffald included five "paste," or pie and tart dough, recipes in *The Experienced English Housekeeper*; Susannah Carter and Hannah Glasse included six such recipes in *The Frugal Housewife* and *The Art of Cookery Made Plain and Easy*, respectively; and Amelia Simmons published nine recipes in her *American Cookery*, six of which were for puff pastry alone. As great as these figures are, they pale in comparison to the quantities of pie and tart recipes that accompanied them, which often numbered in the dozens. To be sure, these authors were committed to sharing as much information as possible with their readers, who undoubtedly understood the importance of preparing proper pastry.

Elizabeth Raffald was fairly succinct in her introductory suggestions, which served as an informative overview of the subject:

> *Raised pies should have a quick oven and [be] well closed up or your pie will fall in the sides. It should have no water put in till the minute it goes into the oven, it makes the crust sad and is a great hazard of the pie running. Light paste requires a moderate oven but not too slow, it will make them sad, and a quick oven will catch and burn it and not give it time to rise. Tarts that are iced require a slow oven or the icing will be brown and the paste not near baked. These sort of tarts ought to be made of sugar paste and rolled very thin.*

Rhubarb & Strawberry Crumb Pie

W hen preparing fruit pies, eighteenth-century bakers not only created flavorful combinations like this classic pairing of tart rhubarb and sweet strawberries but also focused on making high-quality pastry dough. From professional *pâtissiers* to wealthy housekeepers to domestic servants, men and women alike understood that the ability to prepare tasteful, tender pastry was a necessary skill. Whether at home or at school, a girl could learn to combine ingredients, roll the dough, and bake sweet or savory pastries to perfection. This was an art developed with pride.

The *pâte sucrée* in this recipe is a slightly sweet, tender, yet firm crust, which complements the flavor and texture of the cooked fruit.

Makes one 9-inch pie; serves 8

Grease a 9-inch pie pan with butter.

On a lightly-floured surface, roll the Pâte Sucrée into a circle about 10 inches in diameter. Ease the pastry into the prepared pie pan, being careful not to stretch it. Trim the pastry to ½ inch beyond the edge of the pie pan. Fold under the extra pastry and crimp the edge. Refrigerate for 1 hour before using.

Preheat the oven to 350°F.

In a large bowl, mix together the rhubarb, strawberries, brown sugar, sugar, water, cornstarch, and lemon juice. Transfer the filling to the pastry-lined pan. Top with the Streusel topping.

Bake for 35 to 40 minutes, or until the top is golden brown and the filling starts to bubble. Cool completely on a wire rack.

1 pound Pâte Sucrée (page 372), chilled for at least 3 hours

2 pounds fresh rhubarb, cleaned and chopped (about 4 cups)

2 pints (4 cups) fresh strawberries, hulled and quartered

½ cup packed light brown sugar

¼ cup sugar

¼ cup cold water

2 tablespoons cornstarch

½ teaspoon freshly squeezed lemon juice

4 cups Streusel topping (page 376)

Rhubarb and strawberries are a seasonal match made in heaven. Strawberries were abundant in the New World and were used in all types of colonial desserts. As early as 1607, Captain John Smith commented about the uncommonly large strawberries encountered on his expedition. This recipe would have been strictly seasonal, however. In the off-season, pies would have been made with fruit preserves.

Pumpkin Pie

1 pound Pâte Sucrée (page 372), chilled for at least 3 hours

1¾ cups pumpkin purée (see Chef's Note), or about 15 ounces canned pumpkin

1½ cups whole milk

¾ cup sugar

2 large eggs

2½ tablespoons all-purpose flour

1½ tablespoons unsalted butter, melted

½ teaspoon salt

½ teaspoon cinnamon

½ teaspoon ground allspice

½ teaspoon grated fresh ginger

1 teaspoon vanilla

Chantilly Cream (page 375), for serving (optional)

Although pumpkins were available in Britain, they have become synonymous with American foodways. Among the many squashes the Native Americans cultivated, the pumpkin is undoubtedly the most famous, due to the serving of pumpkin pie in 1623 at the Pilgrim's second Thanksgiving celebration. Records, in fact, reveal that early colonists in Connecticut postponed one of their Thanksgiving dinners because they couldn't obtain the molasses necessary for the pie.

From the seventeenth century onward, Americans used pumpkin in numerous dishes besides pie. It is hardly surprising that the gourmet Thomas Jefferson included a stylish soup recipe, complete with buttered croutons, in his collection of recipes.

This version of pumpkin pie is based on period recipes that, while quite simple, were flavorful and rich, due to the use of spices as well as eggs and milk.

Makes one 9-inch pie; serves 8

Grease a 9-inch pie pan with butter.

On a lightly-floured surface, roll the Pâte Sucrée into a 10-inch-diameter circle. Ease the pastry into the prepared pie pan, being careful not to stretch it. Trim the pastry to ½ inch beyond the edge of the pie pan. Fold under the extra pastry and crimp the edge. Refrigerate for 1 hour before using.

Preheat the oven to 375°F.

In a large bowl, mix together the pumpkin purée, milk, sugar, eggs, flour, butter, salt, cinnamon, allspice, ginger, and vanilla; mix well. Transfer the filling to the pastry-lined pan.

Bake for about 40 minutes, or until the filling is nearly set. The top of the pie should be firm but should jiggle slightly. Cool completely on a wire rack. Serve with Chantilly Cream, if desired.

CHEF'S NOTE

Puréeing Fresh Pumpkin: Preheat the oven to 400°F. Cut off the top of a medium-size pumpkin. Remove and the discard seeds. Cut the pumpkin in half and place both pieces, pulp sides down, on a baking sheet sprayed with vegetable cooking spray. Bake about 1 hour, until the inside is soft. Remove from the oven and cool. Remove the skin and place the pulp in a food mill or food processor bowl and purée until smooth.

Chocolate-Pecan Pie

Like many exotic foods, chocolate became fashionable in Europe before gaining popularity in colonial America. Although Columbus might have introduced the Spanish to this unusual ingredient, it wasn't until the Spanish later learned to sweeten the spicy Aztec beverage that chocolate became stylish and much in demand throughout Europe. Although, like coffee and tea, chocolate was fairly expensive in late eighteenth-century America, it was widely available in Philadelphia, sold in a variety of venues from dry goods stores to confectioners' shops.

Native to North and South America, pecans are as "American" as chocolate, although their introduction into regional foodways was arguably more direct than their Aztec counterpart. Thomas Jefferson first cultivated pecan trees in his gardens at Monticello, and his passion for the "Poccon" or "Illinois nut," as it was called, was shared by George Washington, who planted trees at Mount Vernon. Jefferson, in fact, sent the general pecan trees in January 1794 along with instructions concerning when to plant them.

MAKES ONE 9-INCH PIE; SERVES 8

1 pound Pâte Sucrée (page 372), chilled for at least three hours

4 large eggs

1 cup light corn syrup

1 teaspoon vanilla

½ cup sugar

½ cup packed light brown sugar

½ teaspoon salt

3 ounces semisweet chocolate chips

4 tablespoons unsalted butter, melted

2 cups pecan halves

Grease a 9-inch pie pan with butter.

On a lightly-floured surface, roll the Pâte Sucrée into a circle about 10 inches in diameter. Ease the pastry into the prepared pie pan, being careful not to stretch it. Trim the pastry to ½ inch beyond the edge of the pie plate. Fold under the extra pastry and crimp the edge. Refrigerate for 1 hour before using.

Preheat the oven to 350°F.

In the bowl of an electric mixer fitted with the whip attachment, beat the eggs on medium to high speed until pale yellow and thick. Add the corn syrup and vanilla and beat well to combine.

In a separate bowl, mix together the sugar, brown sugar, salt, chocolate chips, and butter. Add to the egg mixture and mix well.

Spread the pecans over the bottom of the chilled pie shell and carefully pour in the egg-chocolate mixture.

Bake for 40 to 45 minutes, or until a knife inserted in the center comes out clean. Cool completely on a wire rack. Refrigerate for 2 hours before serving.

Apple Pie

———◆———

Apples were enjoyed for centuries in England, but it was in the New World that they flourished. Colonists planted European seeds, which grew particularly well in New England and the mid-Atlantic states, and, through grafting, they quickly discovered new varieties. George Washington, Thomas Jefferson, and Benjamin Franklin were among many notable Americans to take an interest in apples, avidly corresponding with European horticulturists and cultivating numerous varieties in their own gardens. Apples made their way into many dishes, including pie. This version is based on the apple puddings and tarts that were prepared in eighteenth-century kitchens.

MAKES ONE 9-INCH PIE; SERVES 8

Grease a 9-inch pie pan with butter.

Divide the Pâte Sucrée in half. On a lightly-floured surface, roll each half into a circle about 10 inches in diameter. Ease one circle of pastry into the prepared pie pan, being careful not to stretch it. Wrap the other circle in plastic wrap. Refrigerate both circles of dough for 1 hour before baking.

Preheat the oven to 375°F.

In a large bowl, combine the apple slices, sugar, and cinnamon. Gently toss to coat. Add the butter and flour. Transfer to the pastry-lined pan.

Use the remaining circle of pastry to cover the apple mixture. Trim the pastry to ½ inch beyond the edge of the pie pan. Fold under the extra pastry and crimp the edge. Prick the top pastry with a fork to allow steam to escape. Using a small knife, make several 1½-inch-long slits in the top crust.

Bake for 30 to 40 minutes, or until the top is golden brown and the filling starts to bubble. Serve warm.

---

2 pounds Pâte Sucrée (page 372), chilled for at least 3 hours

5 Granny Smith apples, peeled, cored, and sliced (about 1½ pounds)

½ cup sugar

1 teaspoon ground cinnamon

2 tablespoons unsalted butter, softened

2 tablespoons all-purpose flour

2 tablespoons cornstarch

Apple pie and apple desserts were very popular in the eighteenth century. In *American Cookery*, Amelia Simmons lists three types of pie—"Apple Pie," "Dried Apple Pie," and "A buttered apple Pie"—in addition to "Apple Tarts," "Apple Pudding," and "An apple Pudding Dumplin." Thomas Jefferson's enthusiasm for apple pie is reflected in his collection of recipes as well. Among the many fruit puddings baked in a crust that he might well have enjoyed serving were "Apple Pudding," "Grated Apple Pudding," and "Sliced Apple Pudding."

Clockwise from top left: Apple, Pumpkin, and Pecan Pies.

Cherry Pie

---

2 pounds Pâte Brisée (page 372), chilled for at least 3 hours

2 (20-ounce) cans dark sweet cherries (4 cups)

2 vanilla beans

¾ cup sugar

Pinch of ground nutmeg

1 teaspoon ground cinnamon

3 tablespoons cornstarch

2 tablespoon kirschwasser (cherry-flavored liqueur)

4 cups Chantilly Cream (page 375), substituting 2 tablespoons kirschwasser for the vanilla

W ild cherries grew plentifully in early America, but, finding them too sour to eat, colonists cultivated sweeter English varieties. Cherries were enjoyed fresh during the spring and summer months, while preserved cherries, cherry wine, and cherry-flavored brandy (or kirschwasser) were consumed year-round.

Both George Washington and Thomas Jefferson grew morello cherries, a sweet and sour variety that yields dark juice.

MAKES ONE 9-INCH PIE; SERVES 8

Grease a 9-inch pie pan with butter.

Divide the Pâte Brisée in half. On a lightly-floured surface, roll each half of the pastry into a circle about 10 inches in diameter. Ease one circle of pastry into the prepared pie pan, being careful not to stretch it. Wrap the other circle in plastic wrap. Refrigerate both circles of dough for 1 hour before baking.

Preheat the oven to 375°F.

Strain the cherries, reserving ½ cup of the canning juice. Put the cherries in a large bowl and the cherry juice in a small bowl.

With a paring knife, cut the vanilla bean in half lengthwise, and scrape out the seeds with the back of the knife. Place the reserved cherry juice, vanilla beans and pods, sugar, and nutmeg in a small saucepan, and bring the mixture to a boil.

In a small bowl, whisk together the cornstarch, kirschwasser, and 2 tablespoons water.

While the cherry juice is rapidly boiling, add the cornstarch mixture and whisk vigorously. Continue to whisk the mixture and boil until the cherry juice is thick and shiny, about 1 minute more. Pour the cherry juice over the cherries and, using a plastic spatula, fold the mixture to combine. Remove the vanilla pods.

Transfer the cherry filling into the pastry-lined pan. On a lightly floured work surface, slice the remaining pastry circle into 1-inch-wide strips and arrange in a lattice on top of the pie. Trim the pastry to ½ inch beyond the edge of the pie pan. Fold under the extra pastry and crimp the edge.

Bake for 20 to 30 minutes, or until the top is golden brown and the filling starts to bubble. Cool completely on a wire rack. Top with the kirschwasser-flavored Chantilly Cream.

Clafouti Tart

⬦

This delicate fruit tart was inspired by the baked French pudding of the same name, traditionally from the Limousin region. Cherries are usually the fruit of choice, but others are often incorporated as well. Although clafouti is traditionally prepared without pastry, this version is based on the eighteenth-century puddings that were commonly baked in pastry-lined pans.

MAKES ONE 10-INCH TART: SERVES 10

Grease one 10 x 2-inch tart pan with butter.

Dust a work surface generously with flour. Roll the Pâte Sucrée to a circle about 12 inches in diameter. Ease the pastry into the prepared pie pan, being careful not to stretch it. Trim the pastry to the edge of the pie plate. Prick the dough all over with a fork, and refrigerate for 1 hour before using.

Preheat the oven to 350°F.

Line the dough with aluminum foil and weigh down with beans or pie weights. Bake for 10 minutes, or until the sides of the tart shell begin to brown. Remove from the oven, and reserve.

In a medium-size bowl, whisk together the eggs, egg yolks, and sugar until light and pale in color. Whisk in the flour.

In a separate bowl, whisk together the milk and sour cream. Add the milk mixture to egg mixture, whisking constantly. Pour into the shell. Arrange the grapes on top and lightly sprinkle with sugar.

Bake 25 to 30 minutes, or until a knife inserted in the center comes out clean.

Cool completely on a wire rack.

Before serving, reheat the tart in a 325°F oven for 5 minutes. To unmold, place a plate over the top of the tart; then invert the pan and plate. Tap lightly on the bottom of the pan, then lift. Place a second plate over the tart, then invert again and remove the top plate. Cut into portions and serve.

1 pound Pâte Sucrée (page 372), chilled for at least 3 hours

4 large eggs

3 large egg yolks

1 cup sugar

¼ cup cake flour

3 cups whole milk

1 cup sour cream or crème fraîche

4 cups red grapes

3 tablespoons sugar

CHEF'S NOTE

Prebaking a pie shell before adding the filling is known as "blind baking." This step usually involves placing aluminum foil into an unbaked shell and adding pie weights to prevent the dough from puffing up while baking. If you don't have pie weights, dried beans or rice can be used for the same results.

Berry Tart

---

1 pound Pâte Sucrée (page 372), chilled for at least 3 hours

2 (¼-ounce) packages unflavored gelatin

2 cups whole milk

1 vanilla bean

⅛ teaspoon freshly grated nutmeg

Pinch of salt

¼ cup sugar

2 large eggs

1 large egg yolk

3 tablespoons cornstarch

2 tablespoons unsalted butter, softened

1 pint heavy cream

1 pint each hulled strawberries, blueberries, raspberries, and blackberries

Confectioners' sugar, for garnishing

Fresh mint sprigs, for garnishing

Because this tart is made up of three basic components—crust, filling, and berries—its success depends on the high quality of each one. The berries that grew in abundance in eighteenth-century Philadelphia would have been enjoyed in sweet dishes similar to this tart during the summer months.

MAKES ONE 10-INCH TART; SERVES 12

Grease a 10 x 2-inch tart pan with butter. Dust a work surface generously with flour. Roll the Pâte Sucrée to a circle about 12 inches in diameter. Ease the pastry into the prepared pie pan, being careful not to stretch it. Trim the pastry to the edge of the pie plate. Prick the dough all over with a fork, and refrigerate for 1 hour.

Preheat the oven to 350°F. Line the crust with aluminum foil and weigh down with beans or pie weights. Bake for 10 minutes, or until the sides of the tart shell begin to brown. Remove from the oven, and set aside to cool.

In a small metal bowl, sprinkle the gelatin over ¼ cup water and whisk to combine. Let stand 10 minutes to "soften."

In a medium pot, combine the milk, vanilla bean, nutmeg, salt, and sugar, and bring to a boil. Meanwhile, in a medium bowl, whisk together the eggs, egg yolk, and cornstarch.

Remove the vanilla bean from the milk mixture. Temper the hot milk mixture into the egg mixture by adding ¼ cup at a time of the hot liquid to the egg mixture, whisking constantly. Once all the milk has been added, return the mixture to the pot and cook until the cream thickens and boils. Allow the cream to boil until the starch "cooks out," about 1 minute. Add the butter and whisk to combine. Transfer the cream to a plastic bowl.

Bring a small pot of water to a simmer. Set the bowl of gelatin over the pot of and stir constantly until it liquefies. Whisk the gelatin into the pastry cream. Cover with plastic wrap, and set aside to cool to room temperature.

In the bowl of an electric mixer fitted with a chilled whip attachment, beat the cream on medium speed until soft peaks form. Add ¼ cup of the pastry cream to the whipped cream and stir to combine. Fold the whipped cream into the pastry cream, and stir until just combined.

Transfer the filling to the crust, and refrigerate for 1 hour. Arrange the berries decoratively atop the tart. Garnish with confectioners' sugar and a sprig of mint.

Custards, Puddings, & Creams

THE MANY CUSTARDS and puddings that were, for centuries, considered staples in Europe remained so as colonists continued Old World culinary traditions in America. Even in the eighteenth century, these were fairly simply prepared, frugal dishes, consisting primarily of milk, sugar, and eggs. They were not always so modest, however; period recipes commonly called for such costly ingredients as raisins, lemon or orange juice, almonds, and a variety of spices. Like other eighteenth-century desserts, the simplicity or elaborateness of these dishes often reflected the wealth of the household that produced them.

Eighteenth-century custards and puddings were similar to contemporary versions, although some of the ingredients and cooking methods have changed over time. Vanilla, so commonly used now to flavor custards and puddings, rarely appears in period recipes, perhaps due to its high cost. The absence of vanilla was countered by the frequency with which cooked fruit and vegetables flavored these dishes. Apples, pears, plums, carrots, and pumpkin were common additions to basic custards and puddings. In addition, nearly all eighteenth-century recipes called for eggs. Custards, by definition, always include them, but today's puddings are usually thickened with flour or cornstarch. Some custard and pudding recipes, however, called for both flour and eggs. One notable exception to this rule appears in recipes for Indian pudding, which were based on neither flour nor eggs but, rather, American cornmeal. As testament to the incorporation of American foodstuffs into traditionally European custards and puddings, Hannah Glasse, in her book *The Art of Cookery Made Plain and Easy*, listed two recipes for "Indian Pudding" and one for cornmeal "Mush" in a chapter entitled "Several New Receipts Adapted to the American Mode of Cooking." In the eighteenth century, it was also common to bake custards and puddings with bread or pieces of cake or in pastry-lined pans. This is less common today, save for today's bread puddings, which remain virtually unchanged from their eighteenth-century predecessors.

Cooking methods have altered slightly as well. Today's custards are often thickened on the stove before baking, while in the eighteenth century this step was omitted, probably to save time. Similarly, puddings, now cooked almost exclusively on the stove, were commonly baked or boiled in cloths.

Vanilla Bean Blanc Mange

lanc mange, also spelled blancmange and blanc manger, dates at least to fourteenth-century Europe. Translated as "white food," this term refers to the colorless, or white, foods that became stylish in France and eventually in England as well. Early cookery books and manuscripts reveal that blanc mange was prepared in many varieties, both savory and sweet, relying on such colorless ingredients as poultry, fish, rice, cream, almonds, and eggs. Eighteenth-century English cookbook authors commonly offered a number of blanc mange recipes, all of which were essentially jellies prepared with "isinglass" (a form of gelatin), ground almonds, sugar, and very little cream. One popular variation, breaking with the "white" tradition, in fact called for spinach juice, which resulted in a bright green jelly. It wasn't until the nineteenth century that blanc mange became an exclusively sweet and creamy dish as it is most commonly known today.

2½ cups heavy cream

1½ cups whole milk

2 vanilla beans

1½ tablespoons unflavored gelatin

5 tablespoons dark rum

½ cup sugar

3 tablespoons honey

Overnight preparation required.

MAKES ONE 1-QUART BAVARIAN MOLD; SERVES 10 TO 12

In a medium-size saucepan, stir together the cream, milk, and vanilla beans. Heat until the cream and milk just start to bubble around the sides of the pan, remove from the heat, and let steep for 20 minutes.

In a small metal bowl, sprinkle the gelatin over the rum and whisk to combine. Let stand 10 minutes to "soften."

Whisk the sugar and honey into the cream and cook over low heat until the sugar has dissolved. Do not boil.

Bring a small pot of water to a simmer. Set the bowl of gelatin over the pan and stir constantly until it liquefies. Whisk the gelatin into the cream.

Prepare an ice bath in a large stainless steel bowl. Pour the custard into a heatproof bowl, and set the bowl in the ice bath. Whisk the mixture slowly until it cools. Pour it into a mold and refrigerate overnight before serving.

CHEF'S NOTE

Making an Ice Bath: If a custard mixture is not iced, the eggs will continue to cook and then scramble, making the mixture unusable. To make an ice bath, fill a large bowl with ice cubes. Place a smaller heat-proof bowl inside the large bowl. Arrange the ice cubes around the bowl. Pour the custard into the smaller bowl and stir constantly—to allow heat to escape—until the mixture has cooled.

Plum Pudding

1 cup chopped dried pineapple

1 cup dark raisins

½ cup golden raisins

½ cup currants

½ cup dried cherries

½ cup freshly grated unsweetened coconut, toasted (see Chef's Note)

¼ cup almonds, toasted (see Chef's Note)

½ cup chopped Candied Apricots (page 349)

¼ cup finely chopped Candied Ginger (page 348)

1 lemon, zest grated

1 lime, zest grated

1½ cups Jamaican gold rum

2 cups chopped suet (¼-inch pieces, available at local butcher's market), or lard

2 cups all-purpose flour

4 cups finely crumbled day-old Sally Lunn Bread (page 318), or any egg bread

1½ teaspoons salt

1 teaspoon ground nutmeg

1 tablespoon ground allspice

1 tablespoon ground cinnamon

Pinch of ground cloves

6 large eggs

1 cup light brown sugar

½ cup plus 2 tablespoons dark beer

Plum pudding, or Christmas pudding, as it came eventually to be known, appeared in many variations in eighteenth-century cookbooks. Some recipes called for plums, while others called for raisins, currants, and candied lemon and orange peels. Some were boiled and others were baked. Some required bread crumbs; others, pieces of bread. Sometimes the puddings were heavily spiced and flavored with liqueur, and other times only a few such ingredients were added.

What is common to most recipes, however, is the care and time that was required to produce such a rich dessert. These puddings not only demanded a lot of preparation, but they baked or boiled for hours at a time as well. In addition, until the nineteenth century, suet, rather than butter, was the fat of choice. Readily available and inexpensive, it not only added flavor but also ensured that the pudding would remain moist through hours of cooking.

Whether baked or boiled, most plum puddings were cooked in molds—some quite decorative. Like other desserts of the period, placed among a multitude of sweet and savory dishes, they were meant to add to the beauty and often luxuriousness of the dining table.

Overnight preparation required.

MAKES ONE 2-QUART CASSEROLE DISH: SERVES 12

In a large bowl, toss together the pineapple, raisins, currants, cherries, coconut, almonds, Candied Apricots, Candied Ginger, and citrus zests. Add 1 cup of the rum and 2 cups water, stir to mix, and soak overnight.

Using a pastry cutter or two knives, cut the suet into the flour until a coarse meal is formed. In a large bowl, stir together the flour-suet mixture with the Sally Lunn Bread, salt, nutmeg, allspice, cinnamon, and cloves. Add the presoaked dried fruit mixture, including any liquid in the bowl, and toss until thoroughly combined.

In another medium-size bowl, whisk together the eggs, brown sugar, the remaining rum, and the beer. Add the liquid ingredients to the dry, and mix until a smooth dough is formed. If the mixture seems too dry, add more beer until the dough is smooth.

Grease a 2-quart casserole dish or decorative mold with butter, and dust it lightly with flour.

Place the batter in the prepared casserole dish or mold, packing it well. Cover it with foil. Place the dish in a large saucepan filled with water halfway up the sides of the dish. Cover the entire pan with foil, and bring the water in the pan to a simmer. Keep the water at a simmer, and steam the pudding for 4 hours, checking the water level regularly and refilling as necessary. The pudding is done when firm and a toothpick inserted in the center comes out clean.

Allow the pudding to cool in the mold at room temperature for about 1 hour. Unmold and serve.

CHEF'S NOTE

To toast freshly grated coconut: Evenly spread out the coconut flakes on a baking pan. Toast in a preheated 375°F oven for 5 minutes, stirring about halfway through the cooking time, until golden.

Plum puddings could be simple or elaborate, depending on the cook's taste and the ingredients he could afford. The following recipes from *American Cookery* and Thomas Jefferson's collection of recipes reveal these contrasts:

. . .

PLUMB PUDDING, BOILED.

Three pints flour, a little salt, six eggs, one pound plumbs, half pound beef suet, half pound sugar, one pint milk; mix the whole together; put it into a strong cloth floured, boil three hours; serve with sweet sauce.

. . .

WYETH'S ENGLISH PLUM PUDDING

Two pounds of best seedless raisins, 1 pound currants, 1 pound sultana raisins, 1 quart grated bread crumbs, 1 quart beef suet chopped fine, ½ pound citron cut fine, 2 ounces candied orange peel, 2 ounces candied lemon peel cut fine, 1 grated nutmeg, 1 teaspoonful of ginger, 1 of salt. Mix all well together. Beat 12 eggs and stir into the first mixture. Add 1 cup of brandy. If not moist enough add as much milk as will make it cling together. Put into tin forms and boil four or five hours. The water must be boiling when the pudding is put in. Plunge into cold water for a few minutes before turning out the pudding

---

Indian Pudding

———

2 cups whole milk

2 (8-ounce) cans creamed corn

¾ cup dark molasses

¾ cup coarse yellow cornmeal

2 teaspoons ground cinnamon

4 tablespoons unsalted butter

¼ cup light brown sugar

1 tablespoon freshly squeezed
lemon juice

3 Gala or Granny Smith apples, peeled,
cored and cut into ½-inch slices

Based on traditional English puddings, Indian pudding was uniquely American, as it was prepared with cornmeal and often molasses. By the third quarter of the eighteenth century, American cookery books included recipes for this dish, as did English cookbooks published in America. Hannah Glasse's American edition of *The Art of Cookery Made Plain and Easy*, for example, added two "Indian Pudding" recipes to the section she referred to as "Several New Receipts Adapted To The American Mode of Cooking." Inexpensive, sweet, and filling, Indian pudding quickly became a favorite of many Americans, including George Washington and Thomas Jefferson.

MAKES ONE 2-QUART CASSEROLE DISH; SERVES 10 TO 12

Preheat the oven to 325°F. Butter a 2-quart casserole dish.

In a small saucepan, combine the milk and corn and bring to a boil. Reduce the heat to low and stir in the molasses, cornmeal, and cinnamon. Continue to cook the mixture, stirring constantly, until thick, about 10 minutes. Reserve.

In a large skillet over medium heat, melt the butter and stir in the brown sugar. Add the lemon juice and cook, stirring occasionally, until the sugar melts, about 1 minute. Stir in the apples and cook until they begin to soften, about 3 minutes more.

Pour the thickened pudding into the casserole dish, top with the sautéed apples, and bake for 15 minutes, or until a knife inserted in the center comes out clean. Serve hot.

Under the heading "Puddings," Thomas Jefferson's collection of recipes included the following instructions for preparing this sweet dish.
When the mould is full of any of the above put into a bowl ¼ teaspoon of either ginger, cinnamon, or mixed spices, or lemon or orange peel. Beat 4 eggs. Add 4 tablespoonfuls of sugar, a pinch of salt and 3 cups of milk. Fill the pudding dish nearly to the rim. It can be either baked, boiled, or set in a saucepan ⅓ full of water, with the lid over, and let simmer for an hour, or until set. Run a knife around the edge of the dish and turn out the pudding. Pour over melted butter mixed with some sugar and the juice of a lemon, or serve with brandy sauce.

Rice Pudding

Although rice was an important southern crop, its economic significance spread north, as did its popularity as a versatile culinary staple. South Carolina became the center of New World rice production in the early eighteenth century; by 1726, the state was exporting 4,500 metric tons annually. This successful campaign halted briefly during the Revolution, when the British, having taken Charleston, sent the entirety of that year's rice crop back to England. Thomas Jefferson clandestinely brought a variety of Italian rice back to the Carolinas in 1787, and, by the turn of the century, southern rice cultivation was again thriving.

MAKES ONE 2-QUART BAKING DISH;
SERVES 6

Preheat the oven to 325°F.

In a 2-quart saucepan, bring 2 cups water to a boil, and add the rice. Simmer, covered, until the liquid is reduced by two thirds and the rice is al dente, about 15 minutes. Let stand, covered, for 5 minutes, and drain, if necessary.

In a separate saucepan, bring the milk to a boil. Stir in the rice and cooking water, and cook for 10 minutes more, or until the grains are soft.

In a large bowl, whisk together the sugar, eggs, butter, vanilla, cinnamon, and orange zest. Gradually stir the hot rice mixture into the egg mixture.

Transfer to a 2-quart ovenproof glass or ceramic dish. Place the dish in a larger high-sided roasting pan, and carefully pour boiling water into the roasting pan around the dish to a depth of 1½ inches. Bake, covered, for 20 to 30 minutes, or until a knife inserted in the center comes out clean.

Sprinkle additional cinnamon on top as garnish. Serve hot, or cool to room temperature, according to personal preference.

¾ cup uncooked long-grain white rice

2½ cups whole milk

½ cup sugar

3 large eggs

1½ tablespoons unsalted butter, softened

2 teaspoons vanilla

1½ teaspoons ground cinnamon, plus more for garnish

Zest of 1 orange

Bread Pudding

⟶•✦•⟵

In the eighteenth century, sweet puddings of many varieties commonly called for using pieces of bread, biscuits, or cake as an enriching base for other ingredients, such as dried or fresh fruit or preserves. Bread pudding simply focused on the bread (in crumbs or pieces) and custard as primary ingredients, with the typical addition of raisins and spices.

Bread was a staple, baked at home as well as in the many bakeries operating in eighteenth-century Philadelphia, and period cookbooks suggest that bread pudding was frequently enjoyed as well. Hannah Glasse's *The Art of Cookery Made Plain and Easy* gave three recipes for the dish, as did Thomas Jefferson's collection of recipes, which also included two sweet butter sauces to accompany them.

MAKES ONE 10 X 3-INCH ROUND BAKING DISH
OR 2-QUART SOUFFLÉ DISH; SERVES 12

In a small bowl, combine the raisins and rum and soak for at least 2 hours.

Preheat the oven to 350°F. Grease a 10 x 3-inch round baking dish or 2-quart soufflé dish with butter.

Add the bread cubes to the prepared dish and sprinkle the raisin-rum mixture on top.

In a large bowl, combine the milk, eggs, sugar, cinnamon, and nutmeg. Stir the egg mixture into the bread-raisin mixture. Cover with foil.

Place the baking dish in a larger high-sided roasting pan. Add boiling water into the roasting pan around the baking dish to a depth of 1½ inches, and reserve for 30 minutes.

Bake, covered, for 45 minutes. Remove the foil. Continue baking, uncovered, for 5 minutes, or until the top is golden brown and a knife inserted in the center comes out clean.

Cool slightly before serving. Serve with the Crème Anglaise flavored with rum to taste, if desired.

CHEF'S NOTE

A water bath, or *bain marie*, is used to cook custard-like desserts. This technique allows delicate egg-based dishes to cook without breaking or curdling.

---

1 cup raisins

½ cup Jamaican gold rum

20 ounces white bread,
crust trimmed and cut into 1-inch cubes
(about 10 cups)

1 quart whole milk

15 large eggs

1½ cups sugar

1 teaspoon ground cinnamon

½ teaspoon ground nutmeg

Crème Anglaise (page 376), flavored with
rum, for serving (optional)

Orange Curd Cake

———◆———

his recipe was inspired by the orange puddings, custards, and fools that were so popular in eighteenth-century colonial America. The addition of candied orange peel and almonds complements the smooth texture and refreshing citrus flavor of this light cake.

This dessert merges two sweet preparations common to eighteenth-century American pâtisserie. Orange curd was most often referred to in the period as "orange pudding" or "orange cream"—recipes that frequently appeared in eighteenth-century cookbooks and called for frugally using the entire fruit (rind, pulp, and juice). Meringue, too, a term so commonly used today, appears mostly to have been used in French cookery and published in French books. In English and American texts, meringue is usually referred to in macaroon recipes not as a distinctive preparation but, rather, as egg whites and sugar "beat to a froth" or "beat . . . till they stand alone."

MAKES SIX 8-OUNCE RAMEKINS; SERVES 6

Preheat the oven to 325° F. Grease six 8-ounce ramekins with butter, and lightly dust with flour.

In a food processor fitted with the blade attachment, grind together the almonds, sugar, flour, salt, and Candied Citrus.

In a medium-size bowl, whisk together the egg yolks, orange zest, citrus juice, butter, and sour cream. Whisk in the mixture from the food processor.

In the clean bowl of an electric mixer fitted with the whip attachment, whip the egg whites to stiff peaks on high speed. Add ½ cup of the base mixture to the egg whites, and gently fold together so as to not deflate them. Add the remaining base and gently fold together.

Divide the batter among the ramekins, filling each half full. Cover each ramekin with foil. Place the ramekins in a high-sided roasting pan. Place the pan in the oven and fill it with hot water halfway up the sides of the ramekins.

Bake for 20 minutes, or until a toothpick inserted in the centers comes out clean. Serve hot.

¼ cup almonds, toasted
(see Chef's Note, page 245)

¾ cup sugar

¼ cup all-purpose flour

Pinch of salt

2 tablespoons finely chopped
Candied Citrus (page 346)

3 large egg yolks

1 orange, zest grated

¼ cup citrus juice
(half freshly squeezed lemon juice
and half orange juice)

3 tablespoons plus 2 teaspoons
melted butter

½ cup sour cream

3 large egg whites

George and Martha Washington loved oranges. From the 1760s until the 1790s, the general regularly ordered them in barrels from the West Indies, where he seems to have first been introduced to them. The couple often received the fruit as gifts as well, and by the late 1790s, oranges were growing at Mount Vernon.

Crème Caramel

———◆◆◆———

Crème caramel is a simple dessert made elegant by cooking a basic custard in caramel-coated molds. When served, the molds are inverted, permitting the custard to glisten with amber-colored caramel.

The fact that this dessert, like its related preparation flan, is widely available today belies its uniqueness in the eighteenth century. Although custard was commonly served, sugar not only remained expensive throughout the 1700s, but also often required time-consuming refining before use. Philadelphia merchants, like those in other major cities, sold sugar in a variety of grades from coarse to fine, and it was priced according to purity.

In order to create a clear caramel like the one for this recipe, sugar would have been boiled with water, skimmed of the scum that accumulated on the surface, and passed through a sieve or flannel bag. This method appeared in most period cookbooks.

1½ cups sugar

6 large eggs

2 cups light cream

½ cup heavy cream

½ teaspoon vanilla

MAKES SIX 3 X ½-INCH (½-CUP) RAMEKINS
OR 6-OUNCE CUSTARD CUPS; SERVES 6

Preheat the oven to 300°F.

To caramelize the sugar, in a large saucepan, heat 1 cup of the sugar over medium heat, until it becomes syrupy and turns golden brown, 2 to 3 minutes, watching closely so it doesn't burn and shaking the pan occasionally to heat the sugar evenly. Do not stir. Once the sugar starts to melt, reduce the heat to low and cook 5 minutes more, until all of the sugar is melted and golden.

Immediately remove from the heat, and pour 1 to 2 tablespoons of the caramelized sugar into the bottom of each ramekin or custard cup, being careful not to burn your skin with the caramelized sugar. Tilt each ramekin to coat the bottom evenly. Let stand 10 minutes.

Place the ramekins or custard cups in a large, high-sided roasting pan. Reserve.

To make the custard, in a large bowl, whisk together the remaining ½ cup of sugar and the eggs.

In a small saucepan, bring the creams and vanilla to a boil over low heat. Slowly pour 1 cup of the hot cream mixture, whisking constantly, into the egg-sugar mixture. Whisk in the remaining hot cream and vanilla mixture.

——————— *(continued)* ———————

Strain the mixture through a fine sieve into an ovenproof bowl.

Pour the custard into the prepared ramekins or custard cups. Fill the roasting pan with boiling water halfway up the sides of the ramekins.

Bake for 30 to 40 minutes, or until set and a knife inserted in the centers comes out clean.

Remove the custards from the water bath. Cool on a wire rack. Cover with plastic wrap and refrigerate for at least 1 hour before serving.

Before serving, remove the custards from the refrigerator and let stand at room temperature for 20 minutes. Run a paring knife around the edge of each custard to loosen. Turn each ramekin or custard cup over onto an individual dessert plate. The caramel will create a syrupy sauce. Serve immediately.

Eighteenth-century custards and puddings were so similar to each other that Hannah Glasse's "Rules to be observed in making Puddings &c.," which appeared in her book *The Art of Cookery Made Plain and Easy*, served as helpful instructions for both:

"*In boiled puddings, take great care the bag or cloth be very clean, not soapy, but dipped in hot water, and well floured. If a bread-pudding, tie it loose; if a batter-pudding, tie it close; and be sure the water boils when you put the pudding in; and you should move the puddings in the pot now and then, for fear they stick. When you make a batter-pudding, first mix the flour well with a little milk, then put in the ingredients by degrees, and it will be smooth and not have lumps; but for a plain batter-pudding, the best way is to strain it through a coarse hair sieve, that it may neither have lumps, nor the treadles of the eggs: and for all other puddings, strain the eggs when they are beat. If you boil them in wooden bowls, or china-dishes, butter the inside before you put in your batter; and for all baked puddings, butter the pan or dish before the pudding is put in.*"

Crème Brûlée

---

1 vanilla bean

1½ quarts heavy cream

1¼ cup sugar

10 large egg yolks

1 large egg

Eighteenth-century cooks prepared custards in a variety of ways. Author John Farley offered many recipes in *The London Art of Cookery*, but his "Plain Custards" appear most similar to modern versions. He offered two methods, the first of which is nearly identical to City Tavern's recipe, although details regarding the baking are woefully absent. One can only assume he meant for them to be baked.

This elegant, creamy, French-titled dessert is really nothing more than basic custard (often called "English custard" or crème anglaise) that is sprinkled with sugar and broiled, caramelizing the sugar. What continues to make this dessert so special is the delightful contrast between the luxurious cream and the crisp sugar layer.

Advance preparation required.

MAKES SIX 8-OUNCE RAMEKINS; SERVES 6

With a paring knife, cut the vanilla bean in half lengthwise, and scrape out the seeds with the back of the knife. Place the pod and seeds, along with the cream, in a medium-size saucepan and bring to a boil over low heat.

Meanwhile, in a medium-size bowl, whisk together 1 cup of the sugar, the egg yolks, and egg.

Remove the vanilla pod from the cream. Temper the hot cream mixture into the egg mixture by adding ¼ cup at a time, whisking constantly.

Refrigerate for at least 2 hours, or overnight.

Preheat the oven to 300°F.

Gently stir the cream mixture to disperse the vanilla seeds throughout. Do not whisk or stir too vigorously as this will incorporate air into the mixture.

Pour the custard into six 8-ounce ramekins. Place the ramekins in a large, high-sided roasting pan, and place the pan in the oven. Fill the roasting pan with boiling water halfway up the sides of the ramekins.

Bake for 25 minutes, or until set and a knife inserted in the centers comes out clean. Turn the oven off, and allow the ramekins to cool in the oven for 30 minutes. Refrigerate for 1 hour.

To assemble the Crème Brûlée, sprinkle ½ tablespoon of sugar evenly across the top of each crème brûlée. Caramelize the sugar with a blowtorch or under the broiler in the oven for 30 to 45 seconds. The sugar will melt and darken quickly, so keep a watchful eye. The caramelized sugar will harden just seconds after you remove the heat. Serve immediately.

Charlotte Russe

—◆—

LADYFINGERS

1 lemon

¾ cup plus 1 tablespoon sugar

1 vanilla bean

6 large egg yolks, at room temperature

1 teaspoon vanilla

3 large egg whites, at room temperature

½ cup plus 2 tablespoons
triple-sifted all-purpose flour

Confectioners' sugar

BAVARIAN

2 (¼-ounce) packets
unflavored gelatin

3 tablespoons dark rum

2 cups whole milk

1 tablespoon vanilla

8 large egg yolks

½ cup sugar

2½ cups heavy cream

1 cup blueberry preserves

2 pints fresh blueberries

This elegant French dessert of light ladyfingers and rich Bavarian cream was surely inspired by eighteenth-century charlottes. These cakes were similar compositions of Naples biscuits (sponge cake) or pieces of bread that were spread with jam or cooked fruit and filled with sweetened, whipped egg whites or sweetened, whipped cream.

Unlike other fillings, Bavarian becomes firm as it chills due to the addition of gelatin. This charlotte is thus easy to slice and maintains its shape once plated.

MAKES ONE 9-INCH CAKE;
SERVES 10

Preheat the oven to 350°F. Line 2 baking sheets with parchment paper. Grease one 9-inch round cake pan with butter, and coat lightly with flour. Fit a pastry bag with a #16 straight tip.

PREPARE THE LADYFINGERS: In a small bowl, zest the lemon over 3 tablespoons of the sugar.

With a paring knife, cut the vanilla bean in half lengthwise, and scrape out the seeds with the back of the knife. Stir the seeds into the sugar.

In the bowl of an electric mixer fitted with the whip attachment, whip the egg yolks, vanilla, and lemon-vanilla sugar on high speed until the mixture is light in color and ribbons form. Transfer the ingredients to a medium-size bowl and reserve.

Clean and dry the mixing bowl and whip attachment immaculately, and whip the egg whites on medium speed until foam begins to form. Decrease the mixing speed to low and add the remaining sugar, 2 tablespoons at a time, waiting until each addition incorporates before adding more. Once all the sugar has been added, increase the mixing speed to high and whip to medium peaks.

Transfer about 3 tablespoons of the whipped egg whites to the yolk mixture, and lightly stir to combine. Using a plastic spatula, fold the remaining whites into the yolk mixture. Fold in the flour gently, so as not to deflate the batter.

Fill the 9-inch cake pan with some of the batter, to a depth of 1 inch. Bake until golden brown, about 7 minutes.

Transfer the remaining batter into the pastry bag, leaving enough room to close and twist the top of the bag. Pipe twenty-five 3-inch-long, 1-inch-wide tubes onto the prepared baking sheets. Lightly sift confectioners' sugar over the raw batter and let stand in the refrigerator for 5 minutes. Bake for 5 to 7 minutes, or until golden.

PREPARE THE BAVARIAN: Prepare an ice bath in a large stainless steel bowl.

In a small metal bowl, sprinkle the gelatin over the rum and whisk to combine. Let stand 10 minutes to "soften."

In a medium-size saucepan, stir together the milk and vanilla and bring to a boil over low heat.

Meanwhile, in a medium-size bowl, whisk together the egg yolks and sugar. Temper the hot milk mixture into the yolk mixture by adding ¼ cup of the hot liquid at a time to the yolks, whisking constantly. Return the custard to the pan and cook, stirring constantly, over low heat until the mixture reaches a temperature of 185°F on a candy thermometer and is thick. Strain this mixture back into the medium-size bowl.

Bring a small pan of water to a simmer. Set the bowl of softened gelatin over the pot of simmering water, stirring constantly until it liquefies. Whisk the gelatin into the custard.

Set the bowl of custard in the ice bath and whisk until the mixture is cool.

In a clean, dry bowl of an electric mixer on high speed, whip the cream until medium peaks form.

Transfer ½ cup of the cool custard into the whipped cream and fold to combine. Fold the remaining custard into the whipped cream.

Spray and line a 10-inch springform pan with plastic wrap. Set the 9-inch cake in the base of the pan. Arrange the ladyfingers around the inside perimeter of the pan. Fill with the cool Bavarian, three fourths of the way full. Freeze for 1 hour.

Once the charlotte is frozen, carefully unmold it. Spread the blueberry preserves evenly atop the Bavarian. Top with the fresh blueberries.

From 1790 to 1800, after the American Revolution, Philadelphia glittered as the new nation's capital: the center of wealth, intellect, and power for America. Balls, parties, and social affairs— many attended by high-ranking visitors from Europe and aristocratic refugees of the revolution in France and the French West Indies—transformed the city into a cosmopolitan scene, with drinking and dining elevated to the loftiest heights.

Floating Islands

Thomas Jefferson was so enamored of French cuisine that when he was dispatched to France as Trade Commissioner in 1784, he brought his cook, James Hemings (Sally's brother), with him to apprentice under the one of the most accomplished *traiteurs*—innkeepers—in Paris. During the three years that followed, Hemings learned how to prepare all of Jefferson's favorites, especially sweets, and eventually took charge of the kitchen at Jefferson's home on the Champs-Elysées.

Oeufs à la Neige, or floating islands, was a particular favorite. Upon their return to the infant United States in 1789, Hemings set about retraining the culinary staff at Monticello, namely, his stocker Peter, who would later take over the kitchens at Monticello after James' manumission. From that time forward, floating islands, among many other French staples, became *de rigeur* on the sweet tables at Monticello.

1 vanilla bean

1 quart milk

8 egg whites

½ cup sugar

3 cups Crème Anglaise
(page 376)

SERVES 8

Cut the vanilla bean in half lengthwise and scrape out the seeds.

In a wide saucepan, stir together the vanilla seeds, pod, and milk, and bring to a gentle simmer over low heat. Remove the vanilla pod.

In bowl of an electric mixer fitted with the whip attachment, whip together the egg whites and sugar on medium to high speed, until they form stiff peaks. Using a large serving spoon, scoop up 2 spoonfuls of the meringue and place them in the simmering milk. Poach for 2 to 3 minutes per side. Using a slotted spoon, carefully remove the meringues and transfer to a plate. Repeat with remaining meringue.

Ladle the Crème Anglaise into a large serving platter or bowl and "float" the meringues carefully in the cream.

In *Thomas Jefferson's Cookbook*, author Marie Kimball offers James Hemings' recipe for Snow Eggs:

Separate 5 eggs and beat the whites until you can turn the vessel bottom upwards without their leaving it. Gradually add 1 tablespoonful of powdered sugar and ½ teaspoonful of any desired flavoring (Jefferson used orange flower or rose water).

Pour 2 cups of milk into a saucepan, add 3 tablespoonfuls of sugar, flavoring, and bring slowly to a boil. Drop the first mixture into the milk and poach until well set. Lay them on a wire drainer to drain.

Beat the yolk of 1 egg until thick, stir gradually into the milk. Add a pinch of salt. As soon as the custard thickens pour through a sieve. Put your whites in a serving dish and pour the custard over them. A little wine stirred in is a great improvement.

Vanilla Bavarian

———◆———

B avarian cream is a dessert based on custard or fruit, enriched with whipped cream, and stabilized with gelatin. Because it becomes firm as it cools, Bavarian cream is not only suitable as a filling for cakes and tortes, but may also be decoratively molded or served in glasses, much as puddings, custards, and creams were in the eighteenth century.

Calves' hooves or calves' feet jelly was the thickener of choice in the period, but, as the nineteenth century progressed, prepared gelatin became an easier, more readily available alternative. It was in the 1800s and early 1900s as well that Bavarian cream became especially popular, due, in large part, to the culinary instruction of French gourmand Auguste Escoffier.

Overnight preparation required.

MAKES ONE 2-QUART BAVARIAN MOLD: SERVES 10

2 (¼-ounce) packets
unflavored gelatin

6 tablespoons Jamaican gold rum

1½ cups whole milk

2 vanilla beans

10 large egg yolks

¾ cup sugar

2½ cups heavy cream

Prepare an ice bath in a large stainless steel bowl.

In a small metal bowl, sprinkle the gelatin over the rum and whisk to combine. Let stand 10 minutes to "soften."

In a medium-size saucepan, stir together the milk and vanilla beans and bring to a boil over low heat.

Meanwhile, in a medium-size bowl, add the egg yolks and sugar, and whisk together. Temper the hot milk mixture into the yolk mixture by adding ¼ cup at a time of the hot liquid to the yolks, whisking constantly. When all of the hot liquid has been added, return the custard to the pan and cook, stirring constantly, over low heat until the mixture reaches a temperature of 185°F on a candy thermometer and is thick. Strain this mixture back into the medium-size bowl.

Bring a small pan of water to a simmer. Set the bowl of softened gelatin over the pot of simmering water, stirring constantly until it liquefies.

Set the bowl of custard in the ice bath and whisk until the mixture is cool.

In a clean, dry bowl of an electric mixer on high speed, whip the cream until medium peaks form. Fold ½ cup of the cool custard into the whipped cream. Fold the remaining custard into the whipped cream.

Pour the Bavarian into the mold, cover with plastic wrap, and refrigerate overnight. To unmold, uncover and hold the mold over a pan of simmering water for 10 to 20 seconds. Place a large serving plate over the top of the mold, invert the plate and mold, gently tap the mold to loosen, and lift off.

Cookies

IN THE EIGHTEENTH CENTURY, the use of the word "cookie" was rare. In fact, Amelia Simmons seems to have been one of the few authors to use the term, including in her cookbook *American Cookery* recipes for "Cookies" and "Another Christmas Cookey." She titled the remaining recipes in this category, however, in the style of her contemporaries: primarily as biscuits, drops, and cakes. Some of these cookies remain familiar in America, such as gingerbread and macaroons, while others, with their English roots, are less so, including Naples biscuits, ratafia drops, Savoy cakes/drops, and Shrewsbury cakes.

Despite the differences in their shapes and textures, most of these cookies were similarly flavored with a variety of spices and other concentrated ingredients, such as rose water and orange and lemon zests. Cinnamon, nutmeg, mace, and cardamom, some of the most celebrated spices of the Middle Ages, continued to be popular in eighteenth-century American baking. Like other imported items, spices were expensive. So desirable were they, however, that home cooks and confectioners alike discovered ways to prudently combine them with American dairy products, fruits, and nuts so as to satisfy the European-influenced, eighteenth-century palate.

Just as cookies are today, colonial American cookies were prepared for special holiday and social occasions as well as daily treats, and were enjoyed with a variety of beverages, including wine, punch, cider, tea, coffee, and hot chocolate.

Apricot Tea Cookies

—◆—

1 pound (4 sticks)
unsalted butter, softened

¾ cup sugar

2 large eggs

5 cups sifted all-purpose flour

2 teaspoons baking powder

½ teaspoon salt

1 cup sliced almonds, toasted
(see Chef's Note, page 245)

1 cup apricot preserves

¼ cup grated unsweetened coconut,
toasted (see Chef's Note, page 275)

Apricots were much appreciated in the eighteenth century, perhaps because of their limited availability. They were cultivated more successfully in the South's temperate climate than in the North. Both George Washington and Thomas Jefferson included apricot trees in their orchards, and they, like many of their contemporaries, must have enjoyed the fruit not only fresh in season but preserved year-round as well.

These German-inspired confections are filled with the sweet-tart flavor of apricots; preserves are incorporated into the dough and jam is spooned decoratively on top of each cookie.

MAKES 3 DOZEN COOKIES

In the bowl of an electric mixer fitted with the paddle attachment, beat the butter and sugar on medium speed until light and fluffy, scraping down the sides of the bowl often. Add the eggs and beat well until combined.

In a separate bowl, combine the flour, baking powder, and salt.

Add the almonds, half of the preserves, and the coconut to the butter mixture, and beat well. Add the flour mixture and mix until just combined. Wrap the dough in plastic wrap and refrigerate for at least 1 hour, or until easy to handle.

Preheat the oven to 350°F.

Shape the chilled dough into 1-inch balls. Place the dough balls 1 inch apart on an ungreased cookie sheet. Press your thumb into the center of each ball. Place ½ teaspoon of the remaining preserves in the center of each impression.

Bake for 12 to 15 minutes, or until the edges are lightly browned.

Transfer the cookies to a wire rack and let cool. To store, place in an airtight container and keep at room temperature.

Anise Biscotti

For centuries, anise has been a traditional addition to biscotti, and it was certainly popular in the eighteenth century. Like many other imported spices and foodstuffs, anise seeds were readily available in local markets.

MAKES ABOUT 24 (3 X ½-INCH) BISCOTTI

Preheat the oven to 350°F. Place parchment paper on a cookie sheet, and grease lightly with butter.

In the bowl of an electric mixer fitted with the paddle attachment, beat the sugar, oil, and eggs on medium to high speed until combined, scraping down the sides of the bowl often. Add the sour cream and vanilla, and beat well.

In a separate bowl, sift together the flour, baking powder, baking soda, and salt. Stir in the anise seed. With the mixer on low, slowly add the dry ingredients to the wet ingredients.

Transfer the dough to a lightly-floured surface, and knead the dough for 1 minute. Shape the dough into a 12-inch roll, about 3 inches in diameter, and place the roll in the center of the prepared cookie sheet.

Bake for 20 to 25 minutes, or until light golden brown.

Remove from the oven and cool on the cookie sheet for about 25 minutes. Using a serrated knife, cut the log into ½-inch-thick diagonal slices.

Arrange the slices, flat sides down, on the same cookie sheet, and put back into the oven for 5 minutes. Turn each slice over and bake 5 minutes more, or until the biscotti are just toasted. Do not overbake.

Transfer the biscotti to a wire rack and let cool. To store, place in an airtight container and keep at room temperature.

1¾ cups sugar

¾ cup vegetable oil

2 large eggs

½ cup sour cream

1 teaspoon vanilla

4½ cups sifted all-purpose flour

1 teaspoon baking powder

1 teaspoon baking soda

½ teaspoon salt

½ teaspoon crushed anise seed

Many shops that stood in the vicinity of City Tavern carried a variety of imported foodstuffs that were incorporated into the dishes served at this stylish establishment. On April 14, 1790, for example, Cadwalader & David Evans advertised in the *Pennsylvania Gazette* that "At their Store, the south side of Market street, the second door below Fifth street" they had for sale imported "Pepper, alspice, ginger, cinnamon [and] cloves," as well as the ever-popular "Anniseed."

Spritz Cookies

————•••————

Buttery flavor and fanciful shapes define these cookies of Northern European origin. The soft dough is pushed through a special cookie press—hence the name, which refers to *spritzen*, German for "to squirt or spray." This press may be fitted with a variety of decorative templates, enabling one to easily create festive cookies so typical of Germany and Scandinavia.

Many varieties of butter cookies existed in the American colonies. The large German population in Philadelphia certainly continued to enjoy this version reminiscent of Old World foodways.

MAKES 2 DOZEN COOKIES

Preheat the oven to 350°F.

In the bowl of an electric mixer fitted with the paddle attachment, beat the butter and sugar on medium speed until light and fluffy, scraping down the sides of the bowl often. Add the egg yolks and vanilla and beat well.

In a separate bowl, sift together the flour, baking powder, and salt. With the electric mixer on low speed, slowly add the dry ingredients and mix until just combined.

Shape the dough into 2-inch-long, finger-sized logs. Place the logs 1 inch apart on an ungreased cookie sheet. Alternatively, you may use a cookie press (spritzer) to form the decorative cookies. Fill the cookie press and shape cookies as per the manufacturer's directions.

Bake for 15 minutes, or until the edges are firm and golden but not brown. (If you are baking cookies you formed with a cookie press, you will probably need to reduce the baking time accordingly; again, see the manufacturer's directions.)

Transfer the cookies to a wire rack and let cool. To store, place in an airtight container and keep at room temperature.

1 pound (4 sticks)
unsalted butter, softened

1½ cups sugar

4 large egg yolks

2 teaspoons vanilla

5 cups sifted all-purpose flour

4 teaspoons baking powder

1 teaspoon salt

Spice Cookies

½ pound (2 sticks)
unsalted butter, softened

¾ cup sugar

½ cup dark molasses

2 large egg yolks

1 teaspoon vanilla

2⅓ cups sifted all-purpose flour

2 teaspoons ground cinnamon

1½ teaspoons ground ginger

½ teaspoon salt

¼ teaspoon ground nutmeg

1 cup confectioners' sugar

1½ tablespoons freshly squeezed and
strained lemon juice

Most eighteenth-century cookies, or "cakes" as they were called in the period, were flavored with spices. Whole or ground caraway and coriander seeds ranked among the most popular, but others were frequently used as well. As in these cookies, nutmeg, ginger, and cinnamon were added to a variety of baked goods to add a taste of the exotic and depth of flavor to simple preparations. This recipe recalls the crisp Shrewsbury cakes and numerous varieties of gingerbread (more closely related to cookies than cake) that filled the kitchens and shelves of many colonial American homes and bake shops.

Makes about 3 dozen cookies

Preheat the oven to 350°F.

In the bowl of an electric mixer fitted with the paddle attachment, beat the butter and sugar on medium speed until light and fluffy, scraping down the sides of the bowl often. Add the molasses, egg yolks, and vanilla, and beat well until combined.

In a separate bowl, sift together the flour, cinnamon, ginger, salt, and nutmeg. With the electric mixer on low speed, add the dry ingredients to the wet ingredients and mix until just combined.

Drop the dough by teaspoonfuls 1 inch apart onto an ungreased cookie sheet.

Bake for 15 to 20 minutes, or until golden.

Transfer the cookies to a wire rack and let cool about 15 minutes.

In a small bowl, whisk together the confectioners' sugar and lemon juice until smooth. When the cookies are cool, use a small spoon to drizzle the glaze over the top of each cookie. To store, place in an airtight container and keep at room temperature.

Oatmeal-Raisin Cookies

Numerous markets and shops in eighteenth-century Philadelphia featured raisins in their advertisements, testament to the popularity and high demand of this dried fruit once considered exotic, sugary jewels. When raisins are combined with the spices and oatmeal in this recipe, the result is a sweet, chewy cookie that is satisfying and comforting.

MAKES ABOUT 28 COOKIES

Preheat the oven to 375°F.

In the bowl of an electric mixer fitted with the paddle attachment, beat the butter, sugar, and brown sugar on medium speed until light and fluffy, scraping the sides of the bowl often. Add the eggs and vanilla and beat well.

In a separate bowl, combine the oats, flour, baking soda, cinnamon, and nutmeg. With the mixer on low speed, gradually add the dry ingredients to the wet ingredients and mix until just combined. Add the raisins and beat well.

Using a 2-inch ice cream scoop, drop the dough 2 inches apart onto an ungreased cookie sheet.

Bake about 15 minutes, or until the edges of the cookies are golden.

Transfer the cookies to a wire rack and let cool. To store, place in an airtight container and keep at room temperature.

¾ pound (3 sticks) unsalted butter, softened

1½ cups sugar

1½ cups packed light brown sugar

4 large eggs

4 teaspoons vanilla

4 cups old-fashioned rolled oats

2 cups sifted all-purpose flour

1 teaspoon baking soda

½ teaspoon ground cinnamon

¼ teaspoon ground nutmeg

1½ cups raisins

Not only is George Washington known to have cultivated grapes at Mount Vernon, which he possibly dried to produce raisins, but he also frequently imported the dried fruit. Between 1758 and 1798, Washington ordered jars of raisins from England. In a letter to his agent in England in November 1762, Washington, placed an order for what were called "best Raisons," adding that "those sent last year were good for nothing." The general must have finally received some acceptable raisins by 1795, however, when, in addition to "puddings, jellies, oranges, apples, nuts, and figs," he served the fruit at a congressional dinner in Philadelphia.

Walnut Crescents

Thomas Jefferson loved walnuts, and experimented with native strains and hybrids at Monticello. As early as 1767 Jefferson notes in his *Garden Book* that he "inoculated English walnut buds into stocks of the Black walnut." Both savory and sweet dishes made with walnuts graced the tables at Monticello with great frequency.

These cookies are from the Piedmont region of Italy, to which Jefferson made a side trip during his tour of French wine producing provinces in 1787.

MAKES 32 CRESCENTS

½ cup shelled walnuts, toasted

1¾ cup plus 2 tablespoons all-purpose flour

1 vanilla bean, split lengthwise

4 cups confectioners' sugar

½ pound (2 sticks) unsalted butter, room temperature

3 large egg yolks

Combine the walnuts and 2 tablespoons of the flour in the bowl of a food processor fitted with the blade attachment and pulse until the nuts are finely ground. Remove to a small bowl.

Carefully scrape the seeds from vanilla bean using a paring knife. Stir together the seeds and ¾ cup of the confectioners' sugar in a small bowl.

Combine the butter and vanilla sugar in the bowl of an electric mixer fitted with the paddle attachment and mix on medium speed until smooth, stopping to scrape the sides of the bowl. Incorporate the egg yolks one at a time, stopping again once or twice to scrape the sides of the bowl. Reduce the mixing speed to low and gradually incorporate the remaining 1¾ cup flour and ground walnuts, mixing until just combined.

Remove the dough to a lightly floured work surface and knead several times until smooth. Roll the dough into three logs about 1 inch wide and 12 inches long, wrap in plastic wrap, and set in the refrigerator to chill for 2 hours.

Line 2 baking sheets with parchment paper. Place the chilled dough on a lightly floured work surface and slice into the 2-inch pieces. Roll each piece into a cylinder, tapering the ends, and curve into a half-moon shape (crescent). (If the dough becomes too soft, set in the refrigerator for several minutes to firm slightly. Avoid using too much flour when rolling the dough to prevent the cookies from becoming tough and dry.) Arrange the crescents about 1 inch apart on the prepared baking sheets and set in the refrigerator to chill for about 30 minutes.

Preheat the oven to 350°F.

Bake the chilled crescents until light golden brown, about 8 minutes. Set on wire racks to cool on the caking sheets for about 2 minutes. Place the remaining confectioners' sugar in a medium bowl. Toss the warm crescents one or two at a time in the sugar, coating them well. Set on wire racks to cool completely and toss again in sugar before serving or storing in airtight containers.

Macaroons

These modest-looking cookies date at least to the seventeenth century and appear in nearly every eighteenth-century cookbook available in Philadelphia and abroad. Often also appearing as "mackroons," "mackeroons," "maccaroons," and "macarons" (the French spelling), they were simple combinations of a few flavorful ingredients. With the occasional substitution of orange water for rose water, eighteenth-century macaroons remained nearly identical to their medieval predecessors. "[T]hese cookies are," as historian Karen Hess writes, "simply baked puffy marchpane [marzipan]," and, as such, they satisfied the eighteenth-century palate's fondness for almonds.

MAKES 2 DOZEN COOKIES

Preheat the oven to 425°F. Line 2 cookie sheets with parchment paper. Fit a pastry bag with a #16 round tip.

Grind the almonds in a food processor. Reserve.

In the bowl of an electric mixer fitted with the paddle attachment, mix the Almond Paste with 1 tablespoon of the egg whites on low speed until soft, scraping down the sides of the bowl often. Add the sugar and mix until light. With the mixer on medium speed, slowly add the remaining egg whites and mix until smooth. Fold in the ground almonds.

Fill the pastry bag one-quarter full with the macaroon batter, leaving enough room to close and twist the top of the bag. Pipe 1-inch rounds of batter, a few inches apart, on the prepared cookie sheets, or drop the batter by the tablespoonful. Put the macaroons in the oven and immediately reduce the oven temperature to 375°F. Bake for 7 to 10 minutes, or until light golden brown.

Cool completely on the cookie sheets before removing. To store, place in an airtight container and keep at room temperature.

½ cup sliced almonds, toasted (see Chef's Note, page 245) and cooled

½ cup Almond Paste (page 246), or 5¼ ounces purchased almond paste

3 large egg whites

1 cup sugar

Hannah Glasse's recipe "To make Mackeroons," published in *The Art of Cookery Made Plain and Easy*, is just one example of how medieval culinary traditions influenced eighteenth-century foodways:

Take a pound of almonds, let them be scalded, blanched, and thrown into cold water, then dry them in a cloth, and pound them in a mortar, moisten them with orange-flower water, or the white of an egg, lest they turn to oil, afterwards take an equal quantity of fine powder sugar, with three or four whites of eggs, and a little musk, beat all well together, and shape them on a wafer-paper, with a spoon round. Bake them in a gentle oven on tin plates.

From left to right: Macarroons, Financiers, and Walnut Crescents N. 299

Shortbread Triangles
with Apple Chutney

Shortbread, a traditionally Scottish holiday treat, is here served with a fragrant, spicy chutney that combines some of the most flavorful ingredients available to eighteenth-century Philadelphians. Molasses, ginger, cinnamon, and raisins were all imported from the West Indies and were available in local shops.

MAKES 6 SERVINGS

PREPARE THE SHORTBREAD: In the bowl of an electric mixer fitted with the paddle attachment, beat the butter, confectioners' sugar, and vanilla on medium speed until light and fluffy.

In a separate bowl, combine the flour and salt. With the mixer on low, slowly add the dry ingredients to the butter-sugar mixture and mix until just combined. Form the dough into a disc shape, wrap in plastic wrap, and refrigerate for at least 1 hour before using.

Preheat the oven to 325°F. Line a cookie sheet with parchment paper.

PREPARE THE FILLING: In a large saucepan over medium heat, melt the butter. Stirring constantly, add the brown sugar, molasses, salt, cinnamon, and ginger. Bring the mixture to a boil.

Reduce the heat to low and add the apples, lime zest, and lime juice. Cook until just the apples start to soften, 3 to 5 minutes.

Add the raisins and walnuts and remove from the heat. Reserve.

On a lightly-floured work surface, roll out the shortbread to ¼ inch thick. Cut the dough into eighteen 3-inch triangle shapes and place them 1 inch apart on the prepared cookie sheet. Sprinkle the sugar over the top of each triangle.

Bake for 15 to 20 minutes, or until golden brown around the edges. Cool on a wire rack.

ASSEMBLE THE TRIANGLES: When the triangles are cool, spoon ½ cup of the warm Apple Chutney onto six of the triangles. Top with another triangle and more chutney. Top with a third triangle. You should have a total of six 3-layer triangles.

Dust the serving plates with confectioners' sugar and, if desired, serve with ice cream.

SHORTBREAD

¾ pound (3 sticks) unsalted butter, softened

1 cup sifted confectioners' sugar, plus extra for dusting

½ teaspoon vanilla

3 cups sifted all-purpose flour

½ teaspoon salt

FILLING

¼ pound (1 stick) unsalted butter, softened

½ cup packed dark brown sugar

¼ cup dark molasses

¼ teaspoon salt

½ teaspoon ground cinnamon

2 teaspoons grated fresh ginger

4 Granny Smith apples, peeled, cored, and sliced into ½-inch cubes

1 medium lime, zest grated and juiced (strained)

½ cup raisins

½ cup chopped walnuts, lightly toasted (see Chef's Note, page 245)

1½ teaspoons sugar, for garnish

Confectioners' sugar, for dusting

Purchased caramel or butter-pecan ice cream, for serving (optional)

Financiers

———

L ike many of the dry sweetmeats of the eighteenth century, financiers are a cross between little cakes and cookies. These cookies are similar to eighteenth-century ratafia cakes (prepared with egg whites and almonds) as well as butter drops (made with eggs, butter, and rose water). Usually prepared with almonds, this recipe may be varied to include pistachios, which Thomas Jefferson cultivated for some years. Flavored with orange, vanilla, nutmeg, and liqueur, these cookies would have appealed to the eighteenth-century palate.

MAKES 2 DOZEN COOKIES

Fill a stainless steel bowl with ice water.

Melt the butter in a small saucepan over medium heat. Continue to cook the butter until it begins to brown. When the butter begins to brown, remove it from the heat and immediately place the pan in the ice water bath. Carefully mix in the vanilla and orange liqueur. Be careful, as the mixture may spatter. Reserve the brown butter at room temperature.

In the bowl of a food processor, add the almonds, flour, 1 cup of the sugar, the orange zest, and nutmeg and process until finely ground. Reserve.

In the bowl of an electric mixer fitted with the whip attachment, whip the egg whites and salt on medium speed until they begin to foam. Slowly add the remaining sugar in a thin steady stream. Once all the sugar has been added, increase the mixer speed to high and whip the meringue to medium peaks. Transfer the meringue to a separate bowl.

Check to make sure the brown butter has cooled to room temperature. If not, refrigerate it for a few minutes. Fold a quarter of the almond-flour mixture into the egg whites. Fold a third of the cooled brown butter into the whites. Proceed with another quarter of the flour mixture and a third of the brown butter until the mixtures are complete and the batter is thoroughly combined and smooth. Chill the batter for 2 hours.

Preheat the oven to 425°F. Grease 24 financier molds or miniature muffin pans with butter and coat lightly with flour.

Fill the prepared molds halfway with the batter, put them in the oven, and immediately reduce the oven temperature to 375°F. Bake 7 minutes, or until golden. Cool briefly on wire racks and unmold the financiers while still warm. To store, place in an airtight container and keep at room temperature.

6 tablespoons unsalted butter, cubed

2 tablespoons vanilla

2 tablespoons orange liqueur (such as Cointreau or Triple Sec)

1 cup almonds, toasted (see Chef's Note, page 245)

1 cup all-purpose flour

1⅔ cups sugar

1 orange, zest grated

Pinch of ground nutmeg

5 large egg whites

Pinch of salt

Madeleines

❖

These French cookies resemble the small sponge cakes prepared so frequently in eighteenth-century America. They are traditionally shell shaped and coated with confectioners' sugar after baking.

MAKES 2 DOZEN COOKIES

¼ cup sugar

1 lemon

1 tablespoon fresh lemon thyme, finely chopped, or substitute fresh thyme

4 large egg yolks

¼ pound (1 stick) unsalted butter, melted

3 large egg whites

¼ cup sifted all-purpose flour

Preheat the oven to 375°F. Grease a madeleine tray, and coat lightly with flour.

In a small bowl, add the sugar and grate the lemon zest over it. Add the lemon thyme and stir to combine.

In the bowl of an electric mixer fitted with the whip attachment, whip the egg yolks and lemon thyme-sugar mixture on medium speed until the mixture triples in volume and ribbons form. Slowly mix in the butter. Transfer the mixture to a medium-size stainless steel bowl.

Clean the electric mixer bowl and whip attachment and dry thoroughly. Add the egg whites and whip to stiff peaks on medium to high speed.

In a medium-size bowl, sift the flour 3 times. Fold the flour into the yolk mixture, about 1 tablespoon at a time.

Transfer one third of the yolk mixture into the whipped egg whites. Fold the egg white mixture into the yolk mixture, being careful not to deflate the batter. With a delicate hand, fold the remaining flour into the batter.

Fill the madeleine molds half full.

Bake for 5 to 7 minutes, or until golden brown and puffed (doubled in size). Unmold the madeleines immediately and cool to room temperature. To store, place in an airtight container and keep at room temperature.

Poppy Seed Squares

These bar cookies pay tribute to the affinity eighteenth-century Americans and Europeans had for exotic, Eastern foodstuffs. For centuries, poppy seeds have been harvested from the opium poppy cultivated in the Middle East and used in sweet and savory dishes throughout Europe. Some period recipes for "surfeit waters" (medicinal waters) call for poppy flowers, but of the "Corn-Rose or wilde" variety rather than the Eastern opium sort. Although these red poppies were renowned for treating headaches, bad breath, and flatulence, they also had a slight sedative effect.

Rather than for any medicinal effect, poppy seeds are used in these cookies to add flavor and texture to the rich filling of nuts, citrus, and honey.

MAKES 24 SQUARES

Grease a 17 x 11-inch baking pan, coat it lightly with flour and refrigerate.

PREPARE THE DOUGH: In the bowl of an electric mixer fitted with the paddle attachment, beat the butter and sugar on medium speed until smooth, scraping down the sides of the bowl often. Add the egg and beat until smooth. Scrape down the sides of the bowl.

Remove the bowl from the mixer and fold in the flour with a rubber spatula or wooden spoon.

Wrap the dough in plastic wrap and refrigerate for 2 hours.

On a lightly-floured work surface, roll out the dough into a rectangle about 12 x 18 inches.

Ease the dough into the prepared pan, being careful not to stretch it. If it breaks, simply patch it together inside the pan. Refrigerate for 1 hour.

PREPARE THE FILLING: In a medium-size saucepan, stir together the poppy seeds, milk, and honey and let the ingredients soak for 1 hour.

Preheat the oven to 350°F.

Add the cream and lemon zest to the poppy seed mixture. Place the saucepan over medium-low heat and cook, stirring constantly until the mixture boils. Continue to cook the mixture, stirring occasionally until the poppy seeds absorb half the milk and the mixture begins to thicken, about 15 minutes.

(continued)

DOUGH

½ pound (2 sticks) unsalted butter, softened

½ cup sugar

1 large egg

1½ cups all-purpose flour

FILLING

½ cup poppy seeds

1 cup whole milk

¼ cup honey

½ cup heavy cream

1 lemon, zest grated

1 teaspoon cornstarch

2 tablespoons orange liqueur (such as Cointreau or Triple Sec)

3 tablespoons unsalted butter

¼ cup ground walnuts

1 large egg

Meanwhile, in a small bowl whisk together the cornstarch and liqueur.

When the milk-poppy seed mixture begins to boil, add the cornstarch mixture, stirring constantly to prevent clumping and cook for 30 seconds.

Remove the pan from the heat, add the butter and walnuts and mix well to combine. Stir vigorously until the mixture cools slightly, then add the egg.

Pour the warm filling into the chilled, dough-lined cookie sheet. Bake for 15 minutes, or until the filling puffs slightly, is firm and the sides brown.

Cool to room temperature and cut into squares.

Like Martha Washington, who included medicinal beverages entitled "To Make Surfit Water of Poppies" and "To Make the Surfit Water" in her cookbook, Hannah Glasse published "To make Cordial Poppy Water" in her book *The Art of Cooking Made Plain and Easy*. It is similar to Washington's waters—spicy, sweet, and strong:

Take two gallons of very good brandy, and a peck of poppies, and put them together in a wide-mouthed glass, and let them stand forty-eight hours, and then strain the poppies out; take a pound of raisins of the sun, stone them, and an ounce of coriander-seed, an ounce of sweet-fennel seeds, and an ounce of liqueurice sliced, bruise them all together, and put them into the brandy, with a pound of good powder sugar, and let them stand four or eight weeks, shaking it every day; and then strain it off, and bottle it close up for use.

Quick Breads

IT IS UNCLEAR just when the term "quick bread" became part of American culinary vocabulary. What is certain, however, is that in the eighteenth century these breads were popularly referred to as cakes and biscuits, some of which were prepared with "emptins" (a fermented leavener based on flour and ale). Unlike yeast breads, which require numerous hours of kneading and fermentation, quick breads rely on fast-acting leaveners, including baking powder, baking soda and, in the case of light batters, eggs. Although chemical leaveners were not widely available until the nineteenth century, eighteenth-century bakers used pearl ash or pot ash (early forms of baking soda) to ensure that their cakes and biscuits would rise quickly.

Indeed, in texture and flavor, quick breads resemble cakes more than yeast breads. Perhaps one of the earliest examples of how cake and bread became linked in name, if not in concept, is Eliza Leslie's 1848 recipe for "Bread Cake," published in *Directions for Cookery, in Its Various Branches*. It called for a combination of wheat-bread dough—"as much of it as would make a twelve cent loaf"— and cake ingredients, including "confectioners' sugar…butter…milk…[and] a beaten egg." Unlike eighteenth-century yeast-leavened breads, cakes, and biscuits, this recipe required only half an hour of rising. As the availability of baking soda and powder increased throughout the nineteenth century, the need for using bread dough and/or yeast in such recipes grew obsolete, and quick breads that resembled eighteenth-century cakes and biscuits became easier than ever to prepare.

Sweet Potato & Pecan Biscuits

5 cups all-purpose flour

1 cup packed light brown sugar

2 tablespoons baking powder

1½ teaspoons ground cinnamon

1 teaspoon salt

1 teaspoon ground ginger

½ teaspoon ground allspice

1 cup vegetable shortening

2 cups cooked, mashed, and cooled
sweet potato (about 2 large potatoes)

1 cup heavy cream

½ cup coarsely chopped pecans

In the eighteenth century, sweet potatoes were plentiful in the southern states, and Thomas Jefferson participated as enthusiastically in their cultivation as other farmers. George Washington was one of his compatriots in this venture. This root vegetable makes a number of appearances in Jefferson's collection of recipes and, consequently, inspired this recipe. Sweet potatoes contribute a sweet flavor and light texture to these biscuits and are complemented by the addition of one of this renowned gardener's other favorite foods, pecans.

MAKES ABOUT 2 DOZEN BISCUITS

Preheat the oven to 400°F.

In a large mixing bowl, stir together the flour, brown sugar, baking powder, cinnamon, salt, ginger, and allspice. Add the shortening and cut in with a pastry cutter or two knives until crumbly. Stir in the sweet potato. Add the cream and pecans and stir until just moistened.

Turn the dough out onto a lightly-floured work surface. Roll the dough out to 1 inch thick and cut out the biscuits with a floured 2-inch biscuit cutter. Place the biscuits 1 inch apart on ungreased baking sheets.

Set the pans in the oven, reduce the oven temperature to 350°F. and bake for 25 to 30 minutes, or until golden brown. Serve warm or cool completely on a wire rack.

CHEF'S NOTE

The biscuit dough freezes beautifully unbaked. Just layer the dough between wax paper and store for up to 3 months. Defrost the dough and follow the baking directions. It pays to make a double batch of these biscuits and freeze half for later.

Clockwise from top left: Sally Lunn Bread (page 318), Anadama Bread (page 319), Sweet Potato and Pecan Biscuits (this page), and French Baguettes (page 320).

Lemon-Poppy Seed Bread

1¼ pounds (5 sticks)
unsalted butter, softened

2 cups sugar

9 large eggs

¼ cup freshly squeezed lemon juice
(about 1 large lemon), strained

2 teaspoons grated lemon zest

1 teaspoon vanilla

4 cups all-purpose flour

2 tablespoons poppy seeds

2 teaspoons baking powder

1 teaspoon salt

This bread represents the intermingling of cultures and foodways that took place throughout the American colonies and especially in cosmopolitan Philadelphia. Lemons were imported from Spain and Portugal, and poppy seeds represent the exotic foodstuffs from Europe and the Orient (the Middle East and India) that influenced stylish eighteenth-century dishes.

Like oranges, lemons are frequently characterized as an elite fruit, so expensive that only the wealthy could afford to display and cook with them. Although their high cost is undisputed, the use of lemons appears to have been fairly widespread. Period cookbooks, even those whose authors focused specifically on domestic frugality, contained numerous recipes that called for lemon juice, peel, oil, and syrup, sometimes in great quantities. If a home cook chose to purchase rather than prepare her own lemon sweetmeats, they were widely available in local shops as well. According to Philadelphia advertisements, "lemmon chips" (candied lemon peel) were among the most popular items sold in confectioners' stores.

MAKES TWO 8-INCH LOAVES

Preheat the oven to 325°F. Butter two 8½ x 4½ x 2½-inch loaf pans.

In the bowl of an electric mixer fitted with the paddle attachment, beat together the butter and sugar on medium speed until light and fluffy, scraping down the sides of the bowl often.

Add the eggs one at a time and beat until combined. Add the lemon juice, lemon zest, and vanilla and beat until just combined.

In a medium-size bowl, stir together the flour, poppy seeds, baking powder, and salt. Add the egg mixture to the flour mixture and mix on low speed until just moistened.

Divide the batter between the prepared pans. Bake about 1 hour, or until golden brown and a toothpick inserted in the center comes out clean.

Cool in the pans on a wire rack for 10 minutes. To remove the breads, flip the pans on their sides and gently pull out the bread. Serve warm, or cool completely on a wire rack.

Cornbread

To Europeans, "corn" has always been a generic name for all grains, and "maize," from the American Indian *mahiz*, has referred specifically to what Americans know as corn. The colonists associated this native grain not only with the New World but also with the Indians who introduced them to it; they, therefore, referred to the grain frequently as "Indian corn" to differentiate it from other varieties.

Not only was cornbread included in period cookbooks, but related corn recipes appeared frequently as well, including baked and boiled Indian pudding, mush, and Johny or Johnny cakes, also known as journey and hoe cakes. These mildly sweet (if they were sweetened at all) dishes called for cornmeal, whole corn, or even, as in the case of Thomas Jefferson's "Corn Pudding" recipe, green (unripened) corn.

Like this version of cornbread, these recipes were flavorful and quick to prepare. In addition, as they were frequently served alongside European-inspired dishes on eighteenth-century dining tables, cornbread and its related preparations certainly represented distinctively American foodways.

2 cups coarse yellow cornmeal

2 cups all-purpose flour

½ cup sugar

2 tablespoons baking powder

1 teaspoon salt

2 cups whole milk

¼ pound lard or margarine

2 large eggs, lightly beaten

SERVES 10 TO 12

Preheat the oven to 400°F. Grease two 8½ x 4½ x 2½ loaf pans with butter.

In a large mixing bowl, add the cornmeal, flour, sugar, baking powder, and salt; stir to combine.

In a medium-size mixing bowl, combine the milk, lard, and eggs. Add to the dry ingredients and stir until just moistened.

Pour the batter into the prepared pans. Bake for 30 to 35 minutes, or until golden brown and a toothpick inserted in the center comes out clean.

Cool in the pan for 30 minutes to prevent crumbling.

Cornmeal, unlike wheat flour, doesn't contain gluten-producing proteins (which, when combined with yeast, trap gases within batters and doughs, causing them to rise), and therefore, does not create a light and airy loaf of bread. North American settlers came to depend on cornmeal out of necessity, mixing cornmeal with eggs and water to make fried corn bread and cake.

Cranberry Bread

———◆·◆·◆———

In the eighteenth century, cranberries were often preserved or baked in tarts and puddings, most likely because, as Lydia Maria Child explained in *The American Frugal Housewife*, "They need a great deal of sweetening." Mrs. Child also recommended that "[a] little nutmeg, or cinnamon, improves them," and Amelia Simmons similarly suggested that after stewing and sweetening the fruit, one should "add spices till grateful."

This recipe calls for a minimal amount of sugar and fresh, rather than cooked, fruit. Even Child and Simmons would agree, however, that the bread is "gratefully," and successfully, flavored with the additions of orange zest and pecans.

MAKES ONE 8-INCH LOAF

9 tablespoons unsalted butter, softened

¾ cup sugar

4 large eggs

2⅓ cups sifted cake flour

1 tablespoon baking powder

1 teaspoon salt

¾ cup whole milk

2 cups fresh cranberries

½ cup chopped pecans

2 teaspoons grated orange zest

Preheat the oven to 350°F. Butter an 8½ x 4½ x 2½-inch loaf pan.

In the bowl of an electric mixer fitted with the paddle attachment, beat together the butter and sugar on medium speed until light and fluffy, scraping down the sides of the bowl often.

Add the eggs one at a time and beat until combined.

In a medium-size mixing bowl, stir together the flour, baking powder, and salt. Fold the dry ingredients into the butter mixture in thirds, alternating with the milk.

In a medium-size mixing bowl, combine the cranberries, pecans, and orange zest. With a rubber spatula, gently fold into the batter.

Pour the batter into the prepared pan. Bake about 45 minutes, or until golden brown and a toothpick inserted in the center comes out clean.

Cool in the pan on a wire rack for 10 minutes. To remove the bread, flip the pan on its side and gently pull out the bread. Serve warm, or cool completely on a wire rack.

Pumpkin-Raisin Bread

This simple but flavorful bread represents the fusion of the New and Old Worlds. Pumpkins grew plentifully in North America and were cultivated first by Native Americans and later by the colonists. Pumpkin, or "pompion," as Americans and Europeans often called it, was not only commonly incorporated into puddings and pies but was also candied, as Harriet Pinckney Horry's recipe "To make Pompion Chips" illustrates. In contrast, raisins were imported to urban areas like Philadelphia, where they were sold as specialty items in local shops among such other exotic ingredients as nutmeg, cinnamon, and chocolate.

MAKES TWO 8-INCH LOAVES

Preheat the oven to 350°F. Grease two 8½ x 4½ x 2½-inch loaf pans with butter.

In a medium-size mixing bowl, mix together ⅔ cup water, the pumpkin purée, oil, and eggs.

In a large mixing bowl, stir together the flour, sugar, baking soda, salt, nutmeg, and cinnamon. Fold the egg mixture into the dry ingredients.

With a rubber spatula or wooden spoon, gently fold the raisins into the batter.

Divide the batter between the prepared pans. Bake about 1 hour or until a toothpick inserted in the center comes out clean.

Cool in the pans on a wire rack for 10 minutes. To remove the breads, flip the pans on their sides and gently pull out the bread. Serve warm or cool completely on a wire rack.

2 cups pumpkin purée
(see Chef's Note, page 362)

1 cup vegetable oil

4 large eggs

3⅓ cups sifted all-purpose flour

3 cups sugar

2 teaspoons baking soda

1½ teaspoons salt

1 teaspoon ground nutmeg

1 teaspoon ground cinnamon

½ cup raisins

Chocolate-Almond Swirl Bread

———◦•◦•◦———

3 ounces semisweet chocolate,
roughly chopped

1 cup Almond Paste (page 246),
or 10½ ounces purchased almond paste

½ pound (2 sticks)
unsalted butter, softened

6 large eggs

1½ teaspoons vanilla

½ cup sifted all-purpose flour

Although chocolate remained costly throughout the eighteenth century in America, it was widely available in various forms in confectioners' shops and stores specializing in imported dry goods and foodstuffs. The panache of chocolate seems to have equaled that of such foods as exotic mustards, whose seeds were in high demand; shopkeepers, in fact, often advertised the two together. Chocolate was sold alongside other imported goods as well. Francis Daymon, on May 14, 1777, advertised in the *Pennsylvania Gazette* that he had many items available "JUST imported in the brig Little Julia." Apropos to this recipe, he listed one after the other "sweet almonds" and "sweeted chocolate."

In this recipe, almond paste complements semisweet chocolate to make a moist and delightfully sweet treat.

MAKES ONE 8-INCH LOAF

Preheat the oven to 350°F. Grease an 8½ x 4½ x 2½-inch loaf pan with butter.

Fill the bottom pan of a double boiler with water to ½ inch below the upper pan and place over low heat. (The water in the bottom of the double boiler should not come to a boil.) Place the chocolate in the upper pan and stir constantly until it is melted. Reserve.

In the bowl of an electric mixer fitted with the paddle attachment, beat the Almond Paste on medium speed until light and fluffy. Add the butter gradually and beat well until combined. Add the eggs and vanilla and beat well until combined. Add the flour and stir until just moistened.

Fold about one-third of the batter into the melted chocolate.

Pour the plain batter into the prepared pan. Spoon the chocolate batter over the top and gently swirl the batter to marbleize. Bake about 50 minutes, or until the loaf is firm on top and pulls away from the sides of the pan and a toothpick inserted in the center comes out clean.

Cool in the pan on a wire rack for 10 minutes. To remove the bread, flip the pan on its side and gently pull out the bread. Serve warm or cool completely on a wire rack.

Apple-Walnut Bread

—•—•—

Apples and walnuts were two foodstuffs that, stored properly, would have remained fresh over extended periods of time in the eighteenth century. In warm months, apples were kept in root cellars, while walnuts required cool, dry pantries or cupboards and were stored whole in burlap. The applesauce in this recipe recalls that prepared in colonial America as the base for rich fruit puddings, similarly flavored with aromatic spices. Applesauce not only lends a subtle sweetness to this bread but also helps to maintain a moist texture, which is nicely complemented by the walnuts.

MAKES TWO 8-INCH LOAVES

Preheat the oven to 350°F. Grease two 8½ x 4½ x 2½-inch loaf pans with butter.

In the bowl of an electric mixer fitted with the paddle attachment, beat together the sugar and shortening on medium speed until light and fluffy, scraping down the sides of the bowl often.

Add the eggs one at a time and beat until combined. Add the applesauce and beat until combined.

In a large bowl, stir together the flour, baking powder, baking soda, allspice, cinnamon, salt, nutmeg, and cloves. Fold the dry ingredients into the egg mixture in thirds, alternating with the milk. With a rubber spatula or wooden spoon, gently fold in the walnuts.

Divide the batter between the prepared pans. Bake about 1 hour or until a toothpick inserted in the center comes out clean.

Cool in the pans on a wire rack for 10 minutes. To remove the breads, flip the pans on their sides and gently pull out the bread. Serve warm or cool completely on a wire rack.

2 cups sugar

1 cup vegetable shortening

4 large eggs

3¼ cups unsweetened, natural-style applesauce

4 cups sifted all-purpose flour

2 teaspoons baking powder

2 teaspoons baking soda

1½ teaspoons ground allspice

1½ teaspoons ground cinnamon

1 teaspoon salt

½ teaspoon ground nutmeg

½ teaspoon ground cloves

½ cup whole milk

1½ cups chopped walnuts, lightly toasted (see Chef's Note, page 245)

Blueberry Muffins

$4\frac{3}{4}$ cups pastry flour

$\frac{3}{4}$ cup sugar

3 tablespoons baking powder

2 teaspoons salt

4 eggs

2 cups milk, at room temperature

12 tablespoons butter, melted

1 teaspoon vanilla

1 pint (2 cups) fresh blueberries

Blueberries were abundantly available to the colonists, who undoubtedly enjoyed them fresh, preserved, and in baked goods. Muffins were included in period cookbooks, especially those dating to the nineteenth century. Resembling English muffins, they were, however, quite different from the sweet little cakes that are so popular today. These light little breads were leavened with yeast and browned on a griddle either free form or in muffin rings, which held their shape.

MAKES 24 STANDARD MUFFINS

Preheat the oven to 400°F. Grease two 12-hole muffin tins with butter.

In a large mixing bowl, stir together the flour, sugar, baking powder and salt.

In a medium-size mixing bowl stir together the eggs, milk, butter and vanilla. Add to the flour mixture and stir until well combined. Gently fold in the blueberries.

Divide the batter among the prepared muffin cups. Bake for 20 minutes, or until golden brown and a toothpick inserted in the centers comes out clean.

Cool in the pans on a wire rack for 10 minutes. To remove the muffins, tilt the tins on their sides and gently pull out the muffins. Serve warm or cool completely on a wire rack.

Blueberries are among the only fruits native to North America. As early as 1616, Samuel de Champlain found the Indians in Lake Huron gathering blueberries for the winter. "After drying the berries in the sun," he wrote in his journal, "the Indians beat them into powder and added this powder to parched meal to make a dish called 'Sautauthig.'" The settlers incorporated blueberries into desserts and breads to satisfy their renowned sweet tooth.

Blueberries were a seasonal fruit prevalent in the heavily wooded outskirts of Philadelphia. No doubt enterprising hucksters sold freshly picked berries at market and directly to inns and restaurants like City Tavern during the summer months.

Buttermilk Scones

A traditional Scottish bread, scones were originally prepared with oats and cooked on a griddle. This version resembles the many variations of yeast-leavened biscuits that appeared in eighteenth-century cookbooks. Some of those yeasts not only helped the bread to rise but also contributed a pleasantly tart flavor to the finished product. In this recipe, that flavor, as well as a tender texture, is achieved through the addition of buttermilk, while the baking powder gives the biscuits a pleasant lightness.

MAKES ABOUT 1 DOZEN SCONES

Preheat the oven to 375°F.

In the bowl of an electric mixer fitted with the paddle attachment, beat together the butter and sugar on medium speed until light and fluffy, scraping down the sides of the bowl often. Add the egg yolks one at a time and beat well until combined.

In a large mixing bowl, stir together the cake flour, bread flour and baking powder. Fold the dry ingredients into the butter mixture in thirds, alternating with the buttermilk, until just combined. Do not overmix. With a rubber spatula or wooden spoon, gently fold in the raisins.

Turn the dough out onto a lightly-floured work surface and roll out to 1½ inches thick.

Cut out the scones with a floured 2-inch biscuit cutter and place 2 inches apart on ungreased baking sheets. Any leftover dough should be chilled for 30 minutes before rolling out again, to prevent overworking and toughening it.

Reduce the oven temperature to 350°F and bake for 30 to 40 minutes, or until golden brown.

Transfer the scones to a wire rack to cool for 10 to 15 minutes. Serve warm with Chantilly Cream or butter.

½ pound (2 sticks) unsalted butter, softened

¼ cup plus 2 tablespoons sugar

3 large egg yolks

2½ cups sifted cake flour

2½ cups sifted bread flour

2¼ tablespoons baking powder

1½ cups buttermilk

1 cup raisins

Chantilly Cream (page 375), for serving (optional)

Although most eighteenth-century biscuit recipes were leavened with yeast, some were simply prepared with flour, milk, and butter, creating a dense, hearty bread. Mary Randolph's recipe for "Cream Cakes" is one such example.

Melt as much butter in a pint of milk as will make it rich as cream, make the flour into a paste with this, knead it well, roll it out frequently, cut it in squares, and bake on a griddle.

Ginger-Raisin Scones

————— ❦ —————

Both ginger and raisins were commonly imported into urban centers like Philadelphia, where the demand for such exotic items was high. Not only were they incorporated into a variety of baked goods, but they were used to prepare specialty items as well. In her book *The Art of Cookery Made Plain and Easy*, for example, Hannah Glasse included recipes for "Ginger Tablets" (a sort of candied ginger) and "The best way to make Raisin Wine." Many eighteenth-century cookery books offered similar instruction, but if home cooks preferred, they could purchase ginger (fresh, preserved, powdered, or candied) as well as jars of raisins in local shops.

MAKES EIGHT 2-INCH SCONES

Preheat the oven to 375°F.

In a large mixing bowl, add the flour, brown sugar, baking powder, cinnamon, ginger, and cloves; stir to combine. Add the butter and mix to combine.

In a medium-size mixing bowl, combine the milk, molasses, egg, and vanilla. Add the egg mixture to the dry ingredients and stir until just moistened. With a rubber spatula or wooden spoon, gently fold in the raisins.

Turn the dough out onto a lightly-floured surface. Roll out the dough to 1 to 1½ inches thick. Cut out the scones with a 2-inch floured biscuit cutter and place 2 inches apart on an ungreased baking sheet. Any leftover dough should be chilled for 30 minutes before rolling out again, to prevent overworking and toughening it.

Reduce the oven temperature to 350°F and bake for 30 to 40 minutes, or until golden brown.

Transfer the scones to a wire rack to cool for 10 to 15 minutes. Serve warm with Chantilly Cream or butter.

2 cups all-purpose flour

⅓ cup packed dark brown sugar

1 tablespoon baking powder

¾ teaspoon ground cinnamon

½ teaspoon ground ginger

⅛ teaspoon ground cloves

6 tablespoons unsalted butter, softened

¼ cup whole milk

3 tablespoons dark molasses

1 large egg

1 teaspoon vanilla

⅔ cup raisins

Chantilly Cream (page 375), for serving (optional)

Yeast Breads

IF THERE IS ONE TYPE of item absent from many period cookery books, it is yeast bread. Eighteenth-century authors gave detailed instructions pertaining to numerous cakes, pies, tarts, and biscuits, many of which relied on leaveners, including yeast. Yet the preparation of bread appears to have been viewed as a baking skill separate from the others. Perhaps this is because in an urban center like Philadelphia bread was sold daily in many bakeries throughout the city. Home cooks could affordably purchase their family's bread while focusing on the preparation of other items that would have been more expensive to buy at local shops, including preserves, puddings, and pastries.

Advertisements from the *Pennsylvania Gazette* ultimately yield more information on bread baking than do period cookery books. Although many confectioners made and sold numerous varieties of baked goods, they specialized in cakes, pastry, and preserved fruits, rather than breads. Some bakeries that specialized in bread, however, also made cakes, although perhaps not as fine as those available in confectioners' shops. In October 1771, an advertisement read, "To Be Sold, Two Brick Houses, each two Stories high, with two Story Brick Kitchens, each House has an Oven, proper for the Baking of Loaf Bread and Cakes, and is very suitable for that Business, which has been carried on there for many Years."

Also telling is an advertisement placed in September 1767 by a woman seeking a position as "House keeper and LadyMaid." In it she listed her abilities, describing herself as "capable of setting off all Kinds of Meat Dishes, and Pastry, in the genteelist Manner; can preserve and pickle, and make any Kind of Collar Beef or Brawn; is well acquainted with all Sorts of Needlework, and can wash and do up any Sort of Lace or Gauze. She has lived in some of the best Families in London, and in this Country, in that Station." With all of this experience, the absence of her skill as a bread baker is striking. One can only assume that she failed to list this ability because it was unnecessary for her to know how to make bread. With the many bakeries in London and in Philadelphia, she could purchase her family's bread and focus on other culinary and domestic duties.

The breads included here vary from dense and substantial to delicate and sweet. They draw on the many varieties that were available in an eighteenth-century Philadelphia that welcomed European baking traditions and offered them opportunities to flourish.

Sally Lunn Bread

1 (¼-ounce package) active dry yeast

2 cups warm water (110° to 115°F)

½ cup sugar

4 tablespoons unsalted butter, softened

¼ cup whole milk

2 large eggs, lightly beaten

1 teaspoon salt

6½ cups all-purpose flour

This golden, rich bread is said to have been named for an eighteenth-century baker, Sally Lunn, of Bath, England, who sold buttery tea cakes to a wealthy clientele. Originally popular in the South, this bread eventually acquired a following in the mid-Atlantic and New England by the nineteenth century. Sally Lunns are traditionally baked as large, individual breads and served with clotted cream (a thick cream from Devonshire, England). This version, prepared in a single, large decorative mold, celebrates the bread's luxurious richness with a fanciful appearance. The slices may be served with clotted cream or, for a lighter but equally elegant accompaniment, with Chantilly Cream (page 375).

MAKES TWO BREADS

Grease 2 Bundt pans or two 7-cup tube molds with butter.

In the bowl of an electric mixer, whisk together the yeast and warm water. Let stand about 10 minutes, until foamy.

Fit the mixer with the dough hook attachment and beat in the sugar, butter, milk, eggs, and salt. Mix in the flour, 1 cup at a time, to make a soft dough. Turn the dough out onto a lightly-floured work surface and knead for 5 minutes, until smooth and elastic, adding only enough flour to prevent sticking.

Transfer the dough to a large bowl coated with vegetable oil and turn the dough to coat all surfaces. Cover with a slightly damp towel and let rise in a warm, draft-free place for 45 minutes to 1 hour, until doubled in size.

Stir the batter to deflate. Divide the dough between the prepared pans. Cover and let rise in a warm place for 40 to 45 minutes, until almost doubled in size.

Preheat the oven to 400°F.

Bake for 30 to 35 minutes, or until golden and the bread sounds hollow when tapped on the bottom.

Remove the bread from the pans. Serve warm or cooled and toasted.

Anadama Bread

This soft, comfortingly sweet, cornmeal-and-molasses bread has a colorful history. For years, New Englanders have passed down two stories that attempt to explain the meaning of this bread's unique name. Both revolve around a fishing village household. The first tells of a Gloucester, Massachusetts, fisherman, whose wife, Anna, prepared nothing for him to eat but a bowl of cornmeal and molasses. Desirous of something different to eat, one day he added yeast and flour to his daily gruel, in an attempt to create a tasteful bread. So frustrated was he in this endeavor that he grumbled, "Anna, damn her!"

A similar but more endearing story tells of a sea captain whose wife, Anna, was quite a good baker and renowned for her cornmeal and molasses bread. New England lore suggests that upon her death her gravestone read, "Anna was a lovely bride, but Anna, damn 'er, up and died."

MAKES 2 LOAVES

In the bowl of an electric mixer, whisk together the yeast and the warm water. Let stand about 10 minutes, until foamy.

Fit the mixer with the dough hook attachment and beat in the cornmeal, molasses, butter, and salt. Mix in the flour, 1 cup at a time, to make a moderately stiff dough.

Turn the dough out onto a lightly-floured surface and knead for 6 to 8 minutes, until smooth and elastic, adding only enough flour to prevent sticking.

Transfer the dough to a large bowl coated with vegetable oil and turn the dough to coat all surfaces. Cover with a slightly damp towel and let rise in a warm, draft-free place for 1 to 1½ hours, until doubled in size.

Punch the dough down. Turn out onto a lightly-floured work surface and divide it in half. Cover and let rest for 10 minutes.

Preheat the oven to 375°F. Grease a large baking pan with butter and sprinkle with cornmeal.

Shape each half of the dough into a ball. Place the balls, smooth sides up, on the prepared baking pans. Flatten each ball into a 6-inch round loaf. Cover and let rise for 30 to 45 minutes, until almost doubled in size.

Bake for 25 to 30 minutes, or until almost doubled in size.

Serve warm or cooled and toasted.

---

2 (¼-ounce) packages active dry yeast

2 cups warm water (110° to 115°F)

¾ cup coarse yellow cornmeal, plus extra for coating pan

½ cup dark molasses

6 tablespoons unsalted butter, softened

1 teaspoon salt

5½ cups bread flour

French Baguettes

SPONGE

1 teaspoon active dry yeast

2 cups water

1 cup plus 2 tablespoons bread flour

Pinch of cumin

BAGUETTE

4¾ cups bread flour

2 teaspoons salt

1 ¼-ounce package active dry yeast

2 cups plus 3 tablespoons
warm water

Baguettes—long, slim breads with crisp, golden crusts and tender interiors—not only epitomize the French bread-baking tradition but also represent French foodways as a whole. As French bakers opened shops in cities like Philadelphia, patrons, who were enamored with French fashion and culture, certainly must have quickly become aware of their great artistry and appreciated the high quality of their products. As for French visitors to America in the eighteenth century, many commented on how little bread Americans consumed and criticized the quality of breads they tasted in American cities. One visitor noted that although "[d]inner . . . is generally . . . composed of a great quantity of meat . . . [Americans] eat very little bread." Another visitor, named Beaujour, remarked, "In France each individual . . . consumes a pound of bread a day and a half a pound of meat . . . An American consumes hardly half a pound of bread, but on the other hand, at least a pound of meat." And yet another visitor, known as Du Bourg, explained that in American cities "they often substitute for bread little biscuits that are easily made and cooked in half an hour." According to historian Charles Sherrill, "Our bread was one of the few American products of which the French consistently vouchsafe no word of praise—for them it was always bad."

Regardless of what the French thought about the American breads that were heartily enjoyed in homes and public eateries like City Tavern, it is undeniable that skillfully prepared baguettes must have been as much appreciated in the eighteenth century as they continue to be today. Note, however, that because they are prepared without any fat, they go stale very quickly and are best consumed the day they are made.

Advance preparation required.

MAKES THREE 14-INCH LOAVES

PREPARE THE SPONGE: In a mixing bowl, add the yeast, water, bread flour, and cumin; stir to combine. Let stand at room temperature for 12 to 15 hours, covered, until the mixture has tripled in volume and begins to sag. *For this recipe, use only ½ cup.* The rest can be stored in the refrigerator for later use.

PREPARE THE BAGUETTE: In the bowl of an electric mixer fitted with the dough hook attachment, add the flour and salt and mix to combine on low speed.

In a separate bowl, whisk together the yeast and water. Whisk in the sponge *(only ½ cup)* a bit at a time. Add the mixture to the flour and mix on low speed for 4 minutes. Turn the dough out onto a floured surface and knead until smooth and elastic.

Transfer the dough to a large bowl coated with vegetable oil and turn the dough to coat all surfaces. In a cool place, allow the dough to double in volume, about 1 hour.

Punch the dough down. Cover and allow the dough to double in volume again, about 45 minutes.

Preheat the oven to 400°F.

Transfer the dough to a lightly-floured work surface and punch down. Divide the dough into 3 equal portions. Shape each portion into a round and cover with a damp cloth. Let the dough relax for 20 minutes.

Roll each round of dough into a 14-inch-long cylinder. Place the baguettes onto a parchment-coated and lightly-floured baking sheet or set them in a greased baguette pan. Allow each baguette to double in volume, about 45 minutes.

Bake the loaves for 20 minutes or until golden. Cool on wire racks for 45 minutes before serving.

CHEF'S NOTE

The extra "sponge" (leavener) can be stored for 2 to 3 days in the refrigerator, but you must "feed" it half of each quantity of water and bread flour six to eight hours before using, and then let it sit at room temperature.

Modern-day City Tavern staff swear there's a ghost in the restaurant—table settings are moved, dishes come crashing off the wall. Who knows? Maybe it's the nameless waiter murdered in the original City Tavern by Col. Craig on January 3, 1781, after a drunken brawl. The murderer was never prosecuted, some say because of the class differences that separated the two men.

Pastries

TTHE SKILLS ASSOCIATED with the preparation of pastry were much admired in the eighteenth century. Home cooks as well as professional bakers were familiar with many doughs and "pastes" and knew just which pastry was suitable for which dish. Not only do the following recipes feature elaborate "pastes" and the desserts made with them, but they are also based on other preparations, such as pâte à choux, meringue, and pancake and fritter doughs.

Although many of the eighteenth-century desserts prepared in Philadelphia reflected the influence of European traditions, pastries of the period seem to have particularly done so. The artistry of German and French *pâtisserie* was especially evidenced in Philadelphia pastry due to the strong cultural influence these groups maintained in the city. Additionally cookbooks published in America included numerous German and French pastry recipes. Fried breads, such as fritters and pancakes, were often associated with German traditions, while desserts based on meringue, puff pastry, and pâte à choux were most often based on time-honored French preparations. William Verral's *A Complete System of Cookery*, published in London in 1757, was virtually a treatise on French culinary arts, with each recipe printed in French and English. Similarly, Eliza Smith's *The Compleat Housewife*, published in 1758, offered readers a combination of English and French dishes. Despite her apparent dislike of French fashion, Smith acknowledged the importance of including French-inspired recipes:

> WHAT you will find in the following Sheets, are Directions generally for dressing after the best, most natural and wholesome Manner, such Provisions as are the Product of our own Country; and in such a Manner as is most agreeable to English Palates; saving that I have so far temporized, as, since we have, to our Disgrace, so fondly admired the French Tongue, French Modes, and also French Messes, to present you now and then with such Receipts of the French Cookery as I think may not be disagreeable to English Palates.

Pastry preparations often numbered in the dozens in eighteenth-century cookbooks. Eliza Leslie published a total of forty pastry recipes in her *Directions for Cookery, in Its Various Branches*. Versions of these often elegant and time-consuming dishes were available to most Philadelphians. It is clear that traditional, skillfully prepared pastries were appreciated and admired as much then as they are today.

Cream Puffs

⬦━━━━⬦

Cream puffs, luxurious combinations of delicate pastry and rich cream filling, are another type of confection that combines British and French baking traditions. It is difficult to say where pastry cream first developed, although it seems to have roots in English pudding and custard preparation. *Pâte à choux*, however, also called "choux paste" and "cream-puff pastry," appears to derive from French pastry traditions. It translates as "cabbage paste," perhaps because as the dough rises in the oven it resembles little cabbages.

MAKES 20 CREAM PUFFS

Preheat the oven to 450°F. Line a 17 x 11-inch baking sheet with parchment paper. Fit a pastry bag with a #16 straight tip.

Prepare the pâte à choux: Sift the flour into a large mixing bowl three times.

In a medium, heavy-bottomed saucepan, combine the milk, butter, sugar, salt, and nutmeg, and bring to a boil. Whisk the mixture for a few seconds. Remove the pot from the heat and stir in the flour with a sturdy wooden spoon. Return the pot to high heat and cook the mixture, stirring constantly, until the mixture pulls away from the sides of the pan and is satiny in appearance, 2 to 3 minutes.

Immediately transfer the dough to the bowl of an electric mixer fitted with the paddle attachment and beat on low speed until the bowl is cool. With the mixer running on medium speed, add 4 of the eggs, one at a time, making sure each egg is incorporated completely before adding the next. Turn the mixer off and run your index finger through the batter. The batter should be wet, but your finger should leave a trail that will pull back on itself to half its original width. (This recipe is subject to variation due to weather changes and the flour's absorbency properties. If the batter is too dry, add the remaining egg and yolk.)

To prepare the pastries, fill the pastry bag one quarter full with the batter, leaving enough room to close and twist the top of the bag. With the bag held at a 75-degree angle 1 inch above the prepared baking sheet, pipe rounds 1 inch wide by ¼ inch high. Allow the batter to fall on top of itself. Applying even pressure to the bag, a quick count to two will leave the right size. When the desired size is achieved, stop applying pressure and quickly pull up and away to the right.

PÂTE À CHOUX

½ cup plus 2½ tablespoons bread flour

1 cup whole milk

¼ pound (1 stick)
unsalted butter, softened

1 tablespoon sugar

¼ teaspoon salt

Pinch of nutmeg

4 large eggs

1 large egg + 1 large egg yolk, if necessary

6 cups Pastry Cream (page 375)

CHOCOLATE SAUCE

1 cup whole milk

8 ounces semisweet chocolate,
finely chopped

4 tablespoons unsalted butter, softened

1 cup heavy cream

━━━━ *(continued)* ━━━━

Transfer the baking sheet to the oven and immediately reduce the temperature to 375°F. Bake until golden brown and puffed, about 15 minutes. Lower the heat to 300°F and bake for 5 to 10 minutes more, until dry and light. The cream puffs will sound hollow when tapped on their bases. Remove the pan from the oven and cool on wire racks.

Prepare the chocolate sauce: In a medium-size saucepan, bring the milk to a boil over low heat, stirring to avoid scorching the bottom. Remove from the heat, add the chocolate and stir until melted completely.

Add the butter and cream, stir to combine, and cool to room temperature.

Using a paring knife, poke a small hole in the sides of each cream puff. Fit a pastry bag with a #10 straight tip and fill the bag a third of the way with Pastry Cream, leaving enough room to close and twist the top of the bag.

Insert the tip of the pastry bag just inside the Cream Puff. Fill the puff with cream by applying steady pressure. When the puff feels heavy and full, stop applying pressure and remove the tip from the puff, pulling quickly down and away from it.

Dip the top of each cream puff in the Chocolate Sauce and reserve. Repeat with remaining puffs.

Although few eighteenth-century English cookbooks included pâte à choux dough, one influential text did so: William Verral's *A Complete System of Cookery*, published in London in 1757. Eighteenth-century Philadelphians almost assuredly had access to Verral's work and therefore would have been exposed to his French recipes, including that entitled "French paste"—undoubtedly pâte à choux. The author suggested filling the pastry with cherry conserve, much in the manner in which cream puffs are filled with pastry cream. The recipe reads:

[Y]our paste make as follows; take half a pint of water, put to it a morsel of fine sugar, a grain of salt and a bit of lemon-peel, an ounce of butter, and boil it a minute or two, take it from your fire, and work in as much fine flour as it takes to a tender paste, put one egg at a time and mould it well till it comes to such a consistence as to pour with the help of a spoon out of the stewpan upon a tin or cover, covered with flour; scrape it off in lumps upon tin with the handle of a large key, and bake them of a nice colour and crispness, cut a hole in the bottom, and fill up with your conserve, sift some sugar over, and dish up. If you make this paste according to the rule before you, it will swell very large and hollow, and makes a genteel "entremets."

Vol-au-Vent
with Berries

This dessert was inspired by the fruit-filled puff pastry pies and tarts of the eighteenth century. In fact, vol-au-vents are said to have first been prepared by the esteemed gastronome and chef Marie Antoine Carême (1784–1833), who cooked for such renowned patrons as Talleyrand, Czar Alexander I, George IV, and Baron Rothschild. If this attribution is to be believed, then it would appear that Carême himself elaborated on the late-eighteenth- and early-nineteenth-century English and French dishes that combined puff pastry with a variety of fillings.

Vol-au-vents are puff pastry shells traditionally filled with creamy, savory combinations of meat and/or vegetables and topped with puff pastry lids. They may be prepared as individual servings or in larger sizes suitable for a table of guests. In modern times, it has become popular to serve these shells for dessert as well, filled with fresh or cooked fruit and whipped cream or crème anglaise. Once the puff pastry is prepared, this dish comes together quickly and elegantly completes any menu.

SERVES 6

Line a 17 x 11-inch baking pan with parchment paper.

Roll out 1 sheet of Puff Pastry to a ⅛-inch thickness. Prick the pastry all over using a fork. Using a 4-inch biscuit cutter, cut the pastry into 6 rounds (Illustration #1). Alternatively, use a 4-inch diameter bowl and cut the pastry with a paring knife. Set these rounds aside; they will be the bases of your vol-au-vents.

Roll out another sheet of Puff Pastry to ½-inch thickness and, using the same 4-inch template, cut 6 more rounds. Take a 3-inch biscuit cutter, or an alternative template, and cut the center from these ½-inch-thick rounds to make rings (Illustration #2).

(continued)

3 pounds Puff Pastry (page 373), or purchased puff pastry sheets

3 large eggs, beaten with 1 tablespoon water and pinch of salt, for egg wash

1 pound semisweet chocolate

FILLING

1 quart heavy cream

½ cup confectioners' sugar, plus extra for dusting

1 tablespoon vanilla

3 tablespoons orange liqueur (such as Triple Sec or Cointreau)

1 pint each raspberries, blackberries, blueberries, and strawberries, cut in half and stems removed

1½ cups Crème Anglaise (page 376)

Fresh mint sprigs, for garnish

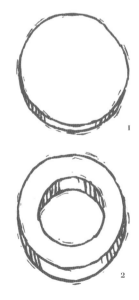

Brush the ⅛-inch-thick bases with the egg wash. Set the ½-inch-thick Puff Pastry rings precisely atop the bases, making certain the edges are aligned (Illustration #3). Brush the vol-au-vents with the egg wash and refrigerate for 30 minutes (Illustration #4).

Preheat the oven to 425°F.

Using a paring knife, make shallow incisions, ¼ inch apart, around the perimeter of each vol-au-vent (Illustration #5). Brush each base with egg wash again.

Place the pastries on the prepared baking sheet. Transfer to the oven and bake for 20 minutes, or until golden. Remove from the oven and allow to cool.

Fill the bottom pan of a double boiler with water to ½ inch below the upper pan and place over low heat. (The water in the bottom of the double boiler should not come to a boil.) Place the chocolate in the upper pan, and stir constantly until it is melted. Remove the melted chocolate from the heat and let cool for a minute. When cool enough to touch, using a pastry brush, paint the inside of the cool vol-au-vents with the melted chocolate.

PREPARE THE FILLING: In an electric mixer fitted with the whip attachment, whip the cream and confectioners' sugar on medium to high speed to form medium peaks. Add the vanilla and orange liqueur and whip to stiff peaks.

Using a large spoon, fill each vol-au-vent with the whipped cream. Top with the berries and serve with Crème Anglaise. Dust with confectioners' sugar and garnish with a fresh mint sprig.

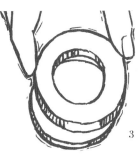

3

4

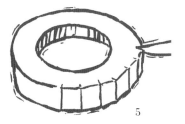

5

Apple & Golden Raisin Turnovers

— · — · —

4 Gala or Granny Smith apples,
peeled and cored

½ lemon, juiced

1 cup golden raisins

4 tablespoons unsalted butter

2 tablespoons honey

2 teaspoons vanilla

1 cup plus 2 tablespoons sugar

¼ cup all-purpose flour

1 tablespoon ground cinnamon

⅛ teaspoon ground nutmeg

3 pounds Puff Pastry (page 373),
or purchased puff pastry sheets

½ cup apple butter

3 large eggs, beaten with 1 tablespoon
water and pinch of salt, for egg wash

½ cup light brown sugar

Pinch of ground cardamom

Based on eighteenth-century fruit and/or cream-filled pies and tarts, turnovers are simply rounds of pastry spread with filling, folded in half, crimped at the edges, and baked. Stuffed with meat and vegetables as well as fruit, these pastries were originally prepared in Europe as complete meals that were consumed conveniently without flatware or plates. Today, turnovers are considered elegant, individual pastries that may be served in place of slices of pies or tarts. The following fillings—prepared with dried and fresh fruits, nuts, spices, and cheese—were inspired by eighteenth-century preserves as well as by pie and tart fillings.

SERVES 6

Line a baking sheet with parchment paper.

Chop the apples into 1-inch cubes and put them in a medium-size bowl. Add the lemon juice and raisins and toss to combine.

In a small saucepan, melt the butter. Remove from the heat and whisk in the honey and vanilla. Pour this mixture over the apples and raisins and toss to combine.

In a separate bowl, whisk together the sugar, flour, cinnamon, and nutmeg. Add this mixture to the apples and stir to combine.

Lightly dust a work surface with flour. With a lightly-floured rolling pin, roll out the Puff Pastry to a ¼-inch thickness. Trim the dough so that you have a 12 x 18-inch rectangle. Cut the sheet of pastry in half lengthwise, then cut each half into thirds.

Place 1 heaping tablespoon of apple butter in the center of each square. Divide the apple mixture evenly among each square and center it. Lightly brush egg wash on the pastry around the filling. Fold the top left corner of the pastry over to the bottom right corner of the pastry, making a triangle-shaped pastry. Seal the edges with a fork. Repeat the process until you have 6 turnovers.

Place the turnovers on the prepared baking sheet. Make three ½-inch incisions on the top of each turnover. Brush the turnovers with egg wash and chill for 30 minutes.

Preheat the oven to 350°F. Brush the turnovers with the egg wash again and sprinkle with the brown sugar and cardamom. Bake the turnovers for 20 minutes, or until golden brown. Serve warm.

Apple Strudel

———•———

Strudel arrived in Philadelphia with the Germans. As the following recipes reveal, the delicate dough may be filled with a variety of fruits, nuts, and creams. Like many other desserts of its type, strudel reflects the mergence of European and American cultures. The golden crust of this pastry is testament to the artistry of German and northern European baking traditions. The sweet fillings, however—prepared with such items as apples, cranberries, cherries, raspberries, peaches, apricots, gooseberries, pears, raisins, citrus, and spices—pay tribute to the rich variety of ingredients available in late-eighteenth-century Philadelphia.

SERVES 10 TO 12

DOUGH

½ pound (2 sticks) unsalted butter, melted and cooled

3 large egg yolks

2 tablespoons white vinegar

½ teaspoon salt

½ cup water

1¼ cups high-gluten flour
4 cups plain, unflavored bread crumbs

FILLING

5 Gala or Granny Smith apples, peeled and cored

1 cup fresh cranberries

½ cup golden raisins

½ cup plus 2 tablespoons sugar

3 tablespoons cake flour

2 teaspoons ground cinnamon

Pinch of ground nutmeg

1 tablespoon cornstarch

3 large eggs, beaten with 1 tablespoon water and pinch of salt, for egg wash

Confectioners' sugar, for dusting

Ice cream, for serving

PREPARE THE DOUGH: In the bowl of an electric mixer fitted with the dough hook attachment, combine 4 tablespoons of the butter, the egg yolks, vinegar, and salt on medium speed. Add the flour and mix on low speed until the ingredients come together. Increase the mixer speed to medium and mix until the dough pulls away from and slaps against the sides of the bowl, about 8 minutes. When the dough is fully and properly developed, it will stretch 3 to 4 inches above the bowl when pulled, without breaking.

Coat a large bowl with cooking spray. Transfer the dough to the bowl. Spray the dough lightly with cooking spray, and place a piece of plastic wrap directly atop the dough. Make certain no part of the dough is exposed to the air. Let the dough relax in a warm, draft-free place for at least 1 hour.

PREPARE THE FILLING: Cut the apples into 2-inch cubes. In a medium-size bowl, toss together the apples, cranberries, and raisins.

In a separate bowl, stir together the sugar, flour, cinnamon, nutmeg, and cornstarch. Add the sugar mixture to the fruit mixture and toss to combine. Set the mixture aside at room temperature.

Preheat the oven to 425°F. Line a baking sheet with parchment paper.

You'll need a 3 x 4-foot working surface. Cover the entire surface with a large, clean linen. Make certain that the table and linen are clean. Lightly dust the linen with flour. Unwrap and place the strudel dough on the center of the linen-covered surface. Dust the dough with flour. Roll the strudel dough out so that it covers three-quarters of the surface. The dough will measure 3 feet 4 inches by 3 feet 2 inches.

Lightly flour the backs of your hands. Place your hands, palm down, under the dough and, working from the center outward, stretch the dough to the length of the table. Stretch the dough until it is transparent and overhangs the table by about 2 inches.

Working lengthwise, brush two thirds of the dough with the remaining melted butter. Cover the remaining third of the dough with bread crumbs (Illustration #1).

Place the filling atop the crumbs in an even, concise strip (Illustration #2), about 3 inches wide and 2 inches high. Lift the overhanging dough and cover the filling (Illustration #3).

Begin to roll the dough by lifting the linen and allowing the dough to fall over itself (Illustration #4). Continue lifting and folding the dough until no excess remains and you have a long tube of dough. Fold the ends under to seal (Illustration #5).

Transfer the strudel to the prepared baking sheet. Brush the strudel with the egg wash and prick it all over with a fork (Illustration #6). Bake for 20 minutes, or until golden brown.

Allow the strudel to cool before slicing. Dust with confectioners' sugar and serve warm, with ice cream.

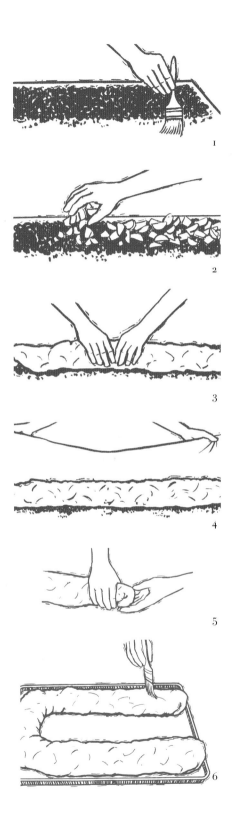

Apple Cakes

◆—◆≡◆—◆

This dish marries the traditions of two preparations: pancakes and what were commonly called "German fritters." American and European cooks of the eighteenth century commonly prepared pancakes of all kinds based on a variety of grains and flavorings. German fritters seem to have generally been prepared with a light batter or simply flour, as well as apples cooked in liquor (often brandy), sugar, butter or lard, and spices. Both of these dishes have significant roots in northern European cooking traditions and were popular in Philadelphia due to the city's large German population. Flavored with nutmeg, cinnamon, apples, and rum, these pancakes pay tribute to the influences of German foodways on English cooking in Philadelphia.

Be sure to make the pancake batter at least 1 hour before cooking the pancakes.

Advance preparation required.

MAKES 1 DOZEN PANCAKES

PREPARE THE BATTER: In a large mixing bowl, stir together the flour, sugar, baking powder, salt, and nutmeg, and slowly pour in the milk, whisking until smooth.

Whisk in the eggs and the egg yolks one at a time, add the rum and set the batter aside to refrigerate for at least 1 hour.

TO ASSEMBLE THE PANCAKES: In a small bowl, toss together the sugar, cinnamon, and nutmeg. Heat a 6-inch omelet or crêpe pan over medium heat, coat it lightly with vegetable spray, and add 1 tablespoon of the melted butter, moving the pan around to coat the bottom.

Add a scant handful of apples and about 2 heaping tablespoons of walnuts. Sprinkle with about 1 heaping tablespoon of the spiced sugar and sauté, stirring until the apples are tender but still firm, about 1 minute.

Using a 3-ounce ladle, pour the pancake batter into the center of the hot pan, tilting the pan to spread the batter evenly. Increase the heat to medium high and cook the pancake until bubbles begin to form, about 45 seconds.

Loosen the edges of the pancake with a spatula, flip it, and lightly brown the second side, about 45 seconds more. Remove the pancake to a plate to keep warm and repeat the assembly process to make about 12 pancakes.

Serve the pancakes with Chantilly Cream and a sprinkling of cinnamon.

BATTER

1⅓ cups all-purpose flour

2 tablespoons sugar

1 teaspoon baking powder

½ teaspoon salt

⅛ teaspoon freshly grated nutmeg

1 cup whole milk

6 large eggs

6 large egg yolks

3 tablespoons light rum

ASSEMBLY

1 cup sugar

½ teaspoon ground cinnamon

⅛ teaspoon freshly grated nutmeg

12 tablespoons (1½ sticks)
unsalted butter, melted

4 apples, peeled, cored,
and cut into thin slices

2 cups walnuts, roughly chopped

Chantilly Cream (page 375), for serving

Ground cinnamon, for garnish

Ice Cream & Sorbet

ICE CREAM AND SORBET, so common today as to be almost ordinary, were among the most celebrated of eighteenth-century confections. By the late 1700s, frozen creams and flavored ices had already been enjoyed for centuries, their beginnings dating back to the ancient world. It was in England and France, however, that these desserts gained their popularity, as the aristocracy enjoyed them served in elegant glasses or elaborate molds.

Perhaps the panache associated with ice cream and sorbet (prepared with fruit or liquor and without milk) during the period can be partially attributed to the arduousness of their preparations. Cooks employed several methods, all of which were time-consuming. Some recipes advocated placing the mixture to be frozen in a tin set in a larger container of ice and salt. It was to be stirred occasionally until uniformly frozen. Then, if desired, the ice cream or sorbet was placed into a mold and set again in the ice and salt until firm, which, according to period recipes, required about four hours. For those who owned them, *sorbetières*, or ice pails, offered another method of preparing the dessert. The concept of freezing the mixture in salt and ice remained the same but, rather than using generic kitchen tins, this tool—a covered pail that was placed in a larger pail—was designed especially for preparing frozen desserts.

By the mid-eighteenth century, confectioners' shops in England and France were regularly serving ice cream and flavored ices. Colonists continued to satisfy their desire for the dessert in Philadelphia, and by the third quarter of the eighteenth century, the city could boast not only about the number of establishments that offered ice cream but about the particularly rich product they sold as well. Frozen desserts were available in specialty shops, like that of Victor Collet on North Front Street, who sold *glaces* (ice creams) and *fromages glacés* (iced cheeses), as well as in larger confectioners' shops.

Describing Martha Washington's parties at Richmond Hill, New York, in July 1790, Abigail Adams wrote to her elder sister, Mary Cranch, that "She gives Tea, Coffe, Cake, Lemonade & Ice Creams in summer."

Chocolate Ice Cream

As are all of City Tavern's ice creams, this version is a variation of the basic French recipe so admired by Thomas Jefferson. The addition of chocolate pays tribute to the popularity of the confection in eighteenth-century Philadelphia.

Advance preparation required.

MAKES 1 QUART

3 cups whole milk

6 tablespoons sugar

8 ounces finely chopped semisweet chocolate

9 large egg yolks

Prepare an ice bath in a large bowl.

In a medium-size saucepan, stir together the milk and sugar; stir to combine and bring to a boil over low heat.

Fill the bottom pan of a double boiler with water to ½ inch below the upper pan and place over low heat. (The water in the bottom of the double boiler should not come to a boil.) Place the chocolate in the upper pan and stir constantly until it is melted. Remove the melted chocolate from the heat and let cool for a minute.

Meanwhile, in a medium-size bowl, whisk the egg yolks.

Temper the yolks by adding ¼ cup at a time of the hot milk, whisking constantly. When all of the milk has been added, return the custard to the saucepan, and cook, stirring constantly over low heat until the mixture thickens and reaches a temperature of 185°F on a candy thermometer. Immediately stir in the chocolate and whisk until completely incorporated.

Strain the mixture back into the medium-size bowl and set the bowl in the ice bath. Once the mixture has cooled, place the mixture in the refrigerator for at least 1 hour or overnight.

Add the cream to an ice cream machine and churn and freeze according to the manufacturer's instructions.

Although Philadelphia was already recognized for its rich ice cream prepared simply with milk or cream, sugar, and flavorings, French-style ice cream, introduced into the country by Thomas Jefferson, quickly gained popularity. Rich and flavorful due to the addition of egg yolks, it was undoubtedly offered by the city's numerous confectioners, much to the pleasure of their patrons. Philadelphian Jane Janvier, who prepared her own French-style ice cream, felt strongly that it was more flavorful than the traditional Philadelphia variety, writing, "It is very poor without any eggs."

French Vanilla Ice Cream

1 vanilla bean

2 cups whole milk

½ cup sugar

1 tablespoon honey

6 large egg yolks

Throughout most of the eighteenth century, ice cream made in Philadelphia and elsewhere in the colonies was prepared with various combinations of sugar, milk and/or cream, and flavorings. Thomas Jefferson was to change this. During his stay in Paris in the mid-1780s, Jefferson appears to have been introduced to ice cream prepared with egg yolks, and it is this rich, silky dessert, which was pale yellow due to the yolks, that Americans came to know as French Vanilla Ice Cream. The following recipe, perfumed with vanilla and sweetened not only with sugar but with honey, is a flavorful variation of Jefferson's own recipe.

Advance preparation required.

MAKES 1 QUART

Prepare an ice bath in a large bowl.

With a paring knife, cut the vanilla bean in half lengthwise and scrape out the seeds with the back of the knife.

In a medium-size saucepan, stir together the vanilla seeds, pod, milk, and sugar and bring the mixture to a boil over low heat. Remove the vanilla pod.

In a medium-size bowl, whisk together the honey and egg yolks.

Temper the egg yolk mixture by adding ¼ cup at a time of the hot milk to the yolks, whisking constantly. When all of the milk has been added, return the custard to the saucepan and cook, stirring constantly, over low heat until the mixture thickens and reaches a temperature of 185°F on a candy thermometer.

Strain the mixture back into the medium-size bowl and set the bowl in the ice bath. Once the mixture has cooled, place the mixture in the refrigerator for at least 1 hour or overnight.

Add the cream to an ice cream machine and churn and freeze according to the manufacturer's instructions.

Raspberry Sorbet

—◦•∗◦—

Eighteenth-century cooks looked for creative ways to use the abundance of fruit picked from summer gardens. The most beautiful raspberries were most likely preserved or eaten fresh and whole, while bruised berries were mashed and used for jams and, perhaps, frozen desserts. This sorbet's vibrant flavor relies on the freshest of ripe berries or the best quality purée available.

Advance preparation required.

MAKES 1 QUART

In a medium-size saucepan, stir together ¾ cup water, the sugar, and lemon juice. Brush the sides of the pan with a pastry brush dipped in cool water, making certain no granules of sugar remain.

With a paring knife, cut the vanilla bean in half lengthwise and scrape out the seeds with the back of the knife. Add the vanilla seeds and pod to the pan and bring the syrup to a boil.

Remove the pan from the heat, add the raspberry purée and stir to combine. Transfer to a bowl and refrigerate for at least 2 hours.

Remove the vanilla pod. Add the sorbet base to an ice cream machine, and churn according to the manufacturer's instructions. Using a rubber spatula, fold in the lemon zest and freeze again.

1 cup sugar

1 lemon, zest grated and juiced

1 vanilla bean

2 cups purchased raspberry purée,
or substitute frozen raspberries, thawed,
puréed, and strained

Sweetmeats

THE TERM "SWEETMEATS" can be quite confusing to present-day students of food history. In some contexts, the term is limited to fruit cooked and preserved in sugar, while in others it expands to include not only these dishes but a variety of baked goods as well. Like many terms, this one, too, has changed over time. Throughout the eighteenth century, "sweetmeats" referred broadly to cakes, biscuits, cookies, nut pastes, chocolates, and candied items such as fruit, seeds, flowers, and nuts (also known as "comfits"), as well as a variety of dishes based on large quantities of sugar and fruit, including jellies, marmalades, jams, preserved fruit (also known as "sucket"), and poached fruit. Martha Washington, for example, listed over 200 sweetmeat recipes in her cookery book. By the nineteenth century, however, the term was limited primarily to fruit cooked and preserved in sugar. In contrast to Washington's manuscript, Eliza Leslie's 1828 edition of *Seventy-Five Receipts, for Pastry, Cakes, and Sweetmeats* includes only sixteen sweetmeats, all of which are preserves, jams, or jellies.

It is the broad definition of sweetmeats that is apropos to the history of City Tavern and the special, sweet dishes that were available in eighteenth-century Philadelphia. So broad is this term, that it could refer to nearly all of the dessert recipes in this book. This chapter, therefore, focuses on those sweetmeats that functioned as colorful additions to the cakes, pies, and pastries that appeared on the eighteenth-century dining table. Today they are known as *petits fours* or *mignardises* and include such items as nut pastes, chocolates, jellies, and candied fruits and nuts.

Over the years, the panache associated with sweetmeats has waned. Items such as candied nuts, chocolate bars, and jam have become so readily available as to be ordinary and even lackluster. Eighteenth-century sweetmeats, however, were some of the most celebrated and elegant items one encountered at the dining table. The following recipes are just some of those that might have been enjoyed in wealthy Philadelphia homes as well as in elegant public eateries like City Tavern.

Young Philadelphian Nancy Shippen often mentioned sweetmeat preparation in her journal. In 1783, she noted: "I passed a most agreeable even'ing—though a large company—which is seldom the case—a most admirable supper—excellent wine an elegant desert of preserv'd fruits & every body in spirits & good humor.—It is now late & I am sleepy." In late summer 1784, she wrote: "I spent the day at home very busy making sweet-meets for the winter." And again on Monday, September 13, 1784, she commented: "This day employ'd as usual in domestic affairs, preserving peaches &c."

Marzipan

By the late eighteenth century, the European tradition of preparing marzipan was already more than three hundred years old. First appearing in fifteenth-century English texts as "march payne" and later as "marchpane," this sweetmeat was so influenced by Germany and Austria that it adopted the northern European spelling and pronunciation, marzipan.

Prepared with almonds, sugar, and rose or orange water, marzipan was one of the most costly confections available in Europe. Although it had been highly prized in England for centuries, the paucity of recipes in American cookery books suggests that its popularity waned in the colonies and that, for those who did desire it, marzipan was mostly available in confectioners' shops.

Two significant texts did include "March-pane" or "Marchpane" recipes, however: Eliza Smith's *The Compleat Housewife* and Martha Washington's cookbook. Washington listed no less than five recipes. Like Smith, she called for shaping the marzipan and then icing and baking it. These last two steps—essentially sugaring and drying—are usually omitted in modern versions and most likely helped to preserve the sweetmeat.

Marzipan was primarily a confection of the wealthy. Not only were the ingredients expensive, but the colorful, fanciful shapes detailed in these recipes reveal that they were also primarily "conceits"—whimsical, elegant sweetmeats that were meant as much to please the eye as the palate. Shining with gold leaf, sparkling with sugar, and decorated with dried fruit, marzipan was probably most enjoyed at dining tables filled with exotic foodstuffs, elaborate sugar figures, and fine wines.

1⅓ cups Almond Paste (page 246), or 14 ounces purchased almond paste

5 tablespoons corn syrup

2 cups confectioners' sugar

3 tablespoons flavored liqueur of your choice (for example, use applejack brandy to make marzipan apples)

¼ cup warm water

3 drops food coloring of your choice (for example, red for making marzipan apples)

MAKES 1½ POUNDS, OR ABOUT 20 PIECES

In the bowl of an electric mixer fitted with the paddle attachment, beat together the Almond Paste and corn syrup on medium speed.

Sift the confectioners' sugar. With the mixer running on low speed, add the sugar in three intervals, incorporating each addition before adding the next. Mix the marzipan until it is smooth. It will be stiff but malleable, about the consistency of Silly Putty. Remove the marzipan from the bowl and knead in the liqueur by hand, 1 tablespoon at a time.

You may shape the marzipan into whatever shape you desire, such as apples, and let them dry on a plate for 1 hour. Stir together the water and food coloring and paint the sides of the marzipan with a small pastry brush. To store, place the marzipan in a plastic storage container, lay plastic wrap directly on top of the marzipan, and cover with a tight-fitting lid.

Chocolate Truffles

———◆———

24 ounces bittersweet
(not unsweetened) chocolate, chopped

4 tablespoons unsalted butter,
cut into pieces

¼ cup heavy cream

1 tablespoon instant espresso powder,
dissolved in 1 tablespoon boiling water

2 tablespoons sambuca
or other flavored liqueur

1 cup unsweetened cocoa powder,
for coating

Although the enthusiasm for some sweet dishes has waxed and waned over the centuries, the desire for chocolate has only strengthened since the eighteenth century. In American homes and confectioners' shops of the mid- to late-1700s, chocolate was most often served as a hot, creamy beverage, sometimes flavored with spices in the South American fashion. It appears, however, that many forms of chocolate were available in the cosmopolitan center that was late-eighteenth-century Philadelphia. Confectioners and chocolatiers opened shops throughout the city, meeting the demands of a stylish public that had grown so fond of this ancient sweet. Surely, chocolate truffles similar to the following version satisfied the cravings of numerous Philadelphians.

MAKES 2 DOZEN TRUFFLES

Fill the bottom pan of a double boiler with water to ½ inch below the upper pan and place over low heat. (The water in the bottom of the double boiler should not come to a boil.) Place 12 ounces of the chocolate, the butter, cream, and espresso in the upper pan and stir constantly until the chocolate is melted and the mixture is smooth.

Remove the upper pan of the double boiler and stir in the liqueur. Transfer to a separate mixing bowl, cool, then refrigerate, covered, for at least 3 hours, or until firm.

Clean the upper pan of the double boiler and place back on the bottom pan. To temper the remaining 12 ounces of chocolate, place 8 ounces of the chocolate in the upper pan, stirring often until melted. Heat the melted chocolate, stirring slowly and constantly until it reaches a temperature of 115°F on a candy thermometer.

Remove the upper pan of the double boiler and add the remaining 4 ounces of chocolate, stirring constantly until the chocolate has melted and it cools to 80°F. Return the upper pan to the bottom pan and heat until it reaches a temperature of 89°F. Remove from the heat and cool slightly, until cool enough to handle.

Remove the chilled chocolate mixture from the refrigerator. With a small ice cream scoop or tablespoon, scoop out walnut-sized portions. Roll each portion into a round ball.

Place the cocoa powder on a large plate.

Pour about 1 tablespoon of the melted chocolate in your hand. Take one of the walnut-sized portions of chilled chocolate and roll it in your hand to thoroughly coat it in the melted chocolate.

Drop the truffles in the cocoa powder and coat, shaking off any excess. Set on a parchment-lined baking pan and let stand in a cool place. Repeat the process until all of the chilled chocolate has been used. (You may have some tempered chocolate left over. It can be stored in the refrigerator, tightly covered, for up to 2 weeks. You can drizzle it on serving plates for another dessert or use it as a topping for ice cream.)

Store the truffles in an airtight container in the refrigerator for up to 2 weeks.

Chocolate was one of Thomas Jefferson's culinary passions. He cultivated his love of the treat while he was in Europe, where chocolate houses had become fashionable as early as 1657. As stated in *Chocolate: An Illustrated History*, Jefferson had predicted in the late 1750s that "the superiority of chocolate, both for health and nourishment, will soon give it the same preference over tea and coffee in America which it has in Spain."

Stuffed Dates

⬥⬥⬥⬥⬥

18 Medjool dates

1½ pounds Marzipan (page 338; use kirschwasser liqueur)

This sweetmeat was inspired by the numerous dried fruits prepared in eighteenth-century home kitchens and available in shops. Sweet, dried dates, delicious and exotic on their own, become even more special when enhanced by the almond flavor of marzipan. Such elegant sweetmeats would have been served on dinner tables and as part of festive dessert displays during tea parties in eighteenth-century Philadelphia.

MAKES 18 PIECES

Slice each date in half lengthwise.

Roll the Marzipan into one long ½-inch log. Cut the log into 2-inch portions, or to the length of each date. Fill each date with marzipan segments and serve. Prepare the stuffed dates no more than 2 to 3 hours before serving and keep at room temperature.

Rum Balls

These small but rich confections bring together some of the most prized flavors in eighteenth-century Philadelphia: chocolate, rum, almonds, and sugar. Given the cost of these ingredients in the period, these rum balls certainly would have been costly. Yet, as with many sweetmeats, they take advantage of items that would have been stocked in eighteenth-century confectioners' shops and probably some wealthy households. Additionally, in keeping with the frugality of the period, chocolate cake that might have been a few days old was (and still is) easily converted into cake crumbs and used in this sort of recipe.

MAKES 20 PIECES

Finely grind the almonds with the confectioners' sugar in a food processor.

In a large bowl, toss together the cake crumbs and almond mixture. Add the Simple Syrup and rum and mix the ingredients with your hands until they clump together. Shape the mixture into 1½-inch balls and arrange the rum balls, spaced 1 inch apart, on a wire screen set atop a baking sheet.

Fill the bottom pan of a double boiler with water to ½ inch below the upper pan and place over low heat. (The water in the bottom of the double boiler should not come to a boil.) Place 1½ pounds of the chocolate in the upper pan and stir constantly until the chocolate is melted and reaches a temperature of 115°F on a candy thermometer.

Remove the chocolate from the heat and add the remaining chocolate. Stir slowly and constantly until the added chocolate has melted and the mixture cools to 80°F. Return the chocolate to the simmering water and heat until it reaches a temperature of 89°F.

Pour the chocolate over the rum balls in one steady sweeping motion. Try to coat each ball completely and evenly. Once all the rum balls have been coated, tap the tray gently against the table a few times to settle the chocolate. Allow the rum balls to cool at room temperature until set. Store in an airtight container in the refrigerator for up to 1 week.

3 cups sliced almonds, toasted
(see Chef's Note, page 245)

½ cup confectioners' sugar

10 cups chocolate cake crumbs

2 cups Simple Syrup
(see Chef's Note)

½ cup dark rum

2 pounds semisweet chocolate,
chopped

CHEF'S NOTE

To prepare Simple Syrup: In a medium-size saucepan, combine 1 cup water and 1 cup sugar. Bring just to a boil, stirring occasionally, until the sugar is dissolved. Remove from the heat and cool to room temperature. Makes 2 cups.

Candied Almonds

---

4 cups whole almonds, toasted
(see Chef's Note, page 245)

Vegetable oil

2½ cups sugar

1 lemon, juiced

1 cup honey

This recipe was inspired by the many candied fruits, flowers, and even spices that were prepared in eighteenth-century homes and confectioners' shops. Today, candied nuts of many varieties are readily available and quite common. In Philadelphia during the mid to late 1700s, however, sugar and almonds were costly and enjoyed sparingly.

These sweet, crunchy almonds are delicious enjoyed on their own as a traditional sweetmeat or as a topping for ice cream.

SERVES 6 TO 10

Preheat the oven to 375°F.

Coat a baking sheet with cooking spray. Lightly brush a wire rack with vegetable oil and set it atop the tray.

In a large saucepan, stir together ¼ cup water, the sugar, and lemon juice. Brush the sides of the pan with a pastry brush dipped in cool water, making certain no sugar crystals remain. Bring the mixture to a boil; then remove it from the heat.

With a wooden spoon, stir in the honey. Return the saucepan to the heat, bring the mixture to a boil and cook until it reaches 320°F on a candy thermometer. Again, wash down the sides of the pot, making certain no sugar crystals remain.

Remove from the heat. With a wooden spoon, carefully stir in the almonds. Immediately pour the almonds over the prepared wire rack and baking sheet. Let cool completely. Store the almonds in an airtight container at room temperature in low humidity for up to 1 week.

Glazed Chestnuts

———•◆•———

Just like fruit, nuts were commonly preserved in the eighteenth century. Home cooks and confectioners cooked whole, shelled nuts in sugar syrup and, as with whole, unblemished fruit, they were stored in jars and served on the dining or sweetmeat table or added to other dessert preparations. Among the nuts most frequently preserved during the period were walnuts and chestnuts, which were abundant and readily available.

Makes 18 pieces

Bring a medium-size saucepan of water to a boil. Prepare an ice bath in a large bowl.

With the point of a small paring knife, make a crisscross cut through the flat side of each chestnut. Add 5 chestnuts at a time to the pot of boiling water and cook for 1 minute. Using a slotted spoon, remove the nuts from the pot, and set them atop a dry kitchen towel. Carefully remove the skins with a paring knife while they're still hot. Let them cool.

In a medium-size saucepan stir together 1 cup water, the sugar, honey, and cream of tartar. Brush the sides of the pan with a pastry brush dipped in cool water, making certain no sugar crystals remain. Bring the mixture to a boil, then remove from the heat.

Add the chestnuts to the syrup, return the pan to medium heat and cook until the mixture reaches a temperature of 260°F on a candy thermometer, 5 to 10 minutes. Set the pot in the ice bath and cool to room temperature.

Transfer the mixture to a plastic container. With a wooden spoon, stir in the rum. Cover and refrigerate the chestnuts in the syrup for 2 days in order to allow them to absorb the syrup.

Strain the chestnuts and set them atop a wire rack to dry at room temperature for half an hour.

Meanwhile, in a small bowl stir together the confectioners' sugar and ¼ cup water until a paste the consistency of yogurt is formed. Pour the glaze over the chestnuts to coat each evenly and completely. Serve immediately, or store in an airtight container in the refrigerator for up to 3 to 4 days.

18 fresh chestnuts (about ½ pound)

2 cups sugar

1 cup honey

1 teaspoon cream of tartar

¼ cup light rum

1 pound confectioners' sugar

Giant chestnut trees once filled East Coast forests and provided builders with exquisite hardwood and everyone with delicious nuts.

Candied Citrus

8 oranges or 12 lemons

10 cups sugar

Iⁿ stylish eighteenth-century cities like Philadelphia, candied lemons and oranges were arguably among the most elegant and desired of sweetmeats. Nearly every cookery book included recipes for them. Confectioners' shops regularly offered these candied jewels to patrons who maintained a great fondness for the costly, imported citrus fruits, which became even more expensive once cooked in sugar. In fact, the great number of recipes for candied lemons and oranges are in keeping with the number of advertisements that mentioned these items. Most were similar to those of Philadelphia confectioner Patrick Wright, who commonly listed "orange and lemon chips" (another oft-used term for the same during the period) among his jams, marmalades, and cakes.

Overnight preparation required.

Makes 4 cups

Using a paring knife, carefully remove the rinds from the oranges or lemons in 2-inch strips. Try to leave as little pith on the rind as possible. Scrape any remaining pith with the back of the paring knife. Save the flesh of the oranges or lemons for another use.

Place the orange or lemon rinds in a medium-size saucepan and cover with cold water. Place the pan over high heat and bring the mixture to a boil. Drain and rinse the rinds under running water. Repeat the boiling, draining, and rinsing process three more times to remove the bitterness from the rinds.

In a medium-size pot, add the rinds, 6 cups of sugar, and 4 cups water; stir to combine. Brush the sides of the pot with a pastry brush dipped in cool water, making certain no sugar crystals remain. Bring the mixture to a boil and cook the syrup until it reaches a temperature of 260°F on a candy thermometer, about 10 minutes. Remove from the heat and allow the mixture to cool to room temperature. Cover the pot with plastic wrap and let the rinds steep overnight at room temperature.

Drain the rinds from the syrup and arrange them on top a wire rack. Cover generously with 2 cups of sugar. Turn the rinds over and repeat the process with the remaining 2 cups of sugar.

Let the sugar-coated rinds sit at room temperature for 8 hours. Store at room temperature in an airtight container for up to 3 weeks.

From top left, clockwise: Candied Lemon, Strawberries, Mango, Orange, Ginger, and Dates

Candied Ginger

---

1 pound fresh ginger, peeled

10 cups sugar

By the eighteenth century, Europeans had been enjoying ginger, usually imported from the East Indies, for about four hundred years. Cooks incorporated the spice into savory and sweet dishes; perhaps candying ginger became a popular method not only of preserving the perishable root but also of taming its fiery flavor.

Ginger can certainly be candied like orange or lemon rinds (by successively boiling it in water and sugar syrup), but Martha Washington wrote a recipe that appears to more closely resemble the dragée method of candying nuts—a process that coats them with hard sugar. Washington instructed the ginger to be soaked in water overnight. She then explained that sugar was to be boiled and cooled, and the ginger added to it, stirring until the lot was "hard to ye pan." The ginger was then removed, dried, and placed again in a hot pan, where, as it cooled, one was to "stir it about roundly, and it will be A rock Candy in A very short space."

Overnight preparation required.

MAKES 4 CUPS

Place the ginger in a medium-size saucepan and add enough cold water to cover completely. Place the pan over high heat and bring the mixture to a boil. Immediately remove from the heat, drain, and rinse the ginger under cool running water. Allow the ginger to cool to room temperature.

Using a mandoline, or carefully with a chef's knife, slice the cooled ginger into ¼-inch-thick slices. Place the slices in a pot and cover with cold water. Bring to a boil. Drain and rinse the ginger under cool running water. Repeat the boiling, draining, and rinsing process four more times to remove the bitterness from the ginger.

In a medium-size pot, add the ginger, 6 cups of sugar, and 4 cups water; stir to combine. Brush the sides of the pot with a pastry brush dipped in cool water, making certain no sugar crystals remain. Bring the mixture to a boil and cook until the syrup reaches a temperature of 260°F on a candy thermometer, about 10 minutes. Remove the pot from the heat and allow it to cool to room temperature. Cover the pot with plastic wrap and let the ginger steep overnight at room temperature.

Strain the ginger slices from the syrup and arrange them on top a wire rack. Cover generously with 2 cups of sugar. Turn the ginger slices over and repeat the process with the remaining 2 cups of sugar.

Let the sugar-coated ginger sit at room temperature for 8 hours. Store at room temperature in an airtight container for up to 3 weeks.

Candied Apricots

Apricots, cultivated with difficulty in the northern states but with greater success in the South, where George Washington and Thomas Jefferson enjoyed fertile crops, were much appreciated up and down the East Coast of eighteenth-century America. Delicate and fragrant when fresh and perfectly ripe, this fruit transforms into a translucent jewel when candied.

SERVES 10 TO 12

Fill a large stainless steel bowl with ice water. Bring a medium-size pot of water to a boil. Using a paring knife, score the bottoms and tops of each apricot with an "X." Drop 5 apricots at a time into the boiling water and cook for 30 seconds. Remove the apricots from the pot and immediately submerge them in the ice water. Quickly peel the skin from the fruit. If the skin isn't easily peeled, return them to the pot for another 30 seconds. Save the ice bath for later use.

In a medium-size pot, add 2 cups water, the sugar, orange juice, and honey and stir to combine. Brush the sides of the pot with a pastry brush dipped in cool water, making certain no sugar crystals remain. Bring the sugar mixture to a boil. Remove the pot from the heat. Add the apricots, cream of tartar, and cinnamon stick to the pot. Return the mixture to medium-high heat and cook until it reaches a temperature of 260°F on a candy thermometer, about 10 minutes. Remove the pot from the heat, set it in the ice bath and allow the apricots and syrup to cool to room temperature.

Transfer the mixture to a plastic container. Cut the lemon in half, squeeze the juice over the apricots and stir to mix. With a wooden spoon, stir in the liqueur. Cover and refrigerate the apricots in the syrup for 2 days in order to allow them to absorb the syrup. Serve, or store at room temperature in an airtight container for up to 2 weeks.

10 apricots

4 cups sugar

½ cup orange juice

2 tablespoons rose honey, or substitute regular honey

1 teaspoon cream of tartar

1 cinnamon stick

1 lemon

¼ cup orange liqueur (such as Cointreau or Triple Sec)

Martha Washington included a unique recipe for candied apricots in her cookbook. She incorporated "green wheat" into the boiling sugar and fruit, which dyed the apricots a vibrant green, a color much admired during the period:

To Candy Green Apricock Chipps
Take your Apricocks, pare them and cut them into chipps, and put them into running water with A good handfull of green wheat, before it be eard. then boyle them a little, after take them from the fire, and put them in a silver or earthen dish with a pritty quantety of good white sugar finely beat[en]. then set them over the fire till they be dry, and they will look clear and green. then lay them on glas[ses & put] them in a stove A while, & then box ym.

Poached Pears
with Madeira Sabayon

Poached fruit, as this version of poached pears reveals, is generally lighter in flavor and consistency than its baked or stewed counterparts, which become caramelized and softer during longer cooking.

SERVES 4

PREPARE THE PEARS: In a large saucepan, stir together the Madeira, sugar, cinnamon sticks, cloves, and vanilla bean and bring to a boil over medium-high heat. Reduce the heat to low and maintain the poaching liquid at a gentle simmer.

Drop the pears into the poaching liquid; place a plate or piece of cheesecloth overtop to keep them submerged and simmer until a paring knife easily pierces the bases (the thickest part) of the pears, about 15 to 20 minutes. (Be careful not to overcook the pears or they will become mushy.)

Prepare a large bowl with ice water. Remove the pears from the poaching liquid using a slotted spoon and place immediately in the ice water to cool. Drain the cooled pears and allow to warm to room temperature.

PREPARE THE SABAYON: Fill the bottom pan of a double boiler with water to ½ inch below the upper pan and place over low heat. (The water in the bottom of the double boiler should not come to a boil.). Whisk together the egg yolks, sugar, and Madeira in the upper pan and continue to whisk vigorously until thickened and foamy, about 5 minutes. (To prevent the eggs from scrambling, constantly whisk the sabayon and remove the upper pan of the double boiler once or twice if it appears to be cooking too quickly.)

To serve, stand each pear in the center of a dessert plate, trimming the bases if necessary. Drizzle with sabayon and garnish with a cinnamon stick.

> Martha Washington's recipe "To Stew Wardens" (firm New York pears) calls for poaching the fruit and then suggests either stewing or baking the pears to complete the preparation: "Boyle them first in faire water, then pare & stew them between 2 dishes with cinnamon, suger, and rosewater; or with ye same seasoning you may put them in a pie & bake them."

PEARS

3 cups imported Madeira

¾ cup sugar

2 cinnamon sticks

1 tablespoon whole cloves

1 vanilla bean

4 firm Bosc pears, peeled and stems on

SABAYON

8 egg yolks

¼ cup sugar

⅓ cup imported Madeira

4 cinnamon sticks, for garnish

Beverages

BEVERAGES, LIKE EIGHTEENTH-CENTURY taverns themselves, played an integral role in the social life of the early Philadelphians and our Founding Fathers. In colonial times, the consumption of beverages, especially alcoholic, began for reasons of necessity, only later becoming the stuff of creativity, enjoyment, and festivity.

Perhaps the greatest challenge colonists faced was the lack of potable drinking water. The major rivers and streams in and around Philadelphia were as polluted, if not even more so, than they are today, so clean water was a rarity. As a matter of survival, colonials were forced to find alternatives to the brackish, bacteria-infused water available to them. Ale was perhaps the most common solution. When making ale, the process of boiling water with grains and hops eliminated sickening bacteria and created a safe and tasty drink. Because it was relatively easy to make, ale was found not only in taverns, but in many households as well.

Madeira's popularity was the result of simple economics. Upon his marriage to Catherine of Braganza, the daughter of Portuguese King John IV, King Charles II gained valuable trade concessions that allowed the English to dominate the Madeira trade. King George III later enacted laws forbidding the importation of any wine to the colonies other than Madeira. The lack of import duties made Madeira a very cheap and attractive beverage to colonists, even to tea totaling Quakers.

The lack of refrigeration and year-round ice meant that most colonial beverages were served room temperature. During cold winters, with only the heat from the fireplaces to keep them warm, beverages were heated.

As substitutes for drinking water, the amount of alcoholic beverages colonials consumed seems staggering to modern Americans, especially given the relatively high alcohol content of colonial ales (if brewed according to his instructions, George Washington's "small beer" has a rather high alcohol content of 14%). The perfect example of this is the dinner bill for 55 "Light Troop of Horse" hosted at City Tavern on September 14, 1787, by Dr. Edward Moyston which lists "54 Bottles of Madeira, 60 of Claret, 8 of Old Stock, 22 Bottles of Porter, 8 of Cyder, 12 of Beer, 7 Large Bowls of Punch" and another "16 Bottles of Claret, 5 of Madeira, and 7 Bouls of Punch."

Hot Buttered Rum

During colonial times, rum was readily available in the colonies because of the slave trade. Slaves brought from Africa were traded for molasses in the West Indies, the molasses was made into rum in New England, and the rum was used to buy more slaves in Africa. Rum was especially prevalent in New England, and was used in many warming drinks. One of the most popular rum drinks was hot buttered rum, most often enjoyed during the winter months and during elections when it was handed out by candidates to influence voters. In the *Thirteen Colonies Cookbook*, Catherine Moffatt Whipple, a New Hampshire socialite, contributes a recipe for "Hot Buttered Rum in a Single Glass."

SERVES 12

In the bowl of an electric mixer fitted with the paddle attachment, cream together the butter, brown sugar, cinnamon, ½ teaspoon of the nutmeg, cloves, and salt on high speed until smooth.

Transfer to another bowl, cover with plastic wrap and refrigerate until almost firm, about 2 hours.

Wash the mixer bowl and chill for about 30 minutes. Fit the mixer with the whip attachment and whip the cream together with the sugar on high speed until soft peaks form. Reserve chilled.

Divide the butter mixture among individual mugs (about 2 tablespoons each) and pour 3 ounces of rum into each mug.

Fill the mugs up the rest of the way with boiling water and stir well. Top with the whipped cream and a sprinkle of the remaining nutmeg.

¼ pound (1 stick)
unsalted butter, softened

2 cups light brown sugar

1 teaspoon freshly ground cinnamon

1 teaspoon freshly grated nutmeg

⅛ teaspoon freshly ground cloves

⅛ teaspoon salt

1 pint heavy cream

1 tablespoon sugar

1 (750 ml) bottle dark rum

Boiling water, as needed

Grog

1 ounce rum

4 ounces water

2 teaspoons raw sugar

Juice of ½ lime

After the British conquest of Jamaica in the seventeenth century, rum quickly became the drink of choice on ships, as an alternative to ale, which had a tendency to spoil, and water, which grew stagnant. Ships' captains soon discovered, however, that it was difficult to keep the crew out of the rum and many ships were overtaken easily because the sailors were too drunk to fight. Finally, on August 21, 1740, British Rear Admiral Edward Vernon concocted a drink of rum and water with sugar and lime added to cut the bitterness of the water—and grog was born. Grog then replaced rum as the daily ration for sailors in the Royal Navy. The benefits were immediately evident: sailors still had their daily dose of rum to steel their nerves in battle, but were no longer too drunk to fight and the vitamin C in the lime juice prevented scurvy.

SERVES 1

Fill an 8-ounce glass with ice and add all ingredients. Stir to combine and serve.

It was thought that the name *Grog* came from Rear Admiral Vernon's nickname, Old Grog, from Grogram, the coarse material from which his coat was made. However, this is predated by a reference to Grog in a 1718 Daniel Defoe novel, in which a former slave boy from Barbados explains, "the black mans make the sugar, make the grog, much great work, much weary work all day long."

"A mighty bowl on deck he drew.
And filled it to the brink;
Such drank the Burford's gallant crew,
And such the gods shall drink,
The sacred robe which Vernon wore
Was drenched within the same;
And hence his virtues guard our shore,
And Grog derives its name."

—Thomas Trotter, "Written on board the Berwick"

Rum or Cognac Shrub

E ven before the eighteenth century, cooks used vinegar to preserve fruit for the winter months. Once the fruit was used, the remaining flavored vinegar was used in cooking or sweetened and spiked with alcohol or fizzed with carbonated water. Shrub crossed geographic and socio-economic lines to become perhaps the most popular mixed drink in the colonies. Every colonial cook, from Martha Washington to Mary Randolph to Amelia Simmons penned multiple recipes for shrub in their cookbooks.

MAKES ABOUT 14 OUNCES: SERVES 2

Fill a stemmed goblet two-thirds full with ice cubes.

Add the shrub and rum; pour in the Simple Syrup. Stir just to mix. Serve at once.

Ice cubes

⅓ cup shrub (see Resources, page 378)

½ cup dark rum or cognac

1 cup Simple Syrup (page 343)

Champagne Shrub

MAKES 18 OUNCES: SERVES 2

Pour the shrub into a glass. Pour in the Champagne and Simple Syrup, stirring only if the Champagne fails to blend the ingredients thoroughly. Serve at once.

In *The Virginia Housewife*, Mary Randolph shares this recipe for "Cherry Shrub."

"Gather ripe morello cherries, pick them from the stalk, and put them in an earthen pot, which must be set into an iron pot of water; make the water boil, but take care that none of it gets into the cherries; when the juice is extracted, pour it into a bag made of tolerably thick cloth, which will permit the juice to pass, but not the pulp of your cherries; sweeten it to your taste, and when it becomes perfectly clear, bottle it—put a gill of brandy into each bottle, before you pour in the juice—cover the corks with rosin. It will keep all summer, in a dry cool place, and is delicious mixed with water."

⅓ cup shrub (see Resources, page 378)

1 cup Champagne or sparkling wine

1 cup Simple Syrup (page 343)

Hot Cider

2 cups fresh apple cider

2 cinnamon sticks

¼ cup applejack brandy
or Jamaican rum

Cider was another beverage that was a substitute for poor drinking water during colonial times. Cider is believed to have migrated to England from Normandy, France's largest apple-growing province and producer of Calvados, its world-renown apple brandy. Already skilled in the art of making cider, English colonists arriving in New England stumbled upon a bounty of natural apple orchards. Cider was most often drunk immediately after the harvest and warmed during the winter months, but it was also frequently aged, allowing natural fermentation to create a powerful alcoholic beverage, hard cider. Benjamin Franklin was particularly partial to hard cider, quipping to a friend "Give me yesterday's Bread, this Day's Flesh and Last Year's Cider."

MAKES 18 OUNCES; SERVES 2

In a medium-size saucepan, bring the apple cider to a simmer over high heat. Add the cinnamon sticks and simmer for about 5 minutes to infuse the flavor of cinnamon into the liquid. Remove from heat. Stir in the brandy or rum. Serve hot in cups or mugs.

Cider was born of frugality, as it was a means of, literally, squeezing the last precious drop from an apple crop, and even made use of apples that were starting to rot. Likewise, shrub, the liquid left over from the preservation of fruits in vinegar, was sweetened and fizzed with carbonated water—the creative cook's way of using up every single drop of a food product.

The consumption of rum was a result of its availability. New England distilleries made rum from West Indian molasses arriving on the ships that plied the triangle trade route. Whatever wasn't transported to Africa to purchase slaves was sold cheaply in the colonies.

Wassail

———◆———

Wassail dates back to the old English and Germanic customs of wassailing during the Christmas and New Year's season. In those days, a big punch bowl was filled with warm spiced wine, usually made with orange or lemon peel and cloves, and everyone gathered around the "wassail bowl" to toast the season. In Pennsylvania, the Moravians, immigrants of German descent, made their wassail with a roasted orange, port wine, and cinnamon sticks.

MAKES 24 OUNCES; SERVES 6

Place the orange and lemon zest, cloves, and cinnamon sticks into a piece of 100% cotton cheesecloth. Tie up with kitchen twine to make a sachet.

Pour the wine into a saucepan over low heat. Add the brown sugar, nutmeg and sachet. Heat until wine is very warm. Do not let boil (boiling will burn off the alcohol content). Remove and discard the sachet. Serve in a fondue pot or an ovenproof punch bowl.

2 tablespoons grated orange zest
(about 1 medium orange)

2 teaspoons grated lemon zest
(about 1 medium lemon)

10 whole cloves

5 cinnamon sticks

1 bottle (750 ml) red Burgundy wine

¼ cup dark brown sugar

2 pinches freshly grated nutmeg

Wassail originates from the traditional Anglo-Saxon toast "Waes Nael," meaning to "be in good health." The spiced drink was always accompanied by the wassail song:
  "Here we come a-wassailing
  Among the leaves so green,
  Here we come a wand'ring,
  So fair to be seen,
  Love and Joy come to you,
  and to your wassail too,
  And God bless you and send you a happy new year,
  And God send you a happy new year."

Hot Spiced Punch

1 quart fresh apple cider

¼ cup fresh lemon juice (about 1 large lemon), strained

4 cinnamon sticks

1 teaspoon whole cloves (about 6)

½ teaspoon freshly grated nutmeg

I n colonial times, any combination of liquors and juices was called punch, so numerous varieties of punches are found in the cookbooks of the era. Typical colonial punches were based on rum, milk, arrack (a strong spirit whose taste is somewhere between whiskey and rum), or cider, and could be served hot or cold, although hot punch seems to have been most prevalent. This hot punch uses the ubiquitous freshly-pressed apple cider and marries it with the popular West Indian spices of nutmeg, cinnamon, and cloves.

MAKES 34 OUNCES; SERVES 8 TO 10

In a medium-size saucepan, bring the apple cider, lemon juice, and cinnamon sticks to a simmer over medium heat. Do not boil.

Place the cloves in a piece of cheesecloth. Tie up with kitchen twine to make a sachet and add to the cider. Simmer about 10 minutes, until the spices have steeped into cider. Remove and discard the sachet and cinnamon sticks. Add the nutmeg. Serve hot in cups or mugs.

City Tavern Cooler

Ice cubes

2 tablespoons peach brandy

1 tablespoon Jamaican rum

1½ teaspoons whiskey

1 cup fresh apple cider

A lthough Madeira was the drink of choice in the City Tavern, rum from Jamaica, French brandy, and English whiskey were also consumed in healthy quantities. This recipe for a refreshing summer drink is a version of the recipe for Fish House Punch contributed to the *Williamsburg Art of Cookery* by a Mrs. Taylor of Norfolk, Virginia. Mrs. Taylor's recipe, however, calls for pineapple juice instead of cider, but the cider blends better with the flavors of the brandy and rum, and tastes better in the heated version that would have been consumed in the winter months.

MAKES ABOUT 10 OUNCES; SERVES 1

Fill a 12-ounce highball glass with ice cubes. Add the brandy, rum, whiskey, and apple cider.

Eggnog

—•◦•◦•—

E ggnog was quite popular in Philadelphia and its environs, as it was both an English and a German tradition. Usually drunk around the Holidays, eggnog also appeared frequently at the breakfast table. In one of the first documentations of eggnog in Colonial America, in February of 1796, Issac Weld wrote about a small entourage of travelers that stopped in Philadelphia for breakfast and enjoyed eggnog. Betty Washington Lewis, our first president's sister, adapted many of the recipes she kept at Kenmore, her Fredericksburg, Virginia plantation, from Eliza Smith's *The Compleat Housewife*, published in London in 1727. The recipe below is virtually identical to her recipe, except that it calls for bourbon, an American spirit, rather than whiskey, which the English borrowed from the Irish.

MAKES ABOUT 48 OUNCES; SERVES 10 TO 12

In the bowl of an electric mixer, beat together the egg yolks and sugar on high speed about 5 minutes, until thick and pale yellow. Gradually beat in the cream, milk, bourbon, rum, and brandy. Cover and refrigerate until completely chilled. Serve in cups or mugs. Garnish with the nutmeg.

7 large egg yolks

¾ cup sugar

2 cups heavy cream

1 cup whole milk

¾ cup bourbon

¾ cup Jamaican rum

¼ cup brandy

Freshly grated nutmeg,
for garnish

Rather than taking a sip after a toast as we do today, toasters drank an entire glass of their beverage of choice. Following are the thirteen toasts, as given at the second Independence Day celebration at City Tavern on July 4, 1778:

The United States of America.
The protection of the rights of mankind.
The friendly European powers.
The happy era of the independence of America.
The commander in chief of the American forces.
The American arms by land and sea.
The glorious 19th of April, 1775. (Battle of Concord)
The glorious 26th of December, 1776. (Battle of Trenton)
The glorious 16th of October, 1777. (Battle of Saratoga)
The 26th of June, twice glorious, 1776–1778. (1776—Battles of Fort Moultrie, Fort Sullivan, and Sullivan's Island; 1778—Battle of Monmouth)
May the arts and sciences flourish in America.
May the people continue free forever.
May the union of the American states be perpetual.

George Washington's
Beer Recipe

—◆◆◆—

In his 1757 notebook, George Washington committed to paper his recipe for porter, or small beer as it was generally called in colonial times. Unlike the whiskey he made in his distillery at Mount Vernon, Washington never sold his beer for profit, rather, he made it only for his personal consumption and, occasionally, that of his officers.

"To Make Small Beer:
Take a large siffer full of bran hops to your taste—Boil these 3 hours. Then strain out 30 gall n into a cooler put in 3 gall n molasses while the beer is scalding hot or rather draw the molasses into the cooler. Strain the beer on it while boiling hot, let this stand till it is little more than blood warm. Then put in a quart of ye[a]st if the weather is very cold cover it over with a blank[et] let it work in the cask—Leave the bung open till it is almost done working—Bottle it that day week it was brewed."

George Washintong Papers,
Manuscript and Archives Division, The New York Public Library,
Astor, Lenor, and Tilden Foundations.

Until her death in 1782, Martha Jefferson made "small beer" at Monticello. After her death, beer brewing was among the many things that the devastated Thomas Jefferson allowed to fall by the wayside. After a spirited correspondence with Michael Krafft, author of *American Distiller*, and the purchase of Michael Combrune's *Theory and Practice of Brewing*, Jefferson began preparations to brew beer again at Monticello. Brewing began again in earnest in fall of 1813 when Thomas Jefferson engaged Captain Joseph Miller to instruct Peter Hemings, stocker of James and Sally Hemings who took over the kitchens at Monticello after James' manumission, in the art of malting and brewing. In a letter to Joseph Coppinger on April 25, 1815, Thomas Jefferson wrote, "I am lately become a brewer for family use, having had the benefit of instruction to one of my people by an English brewer of the first order." Since he did not grow barley, Jefferson's home brew relied on wheat and, later, corn with just a touch of hops. Ever the aristocrat, he preferred that the ale be transferred immediately to special bottles with the best corks possible, and is rumored to have added two expensive ingredients to the second fermentation—honey and lemon.

Ben Franklin's
Spruce Beer Recipe

—◆·▸◆—

Home brewing is one of the hottest new trends in twenty-first century America, but the idea is far from new. In colonial times, virtually everyone had recipes for ale, which was relatively easy to make because it didn't require cold fermentation like its cousin, lager. One of the most unique recipes for ale comes from Benjamin Franklin, who brewed his ale with essence of spruce. Though the thought of spruce beer may seem strange by modern tastes, similar recipes appear in various cookbooks of the era.

"For a cask containing 80 bottles, take a Pot of Essence (of spruce) and 13 Pound of Molasses—or the same amount of Raw Sugar; mix them well together in 20 Pints of hot Water. Stir until the foam, then pour it into the Cask, which you shall fill with Water: add then a Pint of good Yeast; keep stirring, and let it rest for 2 or 3 Days to ferment, after which you close the Cask, and in a few Days, it will be ready to be put into Bottles, that should be perfectly well-corked. Leave them 10 to 12 Days in a cool Cellar, after which the Beer will be good to drink."

Benjamin Franklin
Book of Recipes

At City Tavern we offer our guests a small taste of each of our "Ales of the Revolution." General Washington Tavern Porter, Thomas Jefferson 1774 Tavern Ale, Poor Richard Tavern Spruce Ale and Philadelphia Pale Ale are served up in hand-blown replicas of the glassware Thomas Jefferson commissioned for service at Monticello.

PANTRY

Beef Stock

MAKES 3 QUARTS

Preheat the oven to 350°F.

Place the bones in a large roasting pan and roast, turning the bones once until the meat and bones are well browned, about 1 to 1½ hours.

Drain the fat from the roasting pan, add the wine to deglaze, stirring with a wooden spoon to loosen any browned bits on the bottom of the pan.

Increase the oven temperature to 375°F. Add the celery, carrots, onion, and garlic to the pan; place back in the oven and roast for 15 minutes.

Remove the pan from the oven, pour in the water and bring to a boil over medium-high heat. Stir in the tomato paste, leek, bay leaves, parsley, thyme, peppercorns, and browned meat and bones and return to a boil. Reduce the heat to low, and simmer, occasionally removing any foam that rises to the surface, until the stock is reduced to 2 quarts, about 4 hours.

Line a large colander or fine mesh strainer with two layers of cheesecloth, set in a large bowl, and strain the stock.

Cool the stock in an ice bath and pour into jars or plastic containers. Refrigerate for up to 1 week.

3 pounds meaty beef
or veal bones, such as neck bones,
shank pieces, short ribs, knuckles,
or leg bones with marrow

3 cups full-bodied red wine,
such as Burgundy

1 celery root, skin on, coarsely chopped

2 carrots, coarsely chopped

1 large white onion, coarsely chopped

6 garlic cloves, lightly crushed

2 gallons water, chilled

1 (6-ounce) can tomato paste

1 leek, trimmed, cut in half lengthwise,
and rinsed thoroughly

3 bay leaves

1 small bunch fresh parsley

4 sprigs fresh thyme

12 white peppercorns

Vegetable Stock

MAKES 2 QUARTS

Combine all of the ingredients in a large (at least 2-gallon) stockpot and bring to a boil over medium-high heat. Reduce the heat to low and simmer until the stock is reduced to 2 quarts, about 4 hours.

Line a large colander or fine mesh strainer with two layers of cheesecloth, set in a large bowl and strain the stock.

Cool the stock in an ice bath and pour into jars or plastic containers. Refrigerate for up to 1 week.

1 gallon water

1 celery root, skin on, coarsely chopped

3 carrots, coarsely chopped

2 medium white onions, coarsely chopped

2 large ripe tomatoes

1 leek, trimmed, cut in half lengthwise,
and rinsed thoroughly

3 bay leaves

6 garlic cloves, lightly crushed

1 small bunch fresh parsley

4 sprigs fresh thyme

12 white peppercorns

Chicken Stock

1 stewing chicken or hen
(about 4½ pounds), whole or
cut into 8 pieces (see Chef's Note)

2½ gallons water

½ celery root, skin on, coarsely chopped

2 carrots, peeled and coarsely chopped

2 medium onions, coarsely chopped

1 leek, trimmed, cut in half lengthwise
and rinsed thoroughly

1 bay leaf

4 sprigs fresh thyme

½ bunch fresh parsley

12 whole black peppercorns, crushed

Rinse the chicken in cold running water and trim off any excess fat. Place the chicken in a 12-quart stockpot and pour in the water. Add the remaining ingredients and bring to a boil over medium-high heat. Reduce the heat to medium and simmer gently, occasionally removing any foam that rises to the surface until fully cooked, about 30 minutes. Remove the chicken and reserve for use in another dish. Continue to simmer the stock until it is reduced to about 5 quarts, about 1½ hours more.

Line a large colander or fine mesh strainer with two layers of cheesecloth, set in a large bowl and strain the stock.

Return the stock to the pan and bring to a boil over medium heat. Reduce the heat to low and simmer until reduced by half to 2½ quarts, about 4 hours.

Cool the stock in an ice bath and pour into jars or plastic containers. Refrigerate for up to 1 week.

CHEF'S NOTE

Stewing chickens (also called hens, boiling fowl, or simply fowl) are usually between 10 and 18 months old and weigh between three and six pounds. Because they are older and larger than roasting chickens, they are more flavorful but also less tender. These qualities thus make them particularly good candidates for stewing and making rich, golden stock. There is an alternative, though, to cooking a whole chicken. Simply use chicken necks and backs, which are certainly inexpensive and full of flavor.

Lobster Stock

Combine all ingredients in an 8-quart stockpot and bring to a boil.

Reduce the heat and simmer, uncovered, for 6 hours, until reduced to about 1 quart.

Line a large colander or fine mesh strainer with two layers of cheesecloth, set in a large bowl and strain the stock.

Cool the stock in an ice bath and pour into jars or plastic containers. Refrigerate for up to 1 week.

1 gallon water

2 pounds lobster heads and shells

3 celery ribs, chopped

1 medium white onion, chopped

1 large ripe tomato, chopped

1 tablespoon tomato paste

1 bay leaf

Court Bouillon

MAKES 3 QUARTS

Combine all of the ingredients in a 10-quart stockpot and bring to a boil.

Reduce the heat to medium and simmer uncovered for about 3 hours, until reduced by about half.

Line a large colander or fine mesh strainer with two layers of cheesecloth, set in a large bowl and strain the stock.

Cool the stock in an ice bath and pour into jars or plastic containers. Refrigerate for up to 1 week.

2 gallons water

1 cup white wine

1 cup diced celery

2 large carrots, peeled and diced

1 large onion, cut into quarters

½ cup sliced leeks, rinsed well

2 teaspoons salt

1 teaspoon whole black peppercorns

½ teaspoon cayenne pepper

1 large bay leaf

1 lemon, cut into wedges

Bouquet Garni

———•◦◦•———

4 whole black peppercorns

3 sprigs fresh thyme

2 sprigs fresh parsley

2 medium garlic cloves, peeled

1 medium shallot, coarsely chopped

1 bay leaf

Place all ingredients in a 6-inch square of cheesecloth and tie with kitchen twine to make a sachet. Place in stock or sauce as directed.

Marinade for
Beef, Pork, Rabbit, or Chicken

———•◦◦•———

1 medium onion, thinly sliced

1 garlic clove, crushed

1 small carrot, thinly sliced

1 celery rib, chopped

2 tablespoons fresh parsley, chopped

3 whole black peppercorns

1 bay leaf

1 sprig fresh thyme

2 cups red Burgundy wine

½ cup red wine vinegar

½ cup brandy or cognac

1 tablespoon vegetable oil

Salt and freshly ground pepper to taste

MAKES 1 QUART

Combine all of the ingredients in a 4-quart stockpot. Marinate choice of meat in the refrigerator overnight. Cook meat as desired.

To use the marinade as a flavor-enhancer for sauces, bring it to a boil first. Otherwise, discard it.

CHEF'S NOTE

For a more intense flavor, add rosemary or sage.

Demi-Glace

Melt 4 tablespoons of the butter in a large saucepan over medium heat, add the shallots and sauté until translucent, about 2 to 3 minutes. Toss in the mushrooms and sauté until any liquid they release has evaporated.

Stir in the tomato paste, then add 1 cup of the wine to deglaze, stirring with a wooden spoon to loosen any browned bits on the bottom of the pan. Simmer until almost dry, then deglaze with 1 more cup of the wine. Simmer until almost dry again.

Add the remaining cup of wine, the stock, tomatoes, leek, and thyme, and bring to a boil. Reduce the heat to low and simmer for about 15 to 20 minutes.

In a medium-size bowl, knead together the flour and remaining butter to form a paste (*beurre manié*). Whisk this paste into the demi-glace and simmer for about 15 to 20 minutes, or until the sauce is smooth and velvety.

Strain through a fine mesh sieve and cool the demi-glace in an ice bath. Pour into a jar or plastic container and refrigerate for up to 1 week.

½ pound (2 sticks) unsalted butter

½ cup chopped shallots

1 cup sliced white button mushrooms

3 tablespoons tomato paste

3 cups full-bodied red wine, such as Burgundy

7 cups Beef Stock (page 363)

3 Roma tomatoes, coarsely chopped

½ cup chopped leek

2 sprigs fresh thyme (or 1 teaspoon dried thyme)

6 tablespoons all-purpose flour

CHEF'S NOTE

When reheating, add a bit of red wine to the demi-glace and bring to a boil over medium heat. Remove from heat and whisk in 1 tablespoon of room-temperature butter per cup of demi-glace before serving to ensure proper consistency and flavor.

Madeira Wine Sauce

MAKES 1 CUP

½ cup imported Madeira

1 teaspoon cracked black peppercorns

1 cup Demi-Glace (page 367)

In a medium-size saucepan, combine the Madeira and peppercorns and bring to a boil. Add the demi-glace. Reduce the heat and simmer, uncovered, for 10 minutes, until reduced to about 1 cup liquid.

CHEF'S NOTE

Sauce may be made ahead of time and reheated. However, you must bring the temperature to 165°F for at least 15 seconds before serving.

Sherry Cream Sauce

MAKES 1¼ CUPS

2 tablespoons unsalted butter

1 large shallot, finely chopped

1 cup dry sherry

1 cup heavy cream

1 small bunch fresh chives, chopped (about 2 tablespoons)

Salt and freshly ground black pepper

Melt the butter in a 2-quart saucepan over medium heat, add the shallots and sauté for 3 minutes, until browned. Add the sherry and continue cooking for 8 to 10 minutes, until reduced to ½ cup liquid. Add the cream and bring to a boil. Reduce the heat and simmer for 5 to 10 minutes, until reduced to about 1¼ cups liquid. Remove from the heat. Stir in the chives. Season to taste with salt and pepper.

Béchamel Sauce

Bring the milk to a boil in a small saucepan over high heat. Remove from the heat and set aside to keep warm.

Melt the butter in a medium-size saucepan over medium heat, add the onion and sauté until softened and translucent, about 3 minutes. Gradually stir in the flour to form a roux and cook, stirring frequently, until well combined, about 1 minute.

Gradually whisk in the warm milk, bring the mixture to a boil and add the salt, clove, bay leaf, and nutmeg. Reduce the heat to low and simmer until thickened, about 20 minutes.

Season with salt and white pepper and strain through a fine mesh strainer. Set aside to keep warm for serving or pour into a jar or plastic container and store in the refrigerator for up to 1 week.

1½ cups milk

2 tablespoons unsalted butter

1 small onion, finely chopped

2 tablespoons all-purpose flour

1 teaspoon salt

1 whole clove

1 bay leaf

⅛ teaspoon freshly grated nutmeg

Freshly ground white pepper

Hollandaise Sauce

Fill the bottom pan of a double boiler with water to ½ inch below the upper pan and place over low heat. (The water in the bottom of the double boiler should not come to a boil.). Whisk together the egg yolks, lemon juice, and wine in the top portion of the double boiler until light yellow and thick, occasionally removing the pan from the heat to prevent overheating and scrambling the eggs.

Add the cayenne pepper and, in a slow, steady stream add the clarified butter, whisking until the sauce is emulsified. (Add a few drops of wine if the sauce is too thick.)

Season with salt and white pepper and set aside to keep warm or serve immediately.

4 large egg yolks

Juice of 1 large lemon
(about 3 tablespoons)

1 tablespoon dry white wine,
such as Sauvignon Blanc

About ⅛ teaspoon cayenne pepper

1 cup clarified butter
(see Chef's Note, page 54)

Salt and freshly ground white pepper

Mustard Sauce

MAKES 1½ CUPS

3 tablespoons unsalted butter

1 tablespoon vegetable oil

2 medium onions, finely chopped

3 medium shallots, finely chopped

1 tablespoon all-purpose flour

2 cups white wine

½ cup cider vinegar

2 tablespoons tomato paste

2 tablespoons Dijon mustard

Salt and freshly ground white pepper

2 tablespoons finely chopped
fresh parsley, for serving

Heat the butter and oil in a 2-quart saucepan over medium heat; add the onions and shallots and sauté for 3 minutes, until translucent. Sprinkle the flour over the onion mixture and cook, stirring frequently, until well combined.

Stir in the wine, vinegar, tomato paste, and mustard. Reduce the heat and simmer, uncovered, for 30 minutes, until reduced by one fourth. Season with salt and white pepper and set aside to keep warm or serve immediately. Just before serving, stir in the parsley.

Homemade Mayonnaise

---

3 large egg yolks

1 teaspoon lemon juice

1 tablespoon white wine vinegar

1 teaspoon sugar

1½ cups vegetable oil

Salt and freshly ground white pepper

MAKES ABOUT 1½ CUPS

Combine the egg yolks, lemon juice, vinegar, and sugar in a blender or in the bowl of a food processor fitted with the blade attachment. Begin blending on high speed and whip until thick and light yellow in color. Pouring in a slow, steady stream, add the oil, continuing to blend until thickened and emulsified.

Season with salt and white pepper and transfer the mayonnaise to a storage or serving bowl. Cover and store in the refrigerator for up to 3 days.

Horseradish Sauce

In a small mixing bowl, combine the sour cream, horseradish, parsley, lemon juice, and paprika.

Season with salt and white pepper and transfer the sauce to a storage or serving bowl. Cover and store in the refrigerator for up to 3 days.

¾ cup sour cream

¼ cup grated fresh horseradish

1 teaspoon chopped fresh parsley

1 teaspoon fresh lemon juice, strained

½ teaspoon sweet paprika

Salt and freshly ground white pepper

Herb Croutons

Makes 2 cups; Serves 8

Preheat the oven to 300°F.

Melt the butter in a small saucepan over medium heat, add the shallots and garlic and sauté for 2 minutes, until golden. Transfer to a large mixing bowl. Add the oil, basil, parsley, thyme, and cheese and blend well. Add the bread cubes and toss until well-coated.

Spread the bread cubes in a single layer on a shallow baking sheet and bake for 10 to 15 minutes, until golden brown and crisp and dry. Croutons can be stored, uncovered, for up to 1 week.

4 tablespoons unsalted butter

2 medium shallots, chopped

3 garlic cloves, chopped

¼ cup olive oil

1 small bunch fresh basil, chopped (about ½ cup)

½ bunch fresh parsley, chopped (about 3 tablespoons)

1 sprig fresh thyme, leaves pulled

1 tablespoon grated Parmesan cheese

12 slices white bread (crusts optional), cut into ½-inch cubes

---

Graham Cracker Crust

Makes 1¼ cups; enough for one 9-inch cheesecake crust

In a large bowl, thoroughly combine the graham crackers, butter, and sugar. Cover with plastic wrap and store in the refrigerator.

1½ cups finely crushed graham crackers (about 22)

¼ pound (1 stick) unsalted butter, melted

¼ cup sugar

Pâte Brisée
(Basic Pie Dough)

———— •••• ————

1⅓ cups sifted all-purpose flour

¼ teaspoon salt

4 tablespoons unsalted butter, chilled and cubed

¼ cup vegetable shortening, chilled

4 to 5 tablespoons ice-cold water

In a medium-size bowl, stir together the flour and salt. Using a pastry cutter or two knives, cut in the butter and shortening until the mixture resembles coarse crumbles.

Sprinkle the water, 1 tablespoon at a time, over the flour mixture and toss together with a fork, until a dough starts to form. It will be a little sticky or tacky.

Form the dough into a disc shape, wrap in plastic wrap and chill in the refrigerator for at least 30 minutes before using.

Pâte Sucrée
(Rich Pie Dough)

———— •••• ————

3 cups sifted all-purpose flour

¼ cup sugar

½ pound (2 sticks) cold unsalted butter, cubed

2 large eggs

In a food processor fitted with the steel blade, process the flour and sugar with on/off pulses until the mixture is combined. Add the butter and process with on/off pulses until most of the mixture is crumbly.

With the processor running, quickly add the eggs through the feed tube. Stop the processor when all eggs have been added and scrape down the sides of the bowl.

Process with two more on/off pulses (all of the mixture may not be moistened). Remove the dough from the bowl. Form the dough into a disc shape, wrap in plastic wrap, and chill in the refrigerator for at least 1 hour before using.

Puff Pastry

————◆◆◆————

In the bowl of an electric mixer fitted with the paddle attachment, combine 2 cups of the bread flour, 1 pound of butter, and the salt. Mix until the mixture becomes fine and crumbly. Remove the paddle attachment and replace with the dough hook.

In a separate mixing bowl, whisk together the water and the egg yolks. Make a well in the center of the flour mixture and add the egg mixture. Mix on low speed until just a dough forms, about 5 minutes.

Remove the dough from the bowl and roll it out into a 17 x 11-inch rectangle. Wrap in plastic wrap and refrigerate for 30 minutes.

Meanwhile, in a medium-size mixing bowl add the remaining 2 tablespoons bread flour, the remaining 6 tablespoons butter, and the cake flour. Stir to combine, making sure that the butter is well incorporated into the flour and that there are no lumps of butter in the mixture.

Line a 17 x 11-inch baking pan with parchment paper. Grease two thirds of the parchment with butter; then refrigerate for about 20 minutes to chill the butter.

Coat a work surface generously with flour. Lay out the chilled dough. Spread the butter mixture on top of the dough, covering the left two thirds of the dough and leaving a 1-inch border of dough uncovered around the edges (see Illustration #1).

Fold the unbuttered third of the dough over, from right to left (Illustration #2); then fold the butter-covered third over, from left to right (Illustration #3). Seal all of the edges so no butter is showing.

Turn the dough so that the seam is facing away from you; then, using a rolling pin, roll the dough out to 33 x 17 inches. Fold the dough in thirds, using the same method as used when folding in the butter. Place the folded dough on a baking sheet, cover with plastic wrap and refrigerate for 30 minutes.

Coat a work surface generously with flour. Lay out the chilled dough so that the seam is facing away from you. Using a rolling pin, roll the dough out to 33 x 17 inches again. Fold the left half of the dough in, and then fold the right half of the dough in, so that they touch in the middle of the dough (Illustration #4). Then fold the two halves together as if closing a book (Illustration #5). Cover with plastic wrap and refrigerate for 30 minutes.

(continued)

2 cups plus 2 tablespoons bread flour

1 pound (4 sticks)
plus 6 tablespoons unsalted butter,
chilled and cubed

1 teaspoon salt

1 cup less 2 tablespoons water

2 large egg yolks

2 tablespoons cake flour

1

2

3

(illustrations continued)

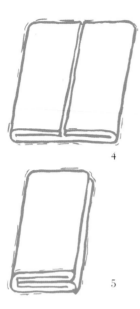

4

5

Turn the dough again so the seam is facing away from you; then roll the dough out to 33 x 17 inches. Fold the dough in thirds. Place the dough on a baking sheet, cover, and refrigerate for another 30 minutes.

Lay out the chilled dough with the seam facing away from you. Roll the dough out to 33 x 17 inches again. Fold the left half of the dough in, and then fold the right half of the dough in, so they touch in the middle of the dough (Illustration #4). Then fold the two halves together as if closing a book (Illustration #5). Cover with plastic wrap and refrigerate for another 30 minutes.

Turn the dough again so the seam is facing away from you; then roll the dough out to 33 x 17 inches. Fold the dough in thirds. Place the dough on a baking sheet, cover, and refrigerate for another 1 hour before use. The final size of the puff pastry sheet will be 11 x 17 inches. The puff pastry will last 3 to 4 days in the refrigerator but can be frozen for up to 2 weeks and defrosted 1 day before use.

Quick Puff Pastry

MAKES 3 POUNDS: ENOUGH FOR 12 MEAT TURNOVERS
OR POTPIE LIDS

4 cups all-purpose flour, sifted

2 teaspoons salt

7 tablespoons unsalted butter, melted

1 cup ice-cold water

1 pound (4 sticks) unsalted butter, chilled and cubed

In the bowl of an electric mixer, beat the flour and salt on low until combined. Add the 7 tablespoons melted butter and beat well. While still beating, slowly add the ice-cold water.

When the dough starts to form, add the cubed butter and beat until just combined. (You should see small specks of butter embedded in the dough—essential for forming a layered effect in the dough. As you roll or shape the dough, these butter specks will blend in.)

Remove the dough from the bowl, form into a disk shape, wrap in plastic wrap and chill in the refrigerator for at least 30 minutes before using.

Pastry Cream

In a 2-quart heavy saucepan over medium heat, bring the milk and ¼ cup of the sugar to a boil, stirring occasionally.

Meanwhile, in a large bowl whisk together the flour, cornstarch, eggs, vanilla, and remaining ¼ cup of sugar.

Slowly pour the hot milk-sugar mixture into the egg mixture, whisking constantly until combined. Pour the mixture back into the saucepan and cook, stirring constantly, until the mixture thickens and just comes to a boil. Cook for 1 minute more to "cook off" the starch.

Remove from the heat. Pour the mixture into a heatproof bowl and stir in the butter. Cover the surface with plastic wrap to prevent a "skin" from forming on the top and let cool at room temperature for 30 minutes.

Chill in the refrigerator for at least 1 hour before using. Pastry cream will keep in the refrigerator for 4 to 5 days if sealed in an airtight container.

> 2 cups whole milk
> ½ cup sugar
> ¼ cup all-purpose flour
> ¼ cup cornstarch
> 3 large eggs
> ½ teaspoon vanilla
> 2 tablespoons unsalted butter, softened

Chantilly Cream

In a clean, dry bowl of an electric mixer on high speed, whip together the cream and sugar until soft peaks form.

Refrigerate until ready to serve. The cream will keep for 2 to 3 days covered, but you will need to rewhip it before using.

> 2 cups heavy cream
> ½ cup sifted confectioners' sugar

Crème Anglaise
(Vanilla Custard Sauce)

MAKES 1½ CUPS

2 cups whole milk

4 tablespoons sugar

1 vanilla bean, split open and seeds scraped out with the back of a knife

4 large egg yolks

2 tablespoons Jamaican gold rum

Fill a large bowl with ice water.

In a 2-quart heavy saucepan over medium heat, combine the milk, 2 tablespoons of the sugar, and the scraped vanilla seeds and pod; bring to a boil.

In a large bowl, whisk together the egg yolks and the remaining 2 tablespoons of sugar.

Slowly pour 1 cup of the hot milk mixture into the egg yolk-sugar mixture, whisking constantly. Do not pour the entire hot milk mixture into the yolk mixture, as it will curdle the eggs. Pour the tempered milk-yolk mixture back into the saucepan with the hot milk, and cook over medium heat, stirring constantly, until the mixture coats the back of a spoon. Do not boil.

Remove from the heat and stir in the rum. Strain the mixture through a fine sieve into a heatproof bowl. Place the bowl in the ice bath.

When cool, transfer the sauce to a bowl. Cover the surface with plastic wrap and chill in the refrigerator until ready to use. The sauce will keep in the refrigerator for 4 to 5 days if well sealed.

Streusel

MAKES 4 CUPS

2 cups all-purpose flour

1 cup packed light brown sugar

¾ cup sugar

1 tablespoon ground cinnamon

12 tablespoons (1½ sticks) unsalted butter, chilled and cubed

2 cups chopped walnuts

In the bowl of an electric mixer on medium speed, mix the flour, brown sugar, sugar, and cinnamon until combined. Add the butter and mix well, until the texture becomes crumbly. With a wooden spoon, stir in the walnuts.

Use immediately, or transfer to a covered container and store in the refrigerator for up to 2 weeks.

Oat Topping

MAKES 2 CUPS

In a medium-size bowl, combine the flour, oats, and brown sugar. Stir to combine.

Transfer the mixture to the bowl of a food processor, add the butter and process until the texture becomes crumbly. You may also do this by hand, cutting the butter into the dry ingredients with two knives. With a wooden spoon, stir in the walnuts.

Use immediately or transfer to a covered container and store in the refrigerator for up to 2 weeks.

½ cup all-purpose flour

½ cup old-fashioned oats

½ cup packed light brown sugar

4 tablespoons unsalted butter, chilled and cubed

½ cup chopped walnuts

Berry Preserves

MAKES 2 CUPS

Fill a large bowl with ice water. Place the berries in a strainer and rinse well with cold water. Pat the berries dry with a paper towel.

Choose a saucepan large enough to hold three times the amount of ingredients being used. Add the sugar, water, and lemon juice; stir to combine. Brush the sides of the pan with a pastry brush dipped in cool water, making certain no sugar crystals remain. Bring the sugar syrup to a boil over high heat, washing down the sides of the pot often. Cook the syrup until it reaches a temperature of 285°F on a candy thermometer.

Remove from the heat. Carefully add a few berries at a time. The mixture will splatter, so add the berries slowly, close to the syrup, stirring constantly. Once all of the berries have been added, return to the heat and continue to stir the mixture until it returns to a boil. Reduce the heat to medium and cook until the mixture is thickened, 8 to 10 minutes.

Once the preserves have reached the desired thickness, transfer them to a stainless steel bowl and set the bowl in the ice bath to cool to room temperature. Store the preserves in an airtight container in the refrigerator for up to 2 weeks.

2 pints berries, such as blackberries, raspberries, strawberries, gooseberries, or blueberries

2 cups sugar

¾ cup water

1 tablespoon freshly squeezed lemon juice

Resources

MAPLE LEAF FARMS
For the finest quality duck and chicken products
800-348-2812   www.mapleleaffarms.com

DIETZ & WATSON
For the world's finest meat delicacies, artisan cheeses,
and one-of-a-kind superior quality sausages.
800-333-1974   www.dietzandwatson.com

MORE THAN GOURMET
For chef-quality demi-glace and all-natural reduction sauces
sold in small portions for home use.
800-860-9385   www.morethangourmet.com

TAIT FARMS
For a refreshing selection of shrubs offered in a variety of flavors,
essential in traditional eighteenth century shrub drinks.
800-787-2716   www.taitfarmfoods.com

ALBERT USTER IMPORTS
For chocolate, pastry and baking equipment, and other pastry baking products
800-231-8154   www.auiswisscatalog.com

PASTRY CHEF CENTRAL
For pastry and baking equipment (such as cookie spritzers)
888-750-2433   www.pastrychef.com

D'ARTAGNAN
For a fresh and exotic selection of game and fowl including venison and pheasant
800-327-8246   www.dartagnan.com

Bibliography

Adams, Abigail. *New Letters of Abigail Adams, 1788-1801.* Edited by Stewart Mitchell. Boston: Houghton Mifflin Co., 1947.

Armes, Ethel, ed. and comp. *Nancy Shippen: Her Journal Book, the International Romance of a Young Lady of Fashion of Colonial Philadelphia.* Philadelphia: J. B. Lippincotte Co., 1935.

Belden, Louise Conway. *The Festive Tradition: Table Decoration and Desserts in America, 1650-1900.* New York: W.W. Norton & Co., 1983.

Bridenbaugh, Carl, ed. *Gentleman's Progress: The Itinerarium of Dr. Alexander Hamilton, 1744.* Pittsburgh: University of Pittsburgh Press, 1948.

Bushman, Richard L. *The Refinement of America.* New York: Alfred A. Knopf, 1992.

Bullock, Helen. *The Williamsburg Art of Cookery.* Williamsburg: The Dietz Press, Inc., 1938.

Carter, Susannah. *The Frugal Colonial Housewife: A Cook's Book wherein The Art of Dressing all Sorts of Viands with Cleanliness, Decency, and Elegance is explained. or Complete Woman Cook.* Edited by Jean McKibbin. Garden City, N.Y.: Doubleday & Co., 1976. Originally published as *The Frugal Housewife or Complete Woman Cook* (London: F. Newbery, 1772; Boston: Edes and Gill, 1772).

Carson, Barbara G. *Ambitious Appetites: Dining, Behavior, and Patterns of Consumption in Federal Washington.* Washington, D.C.: The American Institute of Architects Press, 1990.

Child, Lydia Maria. *The American Frugal Housewife.* Facsimile of the 12th ed., 1833. Bedford, Mass.: Applewood Books, n.d.

Donovan, Mary; Hatrak, Amy; Mills, Frances; Shull, Elizabeth. *The Thirteen Colonies Cookbook.* Montclair: Praeger Publishing, Inc., 1975.

Drinker, Elizabeth Sandwith. *The Diary of Elizabeth Drinker.* Edited by Elaine Forman Crane. Vol. 1. Boston: Northeastern University Press, 1991.

Dubourcq, Hilaire. *Benjamin Franklin Book of Recipes,* Second Edition. London: FlyFizzi Publishing, 2004.

Escoffier, A. *The Escoffier Cookbook: A Guide to the Fine Art of French Cuisine.* New York: Crown Publishers, Inc., 1969. Originally published as Le Guide Culinaire (Paris, 1903).

Faber, Eli. *The Jewish People in America. A Time for Planting: The First Migration, 1654-1820.* Baltimore: The Johns Hopkins University Press, 1992.

Farley, John. *The London Art of Cookery.* Edited by Ann Haly. Introduction by Stephen Medcalf. Lewes, East Sussex, England: Southover Press, 1988.

Glasse, Hannah. *The Art of Cooking Made Plain and Easy.* Facsimile of the 1805, Alexandria ed. Introduction by Karen Hess. Bedford, Mass.: Applewood Books, 1997.

Herbst, Sharon T. *Food Lover's Companion.* New York: Barron's Educational Series, 1990.

Hess, Karen, ed. and transcriber. *Martha Washington's Booke of Cookery.* New York: Columbia University Press, 1995.

Hooker, Richard J., ed. *A Colonial Plantation Cookbook: The Receipt Book of Harriott Pinckney Horry, 1770.* Columbia, S.C.: University of South Carolina Press, 1984.

Kimball, Marie. *Thomas Jefferson's Cook Book.* Richmond, Va.: Garrett & Massie, 1938.

Leslie, Eliza. *Directions for Cookery, in Its Various Branches.* Facsimile of the 1848, Philadelphia ed. Monterey, Ca: Creative Cookbooks, 2001.

——. *Seventy-Five Receipts, for Pastry, Cakes, and Sweetmeats.* Facsimile of the 1st ed., 1828. Bedford, Mass.: Applewood Books.

Leighton, Ann. *American Gardens in the Eighteenth Century, "For Use or for Delight."* Boston: Houghton Mifflin Co., 1976. Reprint, Amherst: University of Massachusetts Press, 1986.

Lowenstein, Eleanor. *Bibliography of American Cookery Books, 1742-1860.* Worcester, Mass.: American Antiquarian Society, 1972.

Mariani, John. *The Encyclopedia of American Food and Drink.* New York: Lebhar-Friedman Books, 1999.

Mount Vernon memos. George Washington's Mount Vernon Estate and Gardens, Mount Vernon, Va.

Nutt, Frederick. *The complete confectioner, or, The whole art of confectionary made easy . . . 1798.* 4th ed. Reprint, New York: Richard Scott, 1807.

Ortiz, Elizabeth Lambert, ed. *The Encyclopedia of Herbs, Spices, and Flavorings: A Cook's Compendium.* New York: Dorling Kindersley, 1992.

Peckham, Howard H., ed. "Journal of Lord Adam Gordon." In *Narratives of Colonial America, 1704-1765.* Chicago: R.R. Donnelley & Sons Co., 1971.

Pennsylvania Gazette, 12 June 1766 to 4 July 1792.

Platt, John D.R. *Historic Resource Study: The City Tavern.* Denver: United States Department of the Interior, 1973.

Raffald, Elizabeth. *The Experienced English Housekeeper.* Facsimile of the 1st ed., 1769. Introduction by Roy Shipperbottom. Lewes, East Sussex, England: Southover Press, 1997.

Randolph, Mary. *The Virginia House-Wife.* Facsimile of the 1st ed., 1824. Historical notes and commentaries by Karen Hess. Columbia, S.C.: University of South Carolina Press, 1984.

Rice, Kym S. *Early American Taverns: For the Entertainment of Friends and Strangers.* Chicago: Regnery Gateway, 1983.

Roberts, Kenneth, and Anna Roberts, eds. *Moreau de St. Mery's American Journey, 1793-98.* Garden City, N.Y.: Doubleday and Co., 1947.

Rundell, Maria Eliza Ketelby. *A new system of domestic cookery: formed upon principles of economy, and adapted to the use of private families throughout the United States.* By a Lady. New York: R. M'Dermut and D.D. Arden, 1814.

Schweitzer, Mary McKinney. "The Economy of Philadelphia and Its Hinterland." In *Shaping a National Culture: The Philadelphia Experience, 1750-1800.* Edited by Catherine E. Hutchins. Winterthur, De.: Henry Francis du Pont Winterthur Museum, 1994.

Sherrill, Charles H. *French Memories of Eighteenth-Century America.* New York: Charles Scribner's Sons, 1915.

Simmons, Amelia. *American Cookery.* Facsimile of the 2nd ed., 1796. Introduction by Karen Hess. Bedford, Mass.: Applewood Books, 1996.

Smith, Andrew F. *The Oxford Encyclopedia of Food and Drink in America.* New York, Oxford University Press, Inc., 2004.

Smith, Eliza. *The Compleat Housewife.* Facsimile of the 1758, London ed. London: Studio Editions, 1994.

Thompson, Mary V. "'Look Into the Milk and Butter': Food Preservation at George Washington's Mount Vernon." Department of the Registrar, Mount Vernon Ladies' Association, Mount Vernon, Va., January 1996.

Verral, William. *The Cook's Paradise being William Verral's 'Complete System of Cookery.'* Published in 1759 with Thomas Gray's cookery notes in Holograph. Introduction and appendices by R. L. Megroz, London: Sylvan Press, 1948.

Weaver, William W., Mary Anne Hines, and Gordon Marshall. *The Larder Invaded: reflections on three centuries of Philadelphia food and drink.* Philadelphia: Library Company of Philadelphia, Historical Society of Pennsylvania, 1987.

Credits

Wood cuts: *Old English Cuts and Illustrations*. Bowles and Carver, Dover Publications, 1970. Originally published in the late 1780s and early 1790s by the firm of Bowles and Carter.

Title page and page 6: Illustration of City Tavern. Courtesy of Concepts by Staib, Ltd.

Page 9: Engraving, *Arch Street, with the Second Presbyterian Church*. Philadelphia. William Birch, 1799.

Page 10: Engraving, *Bank of Pennsylvania, South Second Street*. Philadelphia. William Birch, c. 1800.

Pages 11, 12, 15, 29: Photographs, Frances Soo Ping Chow

Page 18: Engraving, *Arch Street Ferry*. Philadelphia. William Birch, 1800.

Page 20: Engraving, *New Market, in South Second Street*. Philadelphia. William Birch, 1799.

Page 22: Engraving, *Second Street North from Market Street with Christ Church*. Philadelphia. William Birch, 1799.

Page 27: City Tavern East Elevation, drawing #0603-9, and City Tavern West Elevation drawing #0603-11, by Denise Rabzak. Courtesy of National Park Service, Independence National Historical Park. Historic Architect's Office. Scaled Drawings, Plans and Elevations, 1985-1986. Accession #3895.

Page 39: *The compleat housewife*. London, 1737. Courtesy of Winterthur Library: Printed Book and Periodical Collection.

Page 43: T*he Art of Cookery made plain and easy*. Courtesy of Winterthur Library: Printed Book and Periodical Collection.

Page 69: *Le cannameliste Francais,* . . . . Courtesy of Winterthur Library: Printed Book and Periodical Collection.

Page 221: William Deering, *Black Forest Cuisine*. Walter Staib with Jennifer Lindner McGlinn.

Page 277: William Deering, *Black Forest Cuisine*. Walter Staib with Jennifer Lindner McGlinn.

Page 282: William Deering, *Black Forest Cuisine*. Walter Staib with Jennifer Lindner McGlinn.

Page 285: William Deering, *Black Forest Cuisine*. Walter Staib with Jennifer Lindner McGlinn.

Page 298: William Deering, *Black Forest Cuisine*. Walter Staib with Jennifer Lindner McGlinn.

Pages 325, 327, 331, 373, 375: Illustrations, Bill Jones. *Black Forest Cuisine*. Walter Staib with Jennifer Lindner McGlinn.

Page 329: William Deering, *Black Forest Cuisine*. Walter Staib with Jennifer Lindner McGlinn.

Page 332: William Deering, *Black Forest Cuisine*. Walter Staib with Jennifer Lindner McGlinn.

Index